WHATEVER IT TAKES

WHATEVER IT TAKES
MY AUTOBIOGRAPHY

RICHIE HOGAN

WITH FINTAN O'TOOLE

GILL BOOKS

Gill Books
Hume Avenue
Park West
Dublin 12
www.gillbooks.ie

Gill Books is an imprint of M.H. Gill and Co.

© Richie Hogan 2024

9781804581506

Edited by Noel O Regan
Proofread by Natasha Mac a'Bháird
Designed by Typo•glyphix, Burton-on-Trent DE14 3HE
Printed and bound in the UK using 100% renewable electricity at CPI Group (UK) Ltd
This book is typeset in 12.5pt on 18pt Minion Pro.

The paper used in this book comes from the wood pulp of sustainably managed forests.

All rights reserved.
No part of this publication may be copied, reproduced or transmitted in any form or by any means, without written permission of the publishers.

A CIP catalogue record for this book is available from the British Library.

5 4 3 2 1

To Mam, Dad and Anne.
Thank you for everything.

CONTENTS

Prologue ix

Chapter 1 The End of the Road? 1
Chapter 2 Where Are You From? 15
Chapter 3 St Kieran's 37
Chapter 4 Minor Moments 57
Chapter 5 Trying to Make it 77
Chapter 6 Making the Senior Team 101
Chapter 7 The Drive for Five 123
Chapter 8 Back Injuries 135
Chapter 9 2011 Revenge 153
Chapter 10 Setbacks and Successes 191
Chapter 11 Strange Times 215
Chapter 12 Why Is Hurling So Easy? 231
Chapter 13 The Life of an Amateur 249
Chapter 14 Why Is Hurling So Hard? 269
Chapter 15 The Final Red Card 297
Chapter 16 The Road to Redemption 327
Chapter 17 There's More to Life Than Hurling 347

Acknowledgements 375

PROLOGUE

I LOOKED DOWN at my right thumb and inspected the damage. The knuckle had ballooned in size; it smashed on impact when I slipped on the wet court. Having retreated to the dressing room, afforded a 15-minute injury time out, the extent of the injury was clear to see. My hand had swollen up, the glove now welded on to my skin. I tried to bend it but the pain shot through my hand. My knuckle was fractured and will never move freely again, remaining locked in place to serve as a reminder of past battles. I was 15 years of age, playing in a World Handball Championship final in October 2003, and everything was falling apart.

Ken Archbold, a PE teacher in my secondary school, St Kieran's, as well as the Kilkenny team physio, Joe Malone, came out of the crowd and entered the dressing room to help the competition medical team to strap up my hand. It hurt badly, but withdrawing through injury was not an option I was willing to consider.

This may have just been a competition for teenagers, yet as you move away from childhood and get ready to enter adulthood, the importance of everything in sport starts to grow. This was something I already felt.

In the main alley at O'Loughlin Gaels GAA club in Kilkenny, I had been getting the better of Suhn Lee until now; I was 9–4 up in the opening game. But that was all about to change.

Suhn was from Chicago, and was a skilled player. There was a contrast between our styles of play. I liked to attack and be aggressive, which was consistent with the style of most Irish players. I was physically stronger and faster than Suhn, and preferred to finish points as early as possible in the rally. Suhn was more cautious and defensive, content to wait for mistakes and then pounce with the accuracy of his shots. His handball background came from a prestigious academy of USA players who trained under David Chapman, a multiple world champion and undisputed great of the sport.

Suhn's serve was also unusual and difficult to read. It had already caught out some good Irish players on his side of the draw, players who had previously caused me problems in big games. He swooped around the court and controlled every point.

I walked back out with my thumb strapped up, returned to the alley and adjusted to serving with my weaker hand. If

PROLOGUE

a ball came down the right side of the alley, I decided that I would improvise to strike with the back of my left hand and keep it in play. But against one of the best in the world, it wasn't working.

He turned it around quickly and won the opening game 21–14. He was in the driving seat in the second, ahead 19–14. Handball is a best of three contest, the first to 21 in the opening two games wins, and if it goes to a tie-breaker, it's first to 11. Right now the odds were only stacked one way.

Then there was the significance of this event. Handball may be a niche sport but this was still a world final. I was the U-14 All-Ireland title holder, the number one seed, and this championship was being played in my backyard. All week I had been off school, an understanding among teachers as to where I was and what I was doing. The majority of the crowd were there to watch me; I had the backing of that local support and could pick out familiar faces whenever I scanned the benches. My grandmother, Eileen, was in the front row. She had introduced me to the game on those days after school when she'd cart myself and my brother Paddy off to the alley in Kilfane. Jimmy Holden from Thomastown was near her. He'd taken us under his wing at a young age and had coached us ever since.

Living up to all this expectation wasn't easy. Losing the first game in handball is not ideal, but I knew not to completely panic. This had happened before. I generally settled, lifted the intensity, and countered in the second game.

But here I was, struggling with a busted hand, and my hopes of becoming a world champion were all but gone.

Everything pointed to one outcome. The crowd had had little cause for cheer since the middle of the first game, as I'd been playing second fiddle, and so the energy had been completely sapped from the venue. Suhn only needed two more points to win the match.

At 19–14 I took a moment and signalled for a 30-second time out, my last of the game. I already knew the sporting path I was heading down, where I was going to be concentrating my energies. I loved handball but it was an individual sport and a distant second to my priority. My mindset was more geared towards team sports and towards hurling in particular. Still, I reminded myself where I was and urged myself to appreciate the uniqueness of this occasion. I knew I would never play another world championship final again.

A realisation hit me: *I still have one last shot at this.*

There was a release. Any nervous tension I'd tackled beforehand was all gone.

Years later, I read about Johnny Sexton's speech at half-time of the 2011 Heineken Cup final against Northampton. Leinster had been at sea in the first half and were down 16 points at the break. But the game shifted in the second half

PROLOGUE

as they made this incredible turnaround to win by 11. Sexton had assessed things at the break and made this rousing speech. He referenced Liverpool in Istanbul in 2005 – where the Merseyside club came from 0–3 down to win the Champions League final on penalties – and drew parallels to Leinster's situation, talking of their chance to do something really special and come back into the game.

I could relate to that attitude. That day, everyone thought Suhn had the final wrapped up, but this meant that there were no expectations to weigh me down. I could go out and play with a sense of freedom. In this moment, the consequences of defeat remained the same but the incentive to win had increased dramatically. The chance to not just become the world champion, but to do so in the best manner possible: with a miraculous comeback.

I walked back in to the alley and won the next point, then another, and soon fell into a rhythm. The adrenaline started to kick back in and suddenly everything felt a little better. I started serving with my right hand again, ignoring the pain and concentrating only on the opportunity of success. I reeled off seven points in a row to win the second game 21–19.

In the tiebreaker, I took charge. The Richie Hogan who first entered the court that day – a little uncertain but hoping to realise a dream – was unrecognisable from the version who emerged in that tiebreaker with a bulging hand and an unstoppable determination to win.

The whole atmosphere in the venue had changed; the crowd sensed that the momentum in the alley had shifted.

Eleven more unanswered points sealed the deal.

I secured victory, earning that tag of world champion.

It was a hard one to make sense of. I was being beaten out the gate and then suddenly I was walking into the winners' enclosure. It was a testament to the value of willpower when you're caught in a struggle.

I always kept the memory of that day close in the years that followed. When I faced injury hardship and people thought my career was over, when we lost championship games on the biggest days of the hurling year – through all those setbacks, I remembered how it was always possible to turn things around.

That world final in 2003 showed me that the story can always be rewritten.

CHAPTER 1

THE END OF THE ROAD?

R AVELLO IS A resort town, an hour south of Naples, perched high above the Amalfi Coast in Italy. When you land there and gaze out at the Tyrrhenian Sea, it's easy to understand why tourists flock to the area in such numbers. It is a stunning place.

I was there with Anne the Friday after the 2022 All-Ireland hurling final. We had got married the previous December in Kilshane House, before placing our honeymoon trip on hold till after the championship. Anne's patience and support were always a crucial factor to my playing for Kilkenny. Three times previously, we'd had plans laid out for the wedding and on each occasion Covid-19 stepped in to act as the great disruptor.

Life outside hurling had often been interfered with by my absolute commitment of playing for Kilkenny. That was part of the bargain at that level; having to sacrifice important family occasions became common. At times, it was a delicate juggling act keeping all the various balls in the air – when we eventually got the green light to get married that Christmas, I was stuck in the books studying for my MBA at Trinity College, staying up until 2 a.m. before the wedding to get an assignment finished.

Seven months later, we had finally headed off on our honeymoon. The timing was perfect. After losing the final to Limerick, a change of scenery was needed. In the post-mortem after the game, I knew that questions would swirl around about the future of Richie Hogan, on the cusp of his thirty-fourth birthday, and with a body battered from years of competing at the top of the game.

Being abroad meant I could put my mind at ease. Anyway, I had settled on a decision. My time was over as a Kilkenny hurler. It was time to hang up the boots. Even if it wasn't a satisfactory way to finish: with a defeat to Limerick in the All-Ireland final and a miserable 12 minutes of total game time during another injury-ridden season.

How do you define a bad loser? I must come close to being classed as one. I simply detest not winning. But there was still a sense of contentment. I had emptied myself in my pursuit of success with Kilkenny. That meant something. I intended to press pause for a few days while on my honeymoon, then let the world know I was retiring.

By coincidence, my club and inter-county teammate, Paul Murphy, and his wife, Eadaoin, were holidaying in the same area of Italy. The four of us have always been close friends, myself and Paul since childhood, while Anne and Eadaoin had become friends from the years spent at Kilkenny matches. It was a brilliant trip, relaxed and enjoyable.

We pushed away talk of hurling. When myself and Paul have conversations about hurling, they generally tend to go in the same direction. Both of us are always trying to find an extra edge to what we can bring to Kilkenny or our club Danesfort. Paul's army background means he's disciplined and hard working. The ultimate team player. He's also extremely positive, willing to buy into everything he is asked to do.

I'm a far more critical thinker. If a manager walks into our dressing room and announces an ambition to win a county title, my ears will immediately perk up. The next five minutes are a deal-breaker. If the statement is backed up with reasons and a tangible plan, then I'm happy that we are going in the right direction. If it isn't, then I will treat it for what it is – bullshit talk. I've heard it all before, and this game means too much to me to just sit there and blindly trust that if someone can talk the talk, then they can walk the walk.

However, we were forced to break our pact of silence on hurling talk, to address the rumours reaching us from home.

Brian Cody was done, finishing up.

Whatever news people were selling, I wasn't buying it. I had listened to that speculation for years in the quiet downtime after a hurling championship ends.

In conversations on the street or off-season media interviews, my response was always the same. Brian will never leave, his whole life revolves around hurling and he always wants more. He will continue to go to the field until he physically cannot do it anymore. Anyone who has spent significant time around Brian would be of the same opinion.

However, that Friday in Ravello, as I sat in a café, tucking in to another serving of creamy pasta, admiring the sea views and enjoying the sun, David Herity rang.

The former Kilkenny goalkeeper and then Kildare hurling manager knew that I was on honeymoon. Still, he needed to interrupt my coastal idyll.

The news must be big.

'Yeah it's definite, Cody's gone,' he said. 'It's going to be announced tomorrow, be ready for it.'

Herity is a cynical individual; he's heard all this loose talk before as well. If he was adamant about it, then there was something going on.

David always had this incredible ability to read situations when he was in the Kilkenny camp. He regularly seemed to be clued into what management were thinking. Over the years we spent countless evenings together, up and down the M9 motorway, heading to training. David would often have the starting team figured out before the rest of us. As a goalkeeper behind one of the greatest defensive units, he spent a lot of time in training and matches looking at the performances of others and analysing them closely. But it didn't stop there with David; he also had an ability to see things through the eyes of the management.

I remember, in the lead-up to the All-Ireland final replay against Galway in 2012, he gave a group of us a 90-minute debrief in the car on the way back to Dublin after a savagely intense training session.

Most of the time myself, my brother Paddy and Richie Power would be too exhausted to speak. Our level of engagement with Herro often depended on how we'd performed in training that night. If we'd struggled, there would be a level of anger present in the car and the only thing that we craved was for the driver to keep the foot down until we hit our regular pick up spot in Dublin, at the Poitín Stil pub. If we had played well in training, we'd entertain Herro a little more.

That evening, Herro started off by letting us know that Wally Walsh was a dead cert to start against Galway. We couldn't let this one pass without comment.

'Not a chance! I can see him making the panel alright, but he would never start him.'

Wally was going well in training, for sure, and was worthy of consideration. He had thrown Jackie Tyrrell to the ground twice in an internal training match, handing him off like a rugby back row swatting aside an out-half, before firing the ball over the bar. It was clear that he wasn't going to be physically dominated.

Other things didn't add up, though. He was only brought into the training panel before the quarter-final defeat of Limerick, so he lacked that essential early season fitness base. The previous week he had been part of the Kilkenny U-21 team that were beaten comprehensively by Clare in the All-Ireland final in Thurles, and while he'd battled hard, nobody came out of Thurles that day saying Wally needed to start the Senior final replay. Added to that, Wally had never played a minute in a Kilkenny jersey at Senior level before.

'He'll definitely play, he flung Jackie over the line in front of the management team and Cody loves him,' Herro insisted.

On the Friday night before the Galway game, the team was named at a meeting. Wally was parachuted into the full-forward line, alongside myself and Richie Power.

'What did I tell you?' said Herro on the road home.

Herro likes to be right and loves to let me know when I'm wrong.

From that day on I always accepted the fact that Herro was in the know about most things hurling-related and rarely questioned him.

So when he said that Cody was leaving, I was inclined to believe him.

THE END OF THE ROAD?

The following day, that Saturday morning, we got a message to the Kilkenny 2022 WhatsApp group. In it, Brian told us that he was stepping down as manager. He said it had been a tremendous honour managing us, wished us all the best, and to let him know if there was ever anything he could do for us.

It was a seminal moment for the game of hurling, for the county of Kilkenny and for all of us as players. I was 10 years old when Brian took up the role of Kilkenny manager and along with T.J. Reid and Henry Shefflin I had been his longest serving player during his tenure. Sixteen seasons in total.

In typical fashion, Brian made no public announcement about his departure. He kept it low-key, the news relayed to the world that Saturday via a county board-drafted tribute that outlined everything he had done to shape such a successful period.

I'm not sure if any players called him personally after his announcement. It didn't seem like the thing to do. What would we even talk about on the phone? As players, our relationship with Brian had always been strictly business. I doubt words of thanks ever passed between Brian and any of his players over the previous 24 seasons. With the constant focus and drive to achieve more – from both him and the panel – there was never any time to stop, reflect and show gratitude.

Instead, we did what any group of players would do. We replied to him on WhatsApp, with our messages of congrats, thanks and thumbs up salutes.

* * *

Brian always kept his cards close to his chest; often, it was hard to read what he was thinking about you and your form.

After the 2021 championship concluded, my spirits were low.

For the first time since establishing myself as a Kilkenny player, I felt – at the age of 33 – that I was now surplus to requirements. The memory of being stuck in the stand in Croke Park, watching on against Cork as the game drifted away from us, gnawed at me. It had been the eightieth minute, the game in extra time, before I was brought on. Mossy Keoghan had entered the game as a sub at half-time only to be taken off again in the sixtieth minute. As the game went to extra time Mossy was reintroduced from the start of the first period. There couldn't have been a more decisive message than that from my perspective. I may have been togged out and ready to go, but I was at the absolute bottom of the pecking order. I was as deflated as I was baffled.

Shortly afterwards, I was sitting at home in Callan one Saturday afternoon as Kilkenny Community Radio played in the background. Former President of the GAA Nickey Brennan was giving his summation of the year for the Kilkenny team. 'I don't know if we will see Richie Hogan in a Kilkenny jersey again and he certainly doesn't owe anything to anyone. If he does decide to go, I'm happy to see him go out on his own terms, on the field of play, like the greats should.'

I sat and thought about those words. How could things appear so different from the Hogan Stand than from the players' dugout? Could I honestly say that this bit-part ending equated to going out on my own terms?

I knew in my heart that since the Leinster final I had proven my worth on the training pitch, that my fitness and form were both operating at a high pitch. Giving up was not palatable, but it appeared the only card I had left to play.

A few months passed. We reached November and the text came in. Kilkenny training was back, starting with the physical testing of all players. I threw it around in my mind. I was going to go, I decided. See what happens.

We were in the Nowlan Park gym, going through our strength testing, when Brian arrived. He generally didn't get involved in gym sessions, he let the S&C lads run the show while he had a chat with some of the selectors in the corner. There was never anything to see in these sessions that would really interest him. He knew that the real sign of strength and athleticism would show later on the pitch.

As he walked into the gym, I was standing in front of him with a set of dumbbells in my hand. He appeared almost surprised to see me, as if he had forgotten that I was still a Kilkenny hurler.

He looked around at the packed gym. Beckoned me.

'Come out here for a minute.'

We walked into the management dressing room. For a second, I wondered if he was about to tell me that I was no longer required and I could head back to Dublin for myself.

'Come here, Richie, I meant to give you a shout earlier to see what your story is for the year. Sure, what way are you feeling yourself? You obviously want to come back because you wouldn't be here, if you didn't?'

'I do, Brian, yeah. I'm here and I'm ready to go.'

'Well, look, Richie, I won't be telling you whether you can play or can't play. You're one of the greatest players to ever play for Kilkenny. Far be it for me to ever tell you what to do. So we'll just see you next week and go from there.'

After that, we discussed the year ahead and my recent struggles with injuries. But it was clear he now knew that I was hellbent on getting back. I left the room, reassured by the conversation.

From the moment I landed on the Kilkenny panel, I'd idolised Brian Cody. If he said anything good about me, it just raised me to a whole new level. Brian is a brilliant orator, so when you heard him mention your name in a complimentary fashion, it just sends a shot of positivity coursing through your veins. If he said anything bad, of course, it was crushing.

In 2011, we played Wexford in the Leinster semi-final. The previous year had been a nightmare for me due to injury and, as a result, I found myself at 22 years old without having really caught fire in the way that everyone expected me to. But that day down in Wexford Park, I exploded into life. Every single time I got the ball, I was causing carnage. Like when Michael Fennelly blindly struck a cross-field ball into the full-forward line. I broke it down and reacted first to pick it up just as Wexford defender Malachy Travers lined me up for a thumping shoulder. I never saw the tackle coming but I bounced off him anyway and continued to bear down on goal before striking the ball into the top corner.

At half-time, Brian was wound up. We were well on top, but he was determined that we kept our foot on the throat of Wexford. There would be no relenting.

Then he turned and roared, 'Where the fuck is Richie Hogan?'

I was at the other side of the dressing room, caught off guard at being mentioned. All eyes turned to me.

'Richie Hogan, that's how you fucking play hurling. Look at him. Look at what he's doing out there!'

I felt myself almost levitating. My confidence went through the roof; those words of praise made me feel bulletproof. There was a release of pressure from then on that year. I felt certain that I was going to play brilliant hurling, and we were going to win everything.

I often wondered if Brian always appreciated the power that he had to boost the team with positivity. What he was fully aware of was that he had complete control over everybody in that dressing room, the ability to influence their emotions.

In 2009, we played Waterford in the All-Ireland semi-final. It wound up a close game; they tore into us after we'd crushed them in the final the year before.

I came on as a blood sub early in the second half, was only on the field for around 90 seconds but got stuck in straight away, making a couple of tackles and winning the ball back. When I came off, Brian came running over with an order. 'Stay warm. You're going back on.' He was a big believer in body language. It often happened with Brian, if you made an impression as a blood sub, it'd change his thinking. I might have been second or third on his list to come on before that, but he would rip that up, order: 'Get this lad on straight away.' He'd seen that you were in the zone. No time to waste and you're shoved back on.

I was straight into the game again and I thrived. Brick Walsh was operating as a makeshift sweeper for Waterford. He would rise in the centre for puckouts, and I would drift from behind and tap the ball down to collect. On the first occasion, I grabbed a point; on the second, I raced clear and soloed down the middle channel. Typically I would just tap it over the bar, but I spied T.J. Reid alone on my left.

Let's work a goal, I thought.

I drew the man, hit a long handpass to T.J. He caught it, but then slipped and the Waterford backs rushed in to clear.

THE END OF THE ROAD?

After the game as we came off the pitch, content with victory, Brian approached me. 'You know, that pass to T.J. shows that you weren't interested in getting a handy score for yourself. You saw there was a goal on. You did the right thing for the team.'

Right then, I was certain that he wouldn't leave me off the team for the All-Ireland final because I'd played so well during that cameo. It was unusual for Brian to dole out praise one-on-one like that, but those little messages were real confidence boosters, just like it was any time Brian said anything good about you.

It was certainly preferable to having him say or think anything bad about you.

CHAPTER 2

WHERE ARE YOU FROM?

At the back of my grandparents' house in the village of Bennettsbridge, tucked in off the road, just a short walk from the River Nore, is a small yard about 20 metres wide. I turned that patch of concrete into my hurling arena. My Croke Park, a place where I hurled for hours upon hours, practising the game, loving the game, becoming obsessed by the game.

I would get home from school by 3.10 p.m., fire the bag of books into the corner of the kitchen, and would then be straight out the back door. I came alive there, staying out for hours pucking a ball. Often my brother Paddy was with me but if he wasn't it wouldn't deter my enthusiasm. All I needed was a hurl, a ball and a wall. There was no conversation, no laughter – just the constant thud of the ball being hit.

They have an old corporation bungalow with a large back garden. The garage has a door on either side and the wall in between is marked with a white line. It was perfect target practice. Hit the line from 10 yards, 15, 20. Strike, repeat, strike, repeat. I never got tired of it.

Across the yard was the oil tanker for heating the house. When I was nine, they changed it from the classic steel structure to a new plastic container, shaped like a figure of eight with two holes in it. I watched the workmen put it in one day and my mind lit up at the hurling possibilities. I began firing balls off left and right, aiming for the holes in the tanker.

That kept me occupied for hours.

The back of the container led on to the neighbours' house. Mrs Kealy lived there: a lovely, kind old woman. During the summer days when school was out, Paddy, my cousin Denise and I would knock on her door and call in for a chat, knowing that we would each get a Penguin bar in exchange for our company. The odd stray sliotar would fly past a gap between the wall and partitioning leylandiis, travelling directly across her back yard. We would close our eyes in fear, hoping not to hear a yelp from the other side. Later, her daughter came back from England, moved into the house and built an extension out the back, meaning their external bedroom wall was now directly lined up behind the oil tank.

Soon hurling started to be squeezed in before school, often on freezing and wet mornings, although I felt immune to the cold and the rain. Saying that, if you're asleep, that thud, thud, thud of the ball against the wall would quickly wake you up. So it wasn't long before my grandmother got a polite suggestion. Maybe Richie could bang the ball off another wall?

So I started at the other side of yard, going for hours and hours.

The simple joy of striking a ball against a wall never left me. I loved getting into the rhythm of it, repeating that motion, getting my eye in.

When I went to college in St Pat's in Dublin, I lived for two years at Number 20 Home Farm Road, with seven other lads wedged into the terrace house. It was a big sporting environment. Cha Fitz and I were on the Kilkenny Senior team. Niall Tennyson and Shane Campion were classmates of mine from St Kieran's, both of whom went on to win All-Irelands and county titles at various levels over the years. A Clare man, Pa Minogue, played with Tulla, while Declan McKiernan and James Carroll were county U-21 footballers with Cavan and Donegal at the time. Another housemate – Cavan man, David Galligan – was one of the top boxers in St Saviour's Boxing Club in Dublin city.

Every college house is wild, but the crowd of lads packed into ours heightened that. Wherever I could find a small bit of space, though, I'd puck a ball against the wall. I had a spot in the kitchen and another in my bedroom where I could be striking into the early hours of the morning. Everyone gave out about the noise, especially the old lady who lived next door. She couldn't understand what the constant banging was, particularly so late into the night.

Our landlord was a great character, Brian Brady from Cavan, but his patience was tested. He rang his friend, Eddie Nolan – a Conahy man who was heavily involved in the Kilkenny Supporters Club – to vent his frustration. 'Listen, Eddie, I have a house down in Drumcondra. There's a gang of Kilkenny lads in it and they're banging the ball off the wall at all hours of the morning and the neighbours are giving out like mad. Will you go down there please and have a word with them?'

Eddie's intervention didn't work; I kept pucking the ball off the wall at any opportunity.

When I finished college in 2009, I started my first job as a teacher in Belgrove Boys' School in Clontarf. I'd give the kids some Maths or English work to do, then put that 15 minutes to good use, walking around the classroom with a hurl in hand and hopping a tennis ball off the wall, picking spots between the kids' artwork. The big thick walls of the 100-year-old school building were perfect to slam a shot off. The very odd time a ball would go astray and some poor young lad would get it on the forehead, but the kids lapped it all up, telling their parents: 'Mr Hogan plays for Kilkenny and he practises his hurling all the time in the classroom.'

I knew I shouldn't have been doing it in school, but I just couldn't help myself. I was obsessed; any chance I got to hit a ball, I took it. Teaching was how I made money at the time, but hurling was the reason I got up in the morning, and I never wanted to waste a second.

It never really left me – that constant need to practise. I found it therapeutic, saw it as time to think and settle my mind, just swinging the hurl away and connecting with the ball.

It's one of the things that I miss most now; a price I pay for all the wear and tear, all those back injuries that accumulated over the years. I just can't do it to the extent that I used to; my back can no longer stand up to the rotation involved in repeated striking.

It was such a simple thing in my hurling life.

And I miss it.

* * *

'Where are you from, Richie?'

Good question. When I was young, I had to pause before answering. Kilkenny was hardwired into my DNA, so there was no questioning my county allegiances. Drill deeper into my locality, though, and it got trickier.

Identity is a complex thing.

Danesfort GAA club is a few miles off the Dublin–Waterford motorway, stuck on the N10 road that takes you into Kilkenny city. The club is on a crossroads opposite The Harvester Bar. The road past The Harvester leads down to Bennettsbridge. It's two and a half miles long; when you drop down the small hill and cross the bridge, you're into Bennettsbridge village. The water under that bridge is the River Nore, which splits the parishes of Danesfort and Bennettsbridge. I woke up every morning and went to sleep every night in our house in Danesfort, but so many of my waking hours in between were spent in Bennettsbridge.

My mother, Liz, is from Bennettsbridge. My parents were young when Paddy and I were born, as were my grandparents, Mick and Eileen McCarthy. The McCarthy family are steeped in hurling. My grandfather won six county championships with the great Bennettsbridge team of the 1960s. His career with the 'Bridge ended in his early thirties when he lost his eye in a county championship game. My uncle, Richie, maintained the family club tradition, earning a place on underage Kilkenny teams and during his time winning Minor and U-21 All-Ireland medals in the 1980s. His cousins, D.J. Carey and James McGarry, are two of Kilkenny's greatest ever players.

So my mother and father pitched up in Danesfort, in between Bennettsbridge and my father's home town of Callan, after they married at 21 and got their hands on a site.

Paddy was born in May 1987; I arrived the following year, in August 1988. The two girls came later: Rachel in 1994 and Niamh in 2002.

WHERE ARE YOU FROM?

Myself and Paddy, our lives were intertwined from the start. Every morning we made the short walk down the hill to my grandmother's house in Bennettsbridge village, before Mam would get a lift into Kilkenny to the vegetable shop where she worked. Our cousin, Denise, slipped into the same routine, also getting dropped off at our grandparents' house. That house became the centre of our universe, the three of us growing up together along with the other children on that street.

There was a wild streak to myself and Paddy as young lads. Fifteen months apart in age, that sibling rivalry always simmered and regularly boiled over. In that little bungalow and out into the backyard, we would tear around like a whirlwind, causing chaos. Racing after each other, climbing trees, jumping off barrels, pushing, shoving, fighting. We were locked into a constant battle.

Paddy was bigger and stronger than me but that didn't mean that he didn't come off second best from time to time. When it did happen, it tended to be dramatic. One morning Paddy and I were drawing on pieces of paper when a scrap broke out in the room. I sensed what was coming and bolted for safety, running through the hallway, pencil still in hand. As Paddy was tearing after me, he tackled me to the ground. We fell and I accidentally stabbed him in the eye with the pencil, causing him to be shipped off to Waterford University Hospital to have the pencil dislodged and the damage repaired.

WHATEVER IT TAKES

Another time the pair of us were in the back of a trailer, with my father driving the car, when Paddy turfed me out onto the road. Head split open as a five-year-old while the six-year-old brother protested his innocence.

The messing around continued, and our activities often flirted with the blurred lines between harmless and dangerous. One summer's day while out in my grandparents' garden we were playing around with Denise and my other cousin Emer when a shower of rain made us retreat to an open shed in the garden. Paddy soon got bored and decided he was going to climb to the roof by jumping to catch one of the supporting rafters. He grabbed on and was unable to let go as a rusty nail on the other side of the rafter shot through his hand, up through his middle finger. As he was hanging there I decided to try and pull him down, causing the nail to shoot further in, ripping his hand apart. After a few screams and kicks from Paddy, Emer ran in to the house to alert my grandmother. He hung there for a while until my uncle Richie, a carpenter, came to cut him down. He was carted off to A&E where the block of wood and nail were detached from his hand.

Those scrapes tested the patience of our parents. They'd end up separating us a lot. Dad would take Paddy off with him to matches, while Mam would keep me at home. In time, we wised up and settled down. Once we could control ourselves, we both got taken everywhere.

WHERE ARE YOU FROM?

Myself and Paddy were thrown head first into handball without ever having expressed any real interest in taking up the sport. It was a move borne out of necessity on our grandmother's part. If you had your grandsons causing carnage in your house every day, a frenzy of post-school activity, you would get creative too in thinking of ways to get them to expend energy. So she came up with this plan when I was eight and Paddy was nine. Even at that stage we were known as 'the hurling kids', but she added another string to our sporting bows.

We'd be loaded into her car and she'd set off from Bennettsbridge, taking us the 15-minute drive out the road to the handball alley in Kilfane. It was in the middle of the countryside, on the side of a quiet road. The two of us were let loose, playing for hours while our grandmother would watch from the upstairs viewing gallery. Afterwards, once we were wrecked tired after racing around the alley, she'd bring us home.

Paddy was my brother but also my rival. We both dominated our own age groups in Kilkenny competitions so to have one another to compete against gave us the ultimate edge. He was the ideal test against which I could measure myself because he generally won. After all, that extra 15 months in age gave him an edge in size and smarts. As I got older, faster and more skilful, so too did he, meaning that he always stayed that little step ahead. Even though I wasn't looking for it, this was the perfect lesson in continuous improvement for me. I was constantly chasing him as he was getting better. Winning competitions was a welcome by-product.

Winter or summer, we were down at that alley. Anything to get us out of the house where we felt enclosed; all we wanted was to be taken off to somewhere we could roam free.

When we were stuck inside, say on a rainy day, my grandfather, Mick McCarthy, kept me entertained with stories about hurling. It was his primary conversation starter and he had a deep love for Kilkenny hurling in particular. He worked in the railway station, often starting a shift at 4 a.m. and finishing at midday. When he'd get home, he'd rest for an hour on the couch, grab his dinner and tip away then for the day.

There was a little tan leather couch in the bungalow; he'd sit with his back to one side and have the two legs up across it. I was able to squeeze in the other end and I would spend hours there asking him questions about hurling. I never got bored, hanging on his every word, listening to stories of the great Bennettsbridge players of the past– Seamus Cleere, Noel Skehan, the Treacy brothers. He'd often recall games where he watched Christy Ring and Eddie Keher and other legendary forwards play. He was fuelling my hurling imagination every day.

When he did run out of stories, we'd turn to the VCR. RTÉ used to bring out these end of year championship

WHERE ARE YOU FROM?

highlight videos and there was a pile of them stacked up in the living room, covering games from the late '80s and early '90s. I watched them on repeat, studying the main Kilkenny forwards – D.J. Carey, Adrian Ronan and Eamonn Morrissey. The Kilkenny team of the early '90s had a particular influence on me. I would look at the way they moved, the way they struck the ball and their technique in winning possession.

The obsession was growing all the time.

* * *

That was my mother's side. As for my father, Callan has never left Sean Hogan. It is his birthplace and he became a John Lockes GAA diehard early on. The club got a hold of him as a child and never let go. Because Dad was in his early twenties when Paddy and I arrived we got to see him play right throughout our youth, up until my early teenage years. He captained them to win the Junior championship in Kilkenny in 1987, did the same at Intermediate level in 1993, then won another Intermediate title in 1999. His passion for his club never showed any sign of burning out.

Dad went working when he was 17 with Brett Brothers, an animal feeds supplier based in Callan. He started as a lorry driver, trekking around the south-east to farms delivering feed. He could strike up a conversation with anyone, honing in on farming and hurling, the twin currencies in the areas that had the most value. His likeability sparked connections instantly; I have spent years meeting elderly farmers, who tell me tales of his deliveries and chats in their yards. Over five decades later, he is still at the company, having jumped out of the truck and on to directing operations as the manager of the yard.

Through Dad, Callan had a magnetic pull on us as kids. His father, Patsy, won a Minor All-Ireland as a 16-year-old and then headed off to see the world, working with the Merchant Navy. When he came home, he married my grandmother Bea and took over her family's pub in Callan – The Steppes Bar.

Dad grew up there. Paddy was actually born into Callan as well, living there for a year while our house was being built over the road in Danesfort.

Having that Callan dynamic at play added to the identity crisis that myself and Paddy experienced. As Sean Hogan's sons, the Callan people viewed us as two of their own. When we went to see him hurl for John Lockes, we wore the club's blue and gold jerseys in proud support. Dad was an excellent club hurler. Solid as a rock, dependable when given jobs all around defence. His commitment was unwavering; he'd spend long days in the cab of his truck, but would always find a way to park up at the pitch in Callan in the evening, leap out with his gear bag and go training.

People in Callan would say he was unlucky not to get a call-up to the Kilkenny Senior panel. It was a different time, opportunities were scarce, panels were tighter. You didn't have a whole season on a squad to impress a manager. Getting that call was hard.

He was and still is completely obsessed with the game. When he finally hung up his boots, he fell in and did every job going in John Lockes – manager, selector, chairman and treasurer. He even took our club U-16 side in Danesfort when we won the county title. Of the 4–12 the team scored in that final, Paddy hit five points from centre-back and I bagged 4–6 from centre-forward. A few weeks later, we added the Kilkenny Minor Division 3 title to the list, Paddy and I scoring 4–12 between us in that game.

Hurling is his pastime: watching games on TV, listening to them on the radio, or going to them in person. John Lockes games always got the first preference vote when it came to watching one, even if myself and Paddy were playing club for Danesfort the same day.

Growing up, I watched him and learned traits. He was always calm, figured out how to solve problems. And his work ethic was off the charts. We struggle as a family to comprehend how he does it, what energy source fuels him. Always busy and never tired.

* * *

Bennettsbridge was where it was at for us in those early years. Danesfort never crossed our radar. We had no family there, no friends, no connection. It is a large, sprawling parish, with kids around the edges drifting to different schools – Stoneyford, Bennettsbridge, Callan, or into town in Kilkenny. It lacked a central hub like Bennettsbridge village.

Our paths only crossed with Danesfort when we'd thrash them in school matches.

We hurled with Bennettsbridge until we finished primary school. As a 12-year-old, I was togging out for the U-16s. Our local club stalwart was Christy Hayes. He ran everything at underage level during that time with little help. He took every team that I was involved in, organising training sessions and ferrying us to matches. We would have a handful of sliotars and a set of jerseys that would need to be used by all teams from Minor level and below.

Then the whispers started, soon confirmed. The Kilkenny County Board were reinforcing the parish rule. This rule meant that you had to play for either the club in the parish where you were living or the parish where you were born. For me and Paddy, that meant Danesfort. We were the two brightest young hurling talents in the county so the pressure on us to move was greater than on others in the same situation.

We were faced with an ultimatum: play for Danesfort or give up hurling. There was loose talk doing the rounds that if we kept going with Bennettsbridge we would be slapped with suspensions and the club would be barred from entering competitions. That James McGarry, Bennettsbridge's most famous hurling son at the time, might even be stopped from playing in goal for Kilkenny in the 2000 All-Ireland final.

Was it scaremongering or was there substance to it? Even at this remove I don't know, but it caused a world of stress for a 12-year-old. Paddy seemed more relaxed, carrying it in his stride. But it weighed down on me.

I had just started secondary school in St Kieran's, Paddy was a year ahead. We'd get the bus from Bennettsbridge into town with our friends. Was it an act of betrayal to them if we were to leave and go hurling for another crowd up the road? It sure felt like it.

Martin Walsh, Tommy's younger brother, was in my class in first year and we hung around together at lunch. He knew the dilemma we were facing and drew parallels one day with a scenario they had when living on the border of Tullaroan and Ballycallan. 'Oh sure, we sorted all that out when we wrote to the bishop and got him to move the parish boundaries. We could hurl away then with Tullaroan after getting the special dispensation.'

My ears pricked up. I pressed Martin for more information. He won me over.

So I sat down at home one evening, took out pen and paper, and wrote to Bishop Forristal. My predicament was clearly explained: I needed to stay hurling with

Bennettsbridge; he had the power, so could he please redraw the parish boundary on the map. Basically, I wanted him to just nudge my house inside the border.

I folded up the letter, stole a stamp out of my mother's handbag and stuck it on the top corner of the envelope.

There was only one problem.

I had no idea where the bishop lived.

Initially I scribbled down 'Bishop of Kilkenny' and then realised that the diocese was Ossory. Eventually, I settled on: 'The Bishop, Ossory House, Kilkenny'.

The letter stayed in my school bag for a few weeks as I worked up the courage to actually send it. Writing to the bishop was a big deal, after all. Coming home from school one day, I finally decided to just fire it into a letter box.

A few weeks later, post arrived at home. A letter was addressed to me, but my mother spotted the bishop's insignia on the envelope straight away.

She ripped it open.

The bishop's reply was polite: he wished me well in my hurling career, but was afraid to inform me that shifting the parish boundaries was not within his remit. However, he did inform me that the only person with that level of authority was the Pope.

That sparked another idea. As a Professor in Ecumenics, my Aunt Linda had met the Pope a few times. Could she help sort it?

WHERE ARE YOU FROM?

Back out with the pen and paper again, time to write another letter: *Dear Pope John Paul II, My name is Richie Hogan ...*

I never got as far as giving the letter to her.

My mother was absolutely mortified at my actions. Paddy just laughed at me, branding me a complete idiot.

Bishop Forristal had a story for life to regale people with. He kept the letter and the further I progressed in hurling with Kilkenny, the more people he told and the more it spread. The story came full circle back to me on the stage of the Kilkenny All-Ireland medals presentation in 2011 when Mícheál Ó Muircheartaigh recited it to the crowd in Langton's Hotel and at a few other functions since. 'And so, the case of Richie Hogan made it all the way to the Vatican' he'd say in his poetic voice.

Martin Walsh had sold me on an idea that was a pipedream. I'm not sure the Walshes were ever in contact with the bishop, but I certainly had been.

During all this, several delegations from the Danesfort club visited our house making the case for a switch. They never pressured us or demanded anything. They knew this was wrecking our heads and just gave us a core message: 'Look, we'd love if ye came up and hurled with us; we'll help ye in any way we can.'

In the end, we put our hands up and accepted defeat. No cards – or letters – left to play on the table. The love of playing hurling won out and we moved to the Danesfort club.

I knew very few from Danesfort. Robbie Walsh was in my class in St Kieran's and I played soccer for Fort Rangers with Michael Cunningham. The Bennettsbridge soccer club, East End, didn't have a team in my age group, so I went to Danesfort to play. If those links hadn't been forged, I think I would have waited it out, hung tight and said nothing. Robbie and Michael were groomsmen at my wedding 20 years later and without both of them I'm not sure I would have lasted playing with Danesfort in those early years.

Other lads who were instructed to leave their clubs stayed put and threats didn't materialise into action. The key was their family backgrounds. My best friend in Bennettsbridge primary school was Nicky Cleere, a brilliant forward with whom I won an All-Ireland U-21 medal; his father was Bennettsbridge to the core. Whereas our father was from Callan, so those emotional ties didn't exist in the same way. Mam was from Bennettsbridge but in reality she didn't mind what team we played with as long as we were enjoying it.

As it transpired, myself and Paddy were actually the only two to move. Our first game was an U-14 match against Windgap in South Kilkenny. They put Paddy in centre-back, where he lorded it, and stuck me up centre-forward, where I scored 5–09.

They had hit the jackpot. These were not two random young fellas; we helped transform their hurling fortunes.

WHERE ARE YOU FROM?

* * *

It remained a source of conflict for a few years. I constantly wrestled with the answer to that question: 'Where are you from, Richie?' The sense I had betrayed some people lingered in my mind. My friends in school would slag me about the move, while the odd person from Bennettsbridge would remark about it in later years with a bit more meaning. Those Hogan boys should be hurling with Bennettsbridge, they'd say.

About five years after we switched, Bennettsbridge made a push to get us back. A delegation from the club landed at our front door. Paddy and I both had a few successful years behind us as Kilkenny Minors at this stage and our hurling futures were full of promise. The proposition was pretty significant. Some local businessmen had negotiated a deal from a property developer to purchase a house on our behalf. We would live there, have a proper address in the parish, and move seamlessly back. When we were old enough and working, the mortgage would be transferred over to us. This was peak Celtic Tiger time.

We heard them out but it was never even considered. Whatever about being forced to move as a 12-year-old, voluntarily transferring clubs on the cusp of adulthood was a complete non-runner. The decision had been made. This was the path we were on and all we wanted to do now was play hurling.

It was a confusing time. Where did we belong? Were we outsiders? Or were we floating in a hurling no-man's land? As time went on, we adjusted. Being good hurlers was a huge advantage. When you are 12 years old and score 5–09 in your first game acceptance comes quickly and, with that, pride in your achievements.

To further complicate things, when I was 19, my parents moved from our family home and built a house in Callan. The move felt inevitable in a way. The Hogans have always been immersed in life in Callan for generations. My granduncles used to live on Green Street; they ran shops and we owned two pubs. The town is the family's lifeblood.

Niamh was only five at the time, so she would later identify as a Callan native and now plays camogie for John Lockes. Meanwhile, Rachel played for Danesfort, as well as a few years with Kilkenny underage teams. Myself and Paddy were in college in Dublin by then, so the move did not disrupt our lives to any great degree. We regarded ourselves as Danesfort people by now, and our affiliation to Bennettsbridge had faded.

It's all a curious mix. One that doesn't follow the well-worn path of GAA families embedded in one parish where you can trace back generations.

Often, I wanted a family history like that and envied those that had it.

WHERE ARE YOU FROM?

But our situation was different.

As it happened, the girl who would later become my wife was a Danesfort native too, though we wouldn't meet until 2011. Anne and I spent most of our lives living on the same road, our family homes only a mile apart. Anne's brothers Peter and Tommy played with Danesfort and I got to know them both well, but I had no idea that they had a younger sister. She is three years younger than me and because of my Bennettsbridge background, we never came across each other until she came to Dublin to go to college. We finally met on a night out in Coppers where our home connection led to easy conversation, and before I knew it I was making the journey across to the southside to meet her on a regular basis. We got on really well as we both had an interest in sport. Anne played basketball with UCD and camogie with my sister Rachel at home in Danesfort, so my hurling commitments were never questioned.

I would always keep one eye on Bennettsbridge's results. When we won the county Junior championship in 2006, Danesfort and Bennettsbridge played each other in the Northern final. Bennettsbridge were a fading team at the time and we were on an upward trajectory. The aggression levels went up a notch in how we were treated on the pitch. There were plenty of verbals thrown our way but nothing nasty or personal. If there was any hatred there it was only at the fact that we were wearing the wrong club colours.

Myself and Paddy never talked about it much, but the presence of a brother there alongside me meant there was no sense of isolation during those first steps towards playing with Danesfort. Paddy is completely immersed in the club now. He built his house in the parish, carefully choosing the site to ensure his son Páidí would not face a repeat scenario down the line.

When the dust settled after a few years, any trace of doubt in my mind had been removed. I am one hundred per cent a Danesfort man now. I love the place and never regret the time spent coming home from Dublin to hurl for them.

We made the move, things clicked and we fitted in straight away.

We never looked back.

CHAPTER 3

ST KIERAN'S

Before the 2003 All-Ireland Senior Colleges Hurling final, the St Kieran's team bus pulled over to the side of the road outside Clonmel. We were about 10 minutes away from the town, when a video tape was pushed into the recorder underneath a TV at the top of the bus and the 'inch by inch' speech from *Any Given Sunday* flashed onto the screen. The whole bus went silent, eyes glued to Al Pacino addressing his Miami Sharks team.

Ten days before the game, the teachers in charge, Tom Hogan and John Quane, approached me. They were worried about the forwards and wanted another option. As a result, I had been parachuted into the St Kieran's Senior squad. I was 14 years old, a couple of months out from my Junior Cert, but age was no barrier and so I was added to the subs.

It was my first taste of Senior hurling, and while listening to a motivational speech from some American actor on TV, I could see everyone getting fired up around me. The whole thing blew my mind. That's how important this match was, I realised. It turned out that, for the older players, revenge was on their minds. They had lost the final the previous year to St Colman's of Fermoy by a point, so this rematch was a chance to get equal. The Fermoy school had some brilliant players – Andrew O'Shaughnessy and Pat Kirby, for example, had already played Senior league that year with Limerick.

The Clonmel Sportsfield was packed that day. It was one of the unique things about those colleges games: how you'd stand in a club pitch jammed with people, students from both sides singing and chanting, creating a claustrophobic atmosphere.

We destroyed them. Nine clear by half-time, we won by 11 points in the end. It was a recurring theme in the history of St Kieran's: they'd meet Munster teams with big reputations in the All-Ireland series, and usually find a way to win.

I wasn't needed that day but watched and listened and took it all in.

The aura about St Kieran's was easy to detect; wearing that black and white jersey made you feel powerful.

I wanted to develop as a hurler and I knew I was in the right place to do just that.

ST KIERAN'S

✷ ✷ ✷

Everything seemed to go up a notch in St Kieran's: the level of coaching, the way the sport was treated by all the staff, the hours the teachers would put into the preparation and the standard that was expected from players. Up until this point I had never been coached on how to play the game in any significant way. I had come from a rural primary school where numbers were small, and abilities were very mixed. Now I had arrived in an environment where training sessions were not just opportunities to puck around with your friends: they had a purpose, and high standards were expected.

We had some great people over our teams.

The mix of personalities was interesting. Adrian Finan was a big motivating influence. He emptied himself on the sideline during training and matches; afterwards, he'd be drained from the amount of energy he'd poured into it. Tom Hogan was calmer; he'd engage with players on an individual basis and was very shrewd in the things he'd spot.

John Quane was a neighbour across the road at home in Danesfort and would regularly bring myself and Paddy home after school training. He was fascinated by other sports, often trying to import techniques from athletics and basketball into our hurling play. Some of it did not land, but often he discovered gems. His different take on things was a real strength.

Nicky Cashin had been the Kilkenny Minor manager, but didn't oversee any of the hurling teams in the school during my time. He had been coaching for years and had just passed the baton on to others by the time I enrolled. He taught me History and Geography, and for all his vast experience and knowledge on hurling, we never really discussed the sport in the classroom.

Pat Murphy was different. A Carlow man, from St Mullins, he was utterly obsessed with hurling. His passion for the sport amazed me because in my young and uneducated mind I thought that no one in Carlow played hurling. He would gladly put the books away and talk hurling all day in school if he could. Pat was a brilliant storyteller, recalling games and players from the past, bringing that passion into the underage teams of which he took charge.

So even during classes, hurling never strayed far from my thoughts. On the week of a game, a coach would regularly pull me out to sit in the hall for a 10-minute chat, outlining my role or the plan for the team. It might have only been an U-15 schools game in the middle of winter, but nothing was downplayed. And there was never any issue with being taken from the classroom to talk hurling either.

That was the St Kieran's philosophy.

* * *

ST KIERAN'S

I was a good hurler as a child in primary school in Bennettsbridge. But I was a big fish in a small pond – when I moved on to secondary school, and particularly into St Kieran's, I was swimming in deeper waters. After all, the vast majority of good hurlers in Kilkenny went to St Kieran's. A few would go to Kilkenny CBS, or if you were down in the south of the county, you could be drawn over the border to Good Counsel in New Ross. However, most aimed for St Kieran's, and when Paddy did the entrance exam and got into Kieran's, it was nailed down then that that's where I was headed.

Being exposed to good hurlers and a place where the game was taken so seriously accelerated my progress. From that first year alone, when I walked into the school corridors, I could feel myself improve, rising to meet the standards expected. It helped to be surrounded by lads as passionate and as driven about the game as I was. Everyone had a crystal-clear objective: work hard, get better as a hurler and play for Kilkenny.

As first years, we would bring our hurls into school with us every day. There was a small pitch near the front of the school where we would meet at lunch, up to 100 lads. There was one sliotar, maybe two, and no helmets. The ball was lobbed from one end of the pitch to the other, the object being to be the one who caught it.

When it fell from the sky, there was a scene of complete mayhem. A big gang of lads were under the dropping ball, a few focused on getting the hand up to grasp it, while most in there were just trying to make sure nobody else caught it cleanly. There were hurls flying everywhere, lads flinging themselves at each other. Most days, as the school bell rang, it was like a post-war scene, everyone covered in mud, uniforms torn, four or five lads split open, heading into the secretary's office to get patched up and stop the bleeding. To survive, you hardened up and steeled yourself for the contest.

James Dowling was a friend of mine from Muckalee who hurled with St Martin's. He'd later captain our Kilkenny team that won the U-21 All-Ireland in 2008. He was a small fella starting out in St Kieran's but a lack of size didn't deter him from getting involved in this chaos. One day I saw him lurking at the back of this mosh pit of about fifty lads. The ball fell and he made this leap in from behind, on top of everyone, swinging with his left hand to clear hurls out of his way, and catching with his right as everyone else missed it.

My jaw was on the floor. How had he done that? He wasn't tall but he'd risen above everyone to catch it. I had often worried that my height would catch me out when it came to fielding in hurling. Watching James was a lightbulb moment. I started to copy him. Hang out at the back of crowds, time your run in from behind, stay clear until the ball is there. Then grab it and you're away. It's the technique I have used ever since.

ST KIERAN'S

The competition was intense. The sheer volume of talented players in each year meant they had to hold trials for panels and then try to cut that down to a starting fifteen. The team lists would go up on the walls of the school before matches, everyone rushing in to get a look to see who was in and who was out.

I fell in with a great group of like-minded lads, all obsessed with hurling, straight away. I would go on to play on the Kilkenny senior team for years with some of them, like T.J. Reid and 2014 captain Lester Ryan. Others in our group were Robbie Walsh, Nicky Cleere, Martin Walsh, Niall Tennyson and James Dowling, who formed the backbone of our All-Ireland U-21-winning side in 2008. We were all mad into hurling and, in this environment, it felt like the most important thing in the world.

With Danesfort, I hurled in the forwards, focused and consumed by putting as many scores as I could on the board. That's where they first pitched me in the team in St Kieran's, and I was centre-forward when we won a Leinster Juvenile Championship.

But Adrian Finan had a different theory. When he surveyed my range of hurling abilities, he regarded midfield as my best position and didn't want to consider me anywhere else.

Different people would challenge him on it. 'This fella is scoring points and goals for fun, but you want to play him around the middle?'

Adrian's logic was simple. At midfield, I could exert better control on the game and knit things together for the team, he argued. The scores would still flow. It was an early taste of life in the middle of the field.

You'd never challenge your teacher on selections, of course; you just took the jersey you were given.

And I relished the challenges.

We trained hard. We ran in the park in Kilkenny Castle three days a week at lunchtime. Every Monday, Wednesday and Friday, it was the same routine. The bell would ring at one o'clock, we'd go down to the pavilion, tog off and then run down to the park. It might be a couple of laps down there and run back after, so you've pumped a few miles into the legs to build up aerobic capacity. Other times, the focus was on tempo running, moving up through the gears. Plyometrics, shuttle runs, ladder drills, sprint work – all of these were factored in to our training.

That block of work provided us all with a serious athletic foundation. We may not have been aware of it then, but over the years the importance of it became clear.

* * *

When you're a child in Kilkenny, the sight of the Liam MacCarthy Cup being brought into your school fires your imagination. If you're already hooked on hurling, getting to meet the biggest stars in your county while having them show you the biggest trophy in the game is like Christmas morning. I desperately wanted to experience that.

I started secondary school in September 2000, the same week Kilkenny won the All-Ireland against Offaly. After a seven-year wait, it was a big deal in the county. My sister Rachel was six at the time and there's a photo at home of her holding the cup that year in Bennettsbridge school with James McGarry and D.J. Carey. I was wild with envy. It sounds a little pathetic, I know, but in my mind she had experienced something I had been deprived of.

In St Kieran's, when I did finally get to see the cup, the reaction was different. You're in that awkward phase of your teenage years where you don't want to display emotion about anything and make a big deal over something. It's also not as intimate a setting. Hundreds of lads troop out the front of the school. There were so many people present and so many past pupils involved that it felt diluted as an occasion. It just didn't feel as thrilling to see the cup then as I imagine it would have felt in primary school.

Besides, everywhere you looked in St Kieran's, there was hurling royalty. When I started out, the Leaving Cert class included Tommy Walsh and Jackie Tyrrell. Brian Carroll from Offaly was there, and Eoin Kelly from Tipperary had just finished up, but was still spoken of with reverence.

In time, you could see other stars emerge, like Cha Fitzpatrick and Richie Power. Hurlers you knew were on the fast lane to Kilkenny Senior careers. When we were starting out in our Junior Cert year, Kilkenny won the Minor All-Ireland in 2002, crushing Tipperary in the final. Cha and Richie were the top scorers; in fact, the team was backboned by Kieran's lads. They were walking around the same school corridors as us, only now elevated to idols who had shone in Croke Park.

Then there were those who had walked the corridors in the past. In our younger years in St Kieran's, the teachers would feed us stories of the exploits of past students. It was all designed to inspire us to reach those heights. The teachers were creating and adding to the narrative, one that fed into the whole aura that surrounded the school.

Match days for the school Senior team – like that day in Clonmel – were massive events. All the students boarded buses to go watch. In the spring of 2003, there was an All-Ireland semi-final down in Boherlahan in Tipperary against Gort from Galway. Paddy was on the panel and I headed down to watch it.

At every game, the Kieran's supporters would colonise one side of the ground. Plant the flag and mark their territory. The chants would soon start, like a group of soccer ultras on a terrace whipping up an atmosphere. By the time of throw-in, the place would be rocking.

I was walking over to join them that day when I heard a ripple of excitement in the crowd. I looked up and Henry Shefflin was walking past. He was Hurler of the Year at the time. Just one thought crossed my mind: *how big a game must this be if someone as famous as Henry has travelled down to watch it?*

2003 was the first time I sampled an All-Ireland schools final experience, but by 2004 I was properly immersed in it, going from bystander to being centrally involved.

We reached the final that year against St Raphael's from Loughrea. The game was getting the live television treatment on TG4, a rare occurrence at the time. We thrived in the spotlight, winning by 20 points. Paddy was in goal and I was corner-forward. I played one of my best games for Kieran's that day, hitting five points from play.

It was a brilliant feeling to be at the heart of it. I was only in fourth year and was determined to push on, although that would turn out to represent the peak of schools hurling for me. We lost the final in 2005. The previous year we'd beaten St Flannan's in the semi-final, but they flipped it around this time. It was a huge occasion, as we were the curtain-raiser to the league final between Kilkenny and Clare, and although myself and Paddy both scored goals, we couldn't get over the line. I was devastated.

* * *

As part of Transition Year in St Kieran's, we'd get farmed out as students to all sort of places on work experience and to help with community initiatives. One such 'farming out' was to St Patrick's De La Salle. It was a local primary school, just a puck of the ball away from St Kieran's. Myself and a classmate, Alex, were sent down there once a week for a month to do some coaching with their third class.

Their teacher was Brian Cody.

I strolled into the school on the first day with feelings of excitement and nervousness at meeting Brian. Alex went to primary school in De La Salle so he couldn't care less but I had only seen him patrolling the sidelines at games in Croke Park. I kept wondering, what will I call him? Alex called him Mr Cody naturally, but I was wondering should I do the same? Would it be disrespectful to call him Brian? When we arrived, Brian marched straight over to me, hand outstretched.

'Richie Hogan, how are you?'

I was completely floored. I remember thinking: *the Kilkenny hurling manager knows my name. How does he know my name? What is going on?*

My head was spinning as I mumbled a response, trying to process the fact that a man with his top-tier status in Kilkenny hurling was greeting me as if he knew exactly who I was and everything about me.

Matt Ruth was a teacher there as well. He was the Kilkenny U-14 manager at the time and his son, Matt Junior, was around my age. Maybe Matt told him, I reasoned, but I later learned how Brian was always well on top of hurling at all grades in Kilkenny and his son Donnacha was a couple of years older than I was, so he kept a keen interest in anyone showing any kind of promise.

That first day we were trying to figure out how to handle this situation. Coming in to coach Brian Cody's team, what could we as a pair of young lads possibly offer?

We asked Brian what he wanted us to do.

'Lads, ye're the managers here. Ye tell me what's going on.'

He always had that witty side to his character – clever and sharp with remarks. He was loving the awkwardness of two teenagers coming in and telling him how to manage a team.

So he let us take the team for a street league game against St Canice's and stood back. Brian's youngest son, Diarmuid, was playing in the forward line. He was incredible. He was faster, stronger and an all-round better hurler than anyone else on the pitch. He ploughed through the other team and destroyed them on his own. Looking at him as a 10-year-old I imagined that Brian was training him at home, developing him into some kind of Tiger Woods trophy kid who was going to dominate hurling once he came of age. He did make it on to the panel for a few years in his early twenties but he never had a real clear run from injury.

Alex and I were in charge, calling the shots for the few weeks that we were there. If we made a change in the team that was effective Brian would stroll over to us and call us geniuses.

WHATEVER IT TAKES

We were in charge, telling Brian what to do rather than having him order us about. Situations like that make you realise that you're moving outside your own small circle. You're on the cusp of entering a whole new world.

* * *

I continued to play handball right throughout secondary school, picking up multiple All-Irelands and travelling to the US to play international tournaments, but I left it in the sporting rear-view mirror as I entered my late teens. The game never left me, though. I had developed traits which would serve me well in hurling, providing me with advantages that others couldn't keep up with. Handball is a court sport, similar to tennis and squash. In those arenas, your reactions develop at a lightning-fast rate. If you lack the level of speed of thought and footwork to get to the ball, you'll get left behind.

In a straight foot race over a significant distance I was not the fastest, but when it came to the breaking ball in hurling, I knew that my superior agility would get me there first. My balance and vision were also developed from years of playing handball. The goal is not just to get to the ball and hit it back, you must also be correctly balanced in order to send the returning shot in the direction that you want, while also keeping an eye on where your opponent is moving. Your mind, your hands, your feet and eyes are all playing different roles for every shot.

ST KIERAN'S

If a crowd of players were rising for a puckout around midfield and the ball spilled loose, I had that quickness off the mark, the ability to get my feet right and switch direction if needed. Strip it right down and handball is essentially a reaction drill. Do it for four days a week, an hour and a half at a time, over the course of 10 years. You're bound to improve.

When we did speed tests in training with Kilkenny, I consistently scored high in those drills over five-to-ten metres. I simply reacted sharper. Once the distance was increased to 30–40 metres, other players on our squad would take over, the longer stride of a supreme athlete like Cillian Buckley winning out. Timing was critical with my running, having the patience to hold until the last second, then accelerate and lose my marker.

In hurling if you're not alert over the first few yards, you will struggle. Tommy Walsh was built in a similar mould to me. He could shift his legs into gear rapidly, get out in front of his man to win the ball.

And possession is king.

During the start of my career when I played as an inside forward, reacting to the breaking ball was fundamental to my game. Hurling at that time tended not to involve those nice diagonal passes into space that we see now, the ball hopping perfectly for a forward. Back then, the ball fell on top of the full-forward line from on high – these skyscraper deliveries. When it broke, you needed to get to it first if you were going to snap over points.

At midfield, having the ball meant having control. You're in the best section of the pitch to identify everything. I would see the pitch like a clock in my head: twelve o'clock was their goal, six o'clock was ours. I had to put the ball in the best zone for a teammate. My exposure to handball allowed me to react quicker, so I processed and moved the play on while other lads were still trying to figure things out.

The most obvious skill advantage from handball is the ability to handpass the ball accurately and at length from either hand. Your arms are loaded with strength, your hand movement is faster and your connection with the palm is truer. The underarm swing is rooted in the old traditions of Irish handball in the big alleys and gets the name the 'Irish whip' as a result. This swing is the most similar in style to the traditional handpass movement in hurling.

D.J. Carey was the king of handpassing when I was growing up, watching players. I certainly utilised my advantages in handpassing – the accuracy, the distance, the speed at which I could offload to someone moving off my shoulder – while I progressed in hurling. In my later years playing I became particularly frustrated with the lack of enforcement of the handpassing rule in hurling. Handpassing is an incredible skill and takes time to develop. As a result most modern players take the shortcut of just throwing or pushing the ball away. I'm all for using common sense with the rulebook in games in order to protect the physicality or honest tackling. But allowing players to throw the ball is not

ST KIERAN'S

serving to protect any positive part of our game, instead it has eroded the skill level required to compete.

Before half-time in the 2011 All-Ireland final, we got a sideline on the Cusack Stand side. Sheff played a one-two with Eoin Larkin, then he flicked a pass into me after I'd drifted out to get free. The plan was to clip over a point, but at the last second I heard a shout behind me. I swivelled, changed hands and was able to pop a handpass up for Mick Fennelly to barrel through the Tipperary defence and rifle home a goal.

The key was not passing the ball to him, but passing to where he was going to be.

And that ability all came from a handball upbringing.

Despite myself and Paddy terrorising each other in the confines of our nanny's house, I was never a troublemaker in school. I just had no interest in it, so I never caused hassle for anyone. A male school environment can be a tough, intimidating place. Lads are jostling for position, figuring out where they are going in life. There is also an element of searching for recognition and a hard-man attitude can be adopted to get that. It can be an absolutely horrible place for some people who suffer as a result. I steered clear of anything like that. Maybe because hurling was my thing and that was commanding my focus.

In order to evade any negative attention from peers during secondary school you either needed to be the class clown or good at sports. A talented sportsperson was considered the top of the food chain. In an all-boys school environment, strength is measured through displays of athleticism on the sports field. After all, most boys grow up idolising athletes from various sports and dreaming of one day emulating their heroes. So, life in Kieran's was pretty hassle-free for me. I was also pretty mature off the pitch, and I would never have used that sporting clout for popularity gain or utilised my position to bring someone else down. If I had I would actually have felt so shit about myself for picking on another person.

Aside from the hurling, St Kieran's was good for me academically. My motivation increased to study more. The concept of measuring myself against others in exams appealed to me, so I began pushing hard for good results.

Hurling never brought any extra dispensation from studying. It might have provided the benefit of the doubt, at times – a teacher that coached you in hurling, say, could trust you as they knew your character – but you never got away with anything and had to stick to the rules like everyone else. It wasn't always that egalitarian in Kieran's before my time there. My granduncle John Gardiner, who we always refer to as our own uncle because of his close age to my dad, went to Kieran's himself as a boarder in the early '60s. Most students from outside the city were boarders at that time. When the dinner was served in the dining hall every evening the table of hurlers were looked after first. A plate of spuds was then fired down in front of the rest of the boarders and whoever grabbed first would get fed. It wasn't long before John scaled the surrounding walls of the college and thumbed his way back to Callan. That survival-of-the-fittest culture had long gone by the time I had arrived, and the boarding school was also fizzling out.

There was a level of self-motivation that propelled me forward towards the end of my time in school. By Leaving Cert, I was playing handball and hurling almost every evening, so I'd often get up at six in the morning to hit the books for a couple of hours before school. Claire, who is now Paddy's wife, was in my year in the Loreto girls' school across town and we were in the same social circles. She often reminds me that she and her friends thought I needed my head checked at the time.

That work ethic and self-motivation stems from the Hogan side of the family. They're structured, disciplined, and drilled into having a regular routine. My grandad Patsy and both my aunts Linda and Una have written books on a variety of topics including history, ecumenics and human rights. My sister Rachel and I were always really focused and diligent when it came to academic work. Paddy and Niamh needed more of a push.

Above all else, I was determined not to have hurling held up as a reason for failure in exams. I had to get the maximum out of myself, on or off the field.

If you weren't involved in hurling, I'm not sure what St Kieran's was like for students. My memories of the place are warm and comforting; hurling was inextricably linked to the experience, and the passing of the years hasn't loosened the connection I feel whenever I pass by it on College Road.

It was also the time, of course, that I first played for Kilkenny.

CHAPTER 4

MINOR MOMENTS

WHEN MYSELF AND Paddy made the Kilkenny Minor squad together in 2004, Brother Damien Brennan used to pick us up at our home in Danesfort in the afternoons and ferry us to county training. He was the manager, our chauffeur and became a powerful driving force in our lives, constantly striving to help us improve in every way.

Brother Damien was a Christian Brother from Arles in Laois who relocated to Callan in the '90s to teach in the local CBS. The connection with the town, and their shared love of hurling, saw himself and my father become good friends. Brother Damien had an incredible influence on a large number of players who played with Kilkenny over the years. He played several roles such as sports psychologist, masseur, career coach and teacher. But mainly he was a trusted friend.

My relationship with Brother Damien was different to that of others as I knew him from my childhood. He was the John Lockes hurling manager when my dad was playing and because Paddy and I were at most training sessions, we knew him pretty well. Initially we were terrified of him because he had the aura of most Christian Brothers but we knew that Dad respected him and admired him greatly.

Because the whole team were teenagers most of the selectors acted as chauffeurs in the hours before and after training, collecting and dropping players off at their homes around the county. He had other players to collect along our route, so the drive was often a long loop. As a result, we would often strike up conversations with him. There was no tunnel vision with hurling in these conversations. Brother Damien also regularly made enquiries about how our studies were going. When Paddy sat his Leaving Cert, Brother Damien gave him grinds in English, Irish and History. Three days a week for two hours at a time, all designed to give Paddy that extra push to secure the points to study primary teaching in Dublin. With no fee involved, his generosity of time and effort was on full display, something he replicated in his dealings with countless others.

When my turn at sixth year came around Brother Damien sent me a timetable of the support he was going to give me for the year. I didn't feel I needed it and felt guilty taking up six hours of his week. I viewed grinds as a necessity for those that were struggling in a subject or for those whose teacher wasn't up to scratch. However, he viewed it as an opportunity for me to test myself. Halfway through the year I mentioned to him that I was considering doing pass in one subject and focusing on the other six. Brother Damien was having none of it. He wanted to squeeze every last drop out of me, and not only was I to maintain the seven honours subjects, but he insisted that I take up History as well. And, since I wasn't studying it in school, he would be the one to tutor me in it.

It seemed a a little too ambitious six months out from the Leaving Cert. But we ploughed on, getting stuck into this new curriculum, meeting up for History sessions three times a week. When I rang him on results day to tell him I got an A1 I could feel the pride in his voice coming through the phone. 'Good man, Richie. Didn't I tell you it would be easy?'

I wasn't alone in having access to this unique teaching resource. For the brother, it was always a question of a person getting the absolute maximum out of themselves and, if you weren't, that was an injustice. That fuelled his motivation to help others.

* * *

St Kieran's was the shop window to advertise hurling talent for the Kilkenny Minors. When we lifted the Croke Cup in 2004, it vaulted me up the queue. I hadn't participated in trials for the county team but the form I was showing with the school was persuasive. I was now on the panel.

That year was significant for the Kilkenny Minors. There was a chance to complete three in a row of All-Ireland titles. Brother Damien brought the squad down to the Edmund Rice House in Callan for a meeting where he sketched out the shape of our year and spoke about our ambitions. No one needed reminding about the prize we were chasing.

I had my own personal goals. I had watched the older lads in St Kieran's shine for Kilkenny Minor teams. The year before, Richie Power shot the winning point in the All-Ireland final in Croke Park. I had also never played on that pitch. I wanted to shine in the black and amber, to step onto that hallowed turf.

As a Transition Year student, playing Minor for Kilkenny seemed the most important thing in the world. Nothing else mattered.

If Brother Damien was the boss man, Joe Hennessy was like our friend. Joe was a selector, a James Stephens club man and one of Kilkenny's greatest players. He had this charisma which made him so good at interacting with young people and getting them to perform. He was a big child at heart. If we were short a player in training, he would run on with his hurl and his working boots, eager to take part in the game. On our bus journeys back down the road from matches he would wander down to the back, dying to be involved if there was some craic to be had. As a management pair, they were a perfect blend.

We started strongly, beating Offaly in Carlow, and then won comfortably against Dublin in the Leinster final. It was my first day out in Croke Park. I got a couple of points, and Paddy added a few more from midfield. It was one of the good days.

We missed out on serving as the warm-up act for the Kilkenny Seniors that day, however, as they'd been stunned in the Leinster semi-final by Wexford. But we got to experience that warm-up appeal on All-Ireland semi-final day, Kilkenny having come through the back door to play Waterford in that main Senior show, while we played Tipperary in the Minor curtain-raiser.

Lads from that Tipperary team would pop up later in life. Shane Long went on to achieve soccer fame with Ireland and in the Premier League. Darragh Egan managed Wexford against us. Their wing-back, Shane O'Brien – a Clare native – ended up as our Kilkenny team physio.

That All-Ireland Minor semi-final was played on my sixteenth birthday. It was live on TV, played out amid torrential downpours. Whether it was the pressure of the occasion or the weather spoiling the afternoon, I took them all in my stride. I thrived in that environment; I didn't want to be the shy retreating kid in the corner, I demanded to be out front leading the way. I scored four points and set up Gavin Nolan for the only goal of the game. It was tight and tense but we won a low-scoring slugfest by 1–8 to 0–10, with Paddy launching over a long-range missile near the end for a crucial score. We were major underdogs, and my performance that day significantly boosted Brother Damien's opinion of me.

Afterwards, we left the Cusack Stand dressing room and made our way around the pitch to seats in the Hogan Stand. The Senior game had started and we soaked it all in. While walking around the pitchside, Eoin Murphy of Waterford gathered a ball in the corner about two metres away from me and Eddie Brennan floored him with this bone-crunching shoulder. You think you're a great lad playing Minor, but it was sobering to see these Senior giants collide.

It didn't help that there was already an expectation attached to me to bridge that gap. At the time, I had a simple label fastened to me: D.J. Carey's cousin. The comparisons between us were constant, the expectations great that I would reach that benchmark of performance. At first, I had enjoyed that attention, but the novelty soon wore off and I grew to resent it. I wanted to push back against that hype, switching my helmet from black to red specifically to avoid people drawing parallels to our hurling appearances.

I didn't want to be compared to D.J. Carey any more. I wanted to carve out my own reputation, create my own hurling identity.

I even became conscious of it on the pitch – how I ran with the ball, how I struck it, the style of play I adopted. As

MINOR MOMENTS

a Kilkenny Minor, sort of living beneath his shadow and all the associated pressure, I just wanted to escape it.

Later, I would realise that we were in fact quite different hurlers. But during that 2004 Minor campaign, the talk was a heavy weight I had to carry.

* * *

Galway had beaten Cork in the other 2004 Minor semi-final. Joe Canning was their full-forward, but all the hype surrounded Kerril Wade in the corner – their free-taker, their top scorer, their destroyer-in-chief.

My first taste of All-Ireland final day as a player was as part of an epic. The game ebbed and flowed; what was a small crowd at throw-in had swelled to over 50,000 by the second half, as the noise around the ground escalated. I was peripheral in the first half but took off in the second. My only score of the game was the most critical for Kilkenny – dragging us back from one down in injury time to draw the game and prolong our season with a replay.

The feeling that night was anti-climactic as the Kilkenny Seniors had seen Cork crush their three-in-a-row dream. We were shipped off to bed early to get ready for the replay the following Sunday.

We were off to Tullamore for round two. Offaly's county town was wedged with traffic that day, O'Connor Park heaving with people come throw-in. We were pretty well matched once again, neither team budging.

As half-time concluded we burst out of the dressing room and down the tunnel hyped up and ready to blow Galway away in the second half. The Galway team were already on the pitch and their management team were strolling nonchalantly in front of us through the tunnel. I was first in line and waited for a second for them to move aside and let us go out onto the pitch. They continued on strolling at snail's pace and blocking our way, so I lost my patience. I burst out through the middle of them, pushing them aside. One of their management team grabbed me by the jersey and he let me know how he felt. Before I could say anything, our midfielder Pat Hartley sent him flying and we burst out on to the pitch.

Before the ball was thrown in for the second half, I could sense that the Galway players were not going to let me walk off the pitch. Sure enough, as the game unfolded, I began coming in for rough treatment. Running to catch a pass at one point, a Galway player came over and cleaned me out with a shot to the head. I just went blank. I managed to get up and groggily play on but my memory of the rest of the day is fragmented, pieced together by what others have recounted.

We lost by a point and afterwards the field was invaded by supporters. As the trophy presentation was being made, I reasoned – while still on the field – that I was actually in the dressing room and so started removing all my gear, standing with just my Kilkenny shorts on. Adrian Finan, my teacher in St Kieran's, spotted me and escorted me away to the sanctuary of the dressing room. The rest of the lads were distraught over losing, but I was simply dazed.

The team medics checked me out and quickly realised I was concussed. I was carted off to hospital, a short trip as it's located next door to the stadium. I got the all-clear to head home fairly quickly and my parents drove me back to Kilkenny.

The devastation over the result came later. I hadn't contemplated losing; instead, I'd felt that there was a sense of destiny to the whole thing, given that we had worked so hard. Thoughts of that defeat remained with me for a long time. It was my first real experience of significant hurling failure.

I really wanted an All-Ireland Minor medal but that plan fell apart.

* * *

Another consequence of that All-Ireland loss was that we truly felt we had let Brother Damien down.

Anyone fortunate enough to have worked with him, to have reaped the rewards of the time he invested in you, could relate to that feeling. He had that influence on people, that magnetism that draws them in, and makes them seek desperately to repay him for his generosity and selflessness.

In the background of the inter-county hurling game, he had been a dominant figure, crucial for so many players in their preparation. Take the Cadogan brothers from Cork. They read about the work that he was doing with the Kilkenny hurlers and just rang him up. Henry Shefflin was the same. They had no prior relationship, but when Henry sounded him out, I'd say that was one of the happiest days of Brother Damien's life.

He just wanted to help. There was no ego to it. If anybody rang him out of the blue, he'd feel so privileged that someone had reached out that he would get up at six o'clock in the morning to go meet that person every day if that was what was required.

Sometimes he was almost unreasonable in how he tested me.

After a handball trip to Arizona during the Christmas break, I landed home and had a grind the following day. I was meant to have some work completed in advance but jetlag wore me down and I fell asleep. When I attended the grind but hadn't completed the task set for me, Brother Damien was almost offended. Small examples of a lack of commitment were treated seriously by him; it was crucial to address them to avoid any further descent in standards.

He was relentless in how he would challenge players. For example, as Kilkenny Minor hurlers, we were asked not to drink.

MINOR MOMENTS

Firstly because it was illegal when most of us were underage, but also because when we were in the middle of training, alcohol was damaging towards performance.

He would let people go out after a Leinster final, no problem, but during the pre-season training he didn't want anyone drinking.

He got us all into the dressing room in 2006, my last year at Minor level, and asked us to rank ourselves out of 10 in terms of the things that he'd asked.

Again, that question: 'Are you getting the best out of yourself?'

If you gave a mark of 10, it would imply that you could do no more. So you'd have to argue your case. Whatever figure you gave, you needed to justify it.

It came to the drinking question: 'how would you rate yourself out of 10 for sticking to the promise?'

Our full-back Kieran Mooney was beside me. He played for Conahy Shamrocks, and was a brilliant player who Brother Damien really liked. He rated himself seven. Brother Damien turned to me and asked me the same question. I responded with a 10. He jumped on that straight away.

'Why did you say 10, Richie?'

'Because you asked us not to drink and I have never drank. Simple as that.'

He went back to Kieran who immediately knew he was in trouble.

'Why did you rate yourself seven?'

Kieran panicked at the interrogation and tried to sidestep it, but Brother Damien got him to admit that he had gone drinking for a couple of nights earlier in the year.

So, you had to have your wits about you when he threw a question at you.

Everyone was terrified of him, but everybody also loved him – even the subs he wasn't picking. He was the type of character that commanded respect and returned it in spades.

***

Years later, Brother Damien got sick: cancer. He was private about his treatment and the prognosis for his disease. He didn't want it to distract from his work.

I knew he was pushing himself to the limit, surviving on only a few hours' sleep, trying to restore his health, as well as dealing with a lengthy list of Kilkenny hurlers who were seeking his guidance. So I purposely stayed away from him until I really needed him.

While I sometimes struggled with confidence, I never struggled with self-belief. Every player battles confidence to some extent, but I absolutely had the self-belief that as long as I knew what I needed to do at the top level of hurling, I was capable of doing it. In plain language, I always felt I was good enough to succeed. Some of the lads would genuinely be wracked with self-doubt about their hurling, and played with a constant sense of imposter syndrome no matter how great their performances might have been on the pitch. In contrast, I always rationalised that if I trained as hard as I possibly could, that, mixed with my talent, meant I could perform. I always kept in mind the cautionary tales that would go around about the Kilkenny underage star who went off drinking or put on weight or never stepped up to make it. I was terrified of falling into that bracket. I knew I was blessed with bucketloads of talent and so felt a responsibility to match that with an insatiable appetite to train and improve.

Brother Damien was keen to keep checking that I had maintained that mindset. His ultimate goal for me was that I wouldn't rely on him as a crutch but rather have the arrogance to tell him he was no longer needed. He viewed this as a sign that I had power over my hurling life and everyone in it. I never got that far, but I did become far more comfortable making demands of him.

The last months of his life were tough. When he died, it hit hard for those who were close to him and had forged a special bond.

My father spoke at his wake and wrote an obituary afterwards in the *Kilkenny People*: 'He was a preacher, a motivator, a healer and a good friend to all that knew him. We thank this man from County Laois who came to our town and club, for all the good he did and for the people's lives he touched. I don't think I've ever met a finer human being.'

That captured him perfectly. He was the only person I've ever met who would unconditionally do anything for anybody if they asked him.

He was an impossible character to figure out in that way. How anybody is able to give that sort of selfless commitment to anybody else – as long as it meant something to that other person and they were honest with him – is hard to fathom.

I miss him in my life.

He was a truly great friend.

* * *

We never did get to win the All-Ireland Minor title for him. 2005 was disastrous for us in hurling terms as Dublin surprised everyone by winning the Leinster semi-final and shoving us out the exit door. I persuaded Brother Damien to stay on board for the 2006 championship. We breezed through Leinster. My form was good and my scoring tallies were high, but we were undone in the All-Ireland semi-final by a Tipperary team populated with future stars and guided by Liam Sheedy.

There was a sense of devastation at my Minor hurling days being over without the tangible reward of a national medal, although I had already competed for a different

Minor All-Ireland medal earlier that year when I reached the All-Ireland Minor handball final.

The potential prize was huge, as Kilkenny hadn't produced a champion since before I was born. But there was a packed schedule that Sunday: Kilkenny Minor training that morning in St James' Park, and the All-Ireland handball final at lunchtime down in Tuamgraney in East Clare.

My head was wrecked all week in the build-up, incapable of bringing myself to ask Brother Damien if I could skip training. The fear was that he would turn down the request. I couldn't bring myself to call him so Dad ultimately made the call on the Friday night to spell out the dilemma. The solution was a classic Brother Damien move. Come to Kilkenny training for an hour and then leave early to head to Clare.

The rain poured down that morning during training as the clock inched closer towards eleven. I could see my father's car pulled in to collect me, but didn't have the stomach to ask Brother Damien to leave. I was a ball of nerves and settled on the easier option of doing the majority of the training, only asking to break away when the lads were warming down.

I jumped into the car, drowned wet and caked in muck, ready for a cross-country trek. As preparation for an All-Ireland final goes, it was pure madness.

I wolfed down a sandwich my mam had made on the way and landed in Tuamgraney late for the final. My opponent Padraig McGlinchey from Tyrone was already in the alley warming up as I rushed into the dressing room to tog out. The Senior finalists, Eoin Kennedy and Paul Brady, were inside; they broke up laughing at the state of me trying to get my saturated hurling gear off, wipe myself down with a towel, before throwing on the runners and gloves.

There was no warm-up, no pause for thought. I was simply thrown head first into the game.

Padraig had hammered me in the U-16 final two years previously and while that was a surprise at the time, I knew I was completely up against it. I managed to win, scraping through after a tiebreaker in the third game.

To everyone watching on this was crazy and I know some of the handball diehards took it as an insult to their game. My coaches Jimmy and my nanny certainly didn't; they were beaming with pride. In truth, I never stopped to consider it. Days crammed with action were not unusual. One year, I played a Leinster schools final with St Kieran's in Carlow, before being driven straight after to Mullingar for a schools handball All-Ireland semi-final. We drove home that night and headed back to Westmeath the following day for the final. Every Monday morning I would wake up bruised and battered from the weekend, settling my mind to go again for another week. On days off I would come home from school completely shattered and collapse on the couch. I'd wake up a few hours later with a blanket and a hot water bottle that Mam would have slipped over me while knocked out.

MINOR MOMENTS

The action-packed nature of my life didn't stop after losing the Minor hurling semi-final. In fact, the next morning Adrian Finan was on the phone to invite me to join his Kilkenny U-21 squad who were halfway through their All-Ireland campaign.

I jumped at the chance. The squad was filled with hurlers I knew from St Kieran's and I wanted another crack off an All-Ireland.

We won the semi-final against Galway when I was still only fresh on the squad, but for the final with Tipperary, I was shoved on from the bench near the end to try to salvage a game which Kilkenny had been chasing.

The game was in injury time and we were still three points down when we won a free outfield. Usually the ball would be pumped in high in these situations but John Dalton instead tapped it short to Michael Fennelly. He smashed in a shot from 30 yards that was partially blocked; the ball ricocheted near me and my reactions kicked in. I swivelled and whipped a ground shot to the net.

It was a magical feeling. Any worries I had about helicoptering in on the All-Ireland attempt of a squad who had trained all year for it were wiped away. I had contributed; I felt part of it.

For the replay in Thurles, they sent me in from the start. Straight down the middle of the attack at full-forward. My confidence levels never dipped, nor my sense that I belonged at this level.

I settled instantly when I caught a high ball to the square and sent a long handpass to Aussie Murphy who sent it over the bar. I created more scores later in the game and grabbed one myself.

Paddy's goal was the difference maker, though – his clinical shot in the first half after running a mile through the Tipperary team.

We won by three. On the cusp of defeat the previous Sunday, we were now embracing the feeling of success on a Saturday afternoon in Semple Stadium.

It wasn't the underage medal I had craved or envisaged at the start of that summer, but the unexpected nature of the success added to it all the more.

At last, I was an All-Ireland champion with Kilkenny.

* * *

During this time, I was also trying to figure out what to do next with my life. I enjoyed Maths and Economics and the science subjects. Economics was the road I should have first gone down. I was interested in exploring it further, because when I studied it I got this sense that my brain switched into gear. There was something to tap into. But my thought process was consumed by hurling. So I thought: *what can I do that is most advantageous to being a hurler?*

I arrived at the same conclusion most lads in that scenario do: teaching.

MINOR MOMENTS

When you're 17 or 18, personal ambition over mapping out your professional career doesn't enter your consciousness. The goal is to get a few quid in the door, by either getting into the working world straight away, or else head to college to get qualified to do something. I considered P.E. teaching at secondary level, but ultimately settled on the primary option.

After all, the job felt tailor-made for an aspiring inter-county hurler. Finish up at three o'clock every day. Have two months off during the summer, with other holiday breaks dotted throughout the year. Plenty of jobs in every parish in the country. Paddy was already up in the teacher training college, St Pat's, in Drumcondra, so the natural move would be to head there as well. Particularly when a P.E. teaching course would have entailed a move to Limerick.

I didn't mull over it, just arrived at a decision. It would take me a few years to come to the realisation that it had been a mistake.

Before I sat my Leaving Cert, the school honoured me with a Sportsperson of the Year Award. It wasn't to mark any major accomplishments in my final year, but more a wider recognition for the time I'd put into hurling and handball as a student. Ahead of the presentation, one of my teachers, Tom Looby, rang my mother and asked her to gather up all the medals that I'd won while representing the school; they then fitted them onto a board they had got made up and presented it to me. It was a really nice touch.

I left St Kieran's as a player who had been completely transformed, the journey successfully made from a nobody to a somebody.

I was highly motivated and ready to take on whatever came next.

CHAPTER 5

TRYING TO MAKE IT

I LOST MY phone in April 2007.

We hurled a club game against Mooncoin down in Hugginstown on a Sunday and I headed back up to Dublin that night. I went out that Monday, for a typical college night out, and somewhere along the way my phone remained in a pub after I had departed.

Young and carefree and uncontactable, I displayed no particular urgency to get a replacement and, in truth, there was no issue until the following Friday evening when I walked in the door at home in Danesfort and faced my mother.

'Brian Cody has been ringing the house phone here. He's been trying to get on to you all week and you're to ring him back straight away.'

The colour drained from my face. Mortified, I had to compose myself and use our house phone to ring the number Brian had left with my mother.

I heard the click signalling that the call had been picked up.

'Hi, is that Brian?'

'It is.'

'Hi Brian, it's Richie Hogan.'

'Richie Hogan ... It's easier to contact the Pope than it is to contact Richie Hogan.'

My mind was scrambling. He had me on the back foot straight away. Brian had been at our club game the previous weekend and it would have been rather unusual for him to attend an Intermediate game instead of going to watch Senior club games that were on at the same time. He saw something that he liked, though I'd a decent CV built up by then.

He had attempted on several occasions throughout that week to invite me into Kilkenny training but I had gone off the grid. Luckily, the invitation was still open.

There was no ceremony to the discussion. It was simply: here are the details for training. Be there in Nowlan Park.

And that was my introduction as an 18-year-old to the Kilkenny Senior hurling panel.

* * *

The call arrived at a good time for me (apart from the issue with my phone, of course). In secondary school, everything had been planned out for me; the hurling calendar filled itself. Colleges games with St Kieran's in the spring, Minor inter-county action in the summer and then back to Danesfort for the winter. I'd played with the Kilkenny Minor, U-21 and Intermediate teams the previous summer, but by the start of that year – apart from some Fitzgibbon Cup hurling with the college – that cycle had been broken.

The club had kept me busy until March. Danesfort won the Kilkenny Junior championship the previous autumn for the first time in 76 years. It was a magical breakthrough for us. The All-Ireland series in those grades were still in their infancy – it was only the second year that the prestige of playing the final in Croke Park was on offer – but we thrived on the novelty. We cantered through Leinster, then defeated Cork's Kilworth in the All-Ireland semi-final down in Dungarvan, a foul day where the wind came howling in off the estuary.

I had a target on my back by then; Kilkenny underage recognition had seen to that. Tight marking came with the territory, meaning I often had to get used to two players for company at club level. It was a fierce contest but we got over the line, myself and Paddy scoring nine points between us. Robbie Walsh got the other three.

Once we survived that, we were brimming with confidence and it showed in the final against Antrim's Clooney Gaels. Sharp from the start, we were dominant throughout and brought an All-Ireland trophy home to Danesfort.

WHATEVER IT TAKES

Adrian Ronan from Ballycallan was our manager. He was one of the Kilkenny forwards from the early '90s that I knew almost everything about before I ever met him. I had watched his games on my VCR hundreds of times, studying his goalscoring technique, admiring his corner-forward play. He was small and didn't have blistering pace. This meant in order for him to survive he needed to be more skilful and more intelligent than others on the pitch. As I got into my mid-thirties and my own legs began to fail me, the lessons I learned from Ronnie's playing style during that time became invaluable. His track record as a player gave him a status. Bobby Jackman had laid the foundations for us in previous years, but Ronnie had come in and elevated us even further.

He radiated confidence and he immediately inculcated the team with the belief we needed to win. He instilled a structure in our set-up and introduced individuals to his backroom team who were not only technically good, but also possessed the soft skills that were needed to change the culture in the dressing room. One such character was Fergal Purcell. Fergal was in the Defence Forces and was introduced as our S&C coach. This kind of introduction would immediately have spelled groans from club players in the past. The last thing we wanted to do was listen to another army guy screaming at us to do a hundred push-ups and carry guys on our back up and down the pitch. But Fergal was different, he was a press officer in the Defence Forces and he was the ultimate communicator. He didn't make any demands of us; instead he created an environment where we made demands of each other and it worked. After all, this was our team, not his and not Ronnie's. If we were to win anything we would need to do it ourselves. Players doubled down on their commitment regardless of their age or perceived status within the team. Anyone living away in Dublin never questioned the journey home for training.

We had the underage pedigree also. Myself, Paul Murphy, Robbie Walsh and Gavin O'Keeffe had all been on the Kilkenny Minors in 2006. Paddy and I also won U-21 All-Ireland medals with Kilkenny that September. That influx of youthful talent allied to our older core had mapped out our route to victory.

The parish was entranced around the time of our All-Ireland win. Men who had been there for years of toil and struggle were now witnessing unimaginable success. I approached it from a different viewpoint. Namely, we were going to win this championship and the quicker we won it, the quicker we could climb out of this grade and take on the best club teams in the country. I was still only a teenager but I wasn't tolerating the thoughts of playing Junior hurling. My focus was on winning and meeting the expectations I had for myself and the club. Playing for the love of one's homeplace wasn't enough to satisfy me. After all, I had only been playing with Danesfort for five years at this point.

That attitude wasn't rooted in arrogance. It signalled an unwavering belief in our group that we had all the ingredients to be successful. With the potential that we had, not succeeding wasn't an option for us. Myself and my contemporaries brought that mindset to Danesfort, and the club progressed from there.

* * *

At St Pat's in Drumcondra, I quickly found myself in a great group of friends. Familiar faces like Niall Tennyson and Cha Fitzpatrick from Kilkenny were joined by new ones: Declan McKiernan and David Galligan from Cavan, Pa Minogue from Clare and Donall Barry from Navan. This core group lived together and stayed close.

Cha was already a star, having won the All-Ireland at midfield for Kilkenny that year. He'd soon be named Young Hurler of the Year. We played hurling with the college team, but it was more relaxed than competitive. Tom Fitzpatrick, a fantastic character, managed the GAA side of things, handling all the admin and letting the players run the teams. As captain, you also led the training. In my first year, Richie Power, a third-year student, was in charge.

Our player pool was small since the college only offered two courses: Primary Teaching and Arts. We had a decent mix of lads from Kilkenny, Clare, and Wexford, but it was nothing like the bigger colleges with more resources.

TRYING TO MAKE IT

We lived on campus in six-floor buildings that resembled miniature versions of inner-city towers in America. Each floor had six bedrooms, with the bottom floor for the lads and the rest for female students. Our quarters included a shared kitchen and bathroom, and there was a common room for everyone. I turned part of it into a hurling wall, picking a spot between two windows for target practice (I rarely shattered the glass).

Adjusting to this new way of life took time. Days were mostly unstructured: attending lectures, hanging around college, and killing time. We went out a couple of nights a week, sometimes to Quinn's, other times to The Big Tree, or even into town. Coppers became a regular spot from second year on. Hurling seemed to drift away in this lifestyle, and I felt like I needed something to ground me.

That's when Brian Cody reached out, just at the right time.

* * *

That first Kilkenny Senior training session was organised for seven o'clock, but Brian had mentioned that most players liked to arrive early and get on the pitch for 20 minutes to sharpen their touch before the session kicked off. I immediately wanted to make an impression and decided that I would get to Nowlan Park 45 minutes early and be the first one on the pitch.

WHATEVER IT TAKES

That spring, I had damaged my AC joint and spent several weeks out nursing my shoulder. Successfully recuperated, I sought to show the management team that I wasn't just another talented player, I also had the mindset to succeed.

No other players were there when I pulled into Nowlan Park that first evening; it was just the kitman, Rackard Cody.

'Well, Snoz,' he said to me. 'Throw your name on that jersey there and grab a bottle of orange off the table.'

Snoz was the name Rackard used for players whose name or face he didn't know. Rackard had been there since the '70s when his role began as a designated linesman for Kilkenny games and he moved into the role of kitman once neutral linesmen were introduced some time later. He fired over a black marker and instructed me to sign two Kilkenny jerseys for some supporter who had run into him during the week and asked for a favour. I wasn't particularly used to signing anything and I felt a little uncomfortable as I didn't know what my situation was. The last thing I wanted was for Brian to march in and see me settled in signing jerseys and mistake it for a lack of modesty, or over-familiarity. I quickly scribbled my name on it and went looking for a seat. James McGarry was the second player to arrive which made me a little more comfortable. James is my cousin and played for Bennettsbridge with my uncle for years. During the summers when I was a teenager I was still staying in my grandparents' house in Bennettsbridge on weekdays when my parents were at work. Even though I was playing my hurling with Danesfort, I would still go over to the Bennettsbridge field to practise frees and shooting to kill a few hours. James often passed by on his JCB on his way to a local job. If he saw me, he would park up and come in to the pitch and puck the balls back to me. Looking back on it that showed the humility that he had. He was the Kilkenny goalkeeper, and he was standing behind the goal pucking the ball back to a 14-year-old who had just left his club a few years beforehand to play with the local rivals.

Brian came in soon after.

He pulled me aside. 'Look, Richie, what we do here is we invite lads into training when we need to make up numbers so we can have a full 15-a-side game even when we have injuries. But you're going to be involved right through the season. We want you in here every night.'

So there was no guarantee of matchday panels; the onus was more on exposing me to this environment. Push me, prod me, see how I held up. Would I survive the test or wilt under pressure?

That summer Cha and I were based in the Gaeltacht in Galway for three weeks as part of our summer college course. We made the three-hour trek home on weekends to fit in two training sessions. The first round of the championship was coming soon and the intensity of training had stepped up significantly. Brian called us over for a quick chat after training to discuss our travel arrangements.

'Look, lads, ye are up there in Galway and we know you need to be there and that's fine with us. Obviously it's a big ask for ye to make the three-hour drive home and be in a position to train properly on the pitch. We are looking into getting a helicopter to bring you down for a midweek session but we will play it by ear.'

Cha was more established than I was and made a smart Celtic Tiger remark but I stood there quietly and gave a nod of approval.

The helicopter didn't materialise, instead we tore the roads out of it in Cha's new Mitsubishi Lancer which he had won from Michael Lyng Motors the year before for being Kilkenny's Club Hurler of the Year. Cha had one CD in the car, The Killers' album *Samstown*, which he blared at maximum volume the whole way home. Shades on, singing at the top of his voice.

The Friday night, before the first round of the championship against Offaly, I went in for the puck-around. Brian mentioned there was a team meeting upstairs after, and while I wasn't on the squad for the game, I was welcome to come up to the meeting. I took that as my cue to leave and pitched back up the following week once more.

It was an ambiguous situation to grapple with. I was immersed in the set-up, as I was attending training, but felt detached at the same time given my lack of any role on match day. As if to hammer that home, for the All-Ireland semi-final against Wexford, I sat in the Upper Cusack Stand with my father, having paid for our own tickets. Later during my career an extended panel was created with 40–45 players involved right throughout the season, and there was at least a greater sense of involvement from those who were in my situation.

My experience in my first year always made me more sympathetic to those who played similar roles over the years. When Paddy Deegan first joined the training panel, he was in college in Maynooth. Without a car, he had to trek from Maynooth to Drumcondra station by train, then walk to DCU to get a lift from some of the lads on the panel who were in college there. They would drop him back at the station later that night, and he would take the train back to Maynooth. This journey took nearly 12 hours of his day.

When I found out, I was baffled that he wasn't speaking up to the county board about his journey, but he didn't want to make any noise. I lived in Drumcondra and couldn't face dropping him at the station one night, so I offered to take him home. We settled on dropping him to catch the last bus from Lucan to Maynooth, which was only a little out of the way.

As I pulled over at the bus stop and Paddy grabbed his gear, the bus arrived and flew past us. He jumped back in, and we chased the bus, passing it and furiously flagging it down, only for the driver to ignore us again. After several stops, I lost patience and drove him back to the Maynooth campus. That was early 2016. The following year, Paddy was made the captain of the team.

In the summer of 2007 I was also working in Nowlan Park. The Kilkenny County Board would organise for students to come in to help the caretakers Timmy Grogan and Mick O'Neill: line pitches, clean the stand, do whatever odd job was required.

On the Tuesday after the All-Ireland semi-final in 2007 where I had paid in to the game, Brian rang and asked to meet me. He knew I was working in the Park at this point and said he would meet me in the car park at lunchtime.

'Richie, you are going well in training, and we are going to add you to the panel for the final. You won't be listed on the programme but you will be on the team sheet that goes to the referee and that's what matters.'

I was elated. There was no promise of game time, of course, but being involved represented a step forward. Part of me still thought I might feature. Why draft a guy in if you're not going to use him? It was a situation that I was used to by this point. I had been added to the panels of the Kieran's, the Kilkenny U-21s, the Kilkenny Intermediates and now the Kilkenny Senior team in the weeks leading up to All-Ireland finals.

It was a new environment for me. My first time on the Senior bus going to a match, landing at the Langton's Hotel in Kilkenny on the Sunday morning and off we went. Being an All-Ireland final, there were extra trappings involved.

Everyone else had already been fitted for their suits, but my aunt Pearl worked in Paul Menswear in town, so she had my size and was able to fast-track it for me. One of the county board lads was tipped off about my inclusion, and so I got kitted out in the same matchday gear as everyone else.

A pile of tickets were fired at me. At this stage, I hadn't told my family, but they could see the gear coming in at home. They put two and two together. In the end, I just handed the tickets to Mam to distribute to whomever she wanted.

When I ran out onto Croke Park that day, a wave of noise came crashing down to engulf me. It was an assault on the senses. Limerick hadn't won the All-Ireland since 1973 or been in a final since 1996. Their hype machine had cranked into gear all summer, the county in a frenzy of excitement.

And we just blew them away. Eddie Brennan and Henry Shefflin stuck goals inside the first 10 minutes. We won at our ease.

However, as an unused sub, I felt like a bystander. I had trained hard over the previous few months, but it didn't carry the same meaning when I wasn't playing.

It was my first All-Ireland Senior medal, but had I really earned it?

WHATEVER IT TAKES

* * *

I was still finding my way, learning the lay of the land, though I'd picked up some things quickly. There was an in-house squad game the night of my first training session. I was shoved in corner-forward on Jackie Tyrrell.

The ball dropped over on the wing and Jackie went to pick it up. I charged in and lined him up for a shoulder and the two of us just bounced off each other.

Oh, Jesus, these lads are bigger than I thought, I remember thinking.

Still, I knew that something like that would have made a huge impression. Watching me, they'd notice I wasn't just letting this lad waltz out; instead, I was getting stuck in and prepared for the hard graft. Brian would have loved that far more than someone clipping over a few points, I knew even then. That was valued currency in Brian Cody's eyes.

After all, as a Kilkenny player, your whole life revolved around trying to impress Brian. He had full control. When he saw something – and it might just be a small thing in a training session or a match – that would immediately stick in his mind. For example, if a guy was running down the line and a player chased him 50 yards from the far side of the pitch and put him out over the line, that was a big moment. That would stick in Brian's head for months. He wouldn't worry too much about anything else because in his eyes there was now something that he could work with. You could find yourself elevated into the starting fifteen straight away.

The flipside of this was that if he saw something that didn't impress him, well, a red line could be drawn through your name and you could disappear from his thinking.

Years later, in the 2012 Leinster final, we got hammered by Galway. This sparked an inquest into how we had collapsed in such 'un-Kilkenny-like' fashion. While we recovered to beat Limerick in the quarter-final we still weren't motoring as expected. Martin Fogarty had a collection of clips ready to go on the big screen while at a training camp in Carton House after that Limerick game. It made for uncomfortable viewing for all of us but for T.J. in particular. T.J. had been taken off after 50 minutes in the Leinster final. When he was dropped against Limerick he made the mistake of complaining to Martin Fogarty.

The collection of clips mainly featured T.J. and he was roasted for his effort by Fogarty. In one clip, I won a ball in the centre-forward position and turned to run at the defence. Three Galway defenders swarmed around me and I turned desperately, looking for someone to offload the ball to. T.J. was beside me but instead of providing support he moved away from the play and drifted out towards the sideline.

'Now T.J., you think we are being hard on you. But your teammate is being assaulted in the middle of the field and you are the closest man to him.'

WHATEVER IT TAKES

T.J. had been drifting on and off the team for the previous couple of years, but had played his best game in a Kilkenny jersey to date in that year's Leinster semi-final against Dublin. It looked like he would finally nail his place down. We all learned a valuable lesson coming out of the room that day: if you are dropped from the team you need to take your medicine and keep your head down. Those who'd escaped were just thankful they hadn't featured in the post-match montage. My suspension for the All-Ireland semi against Tipp provided T.J. with an unexpected opportunity to get back into the team and he took it, scoring two goals and ending the year with an All-Ireland and an All Star for his efforts.

The decision-making process may sound a little bizarre to those outside the camp but every player knew what they were getting into. It was ruthless. If you shot from an angle that was too tight and it went wide, you were coming off. If you were a little lethargic in your chase of an opponent in training and Brian spotted it, then he made a mental note. There would be no communication or explanation, just another man selected in the offender's place.

**

The jump to Senior hurling with Kilkenny felt significant. Coming from a Junior club, my exposure to the highest level of adult hurling had been limited. Adaptation was required, particularly when I was joining an established group filled with seasoned players who were the best in the country.

Adjusting to the increased heat in that climate was hard, but the flipside was that the scope for learning was enormous. The intensity of the training games for starters. I was accustomed to the fact that, even if I wasn't performing my best, I would still score freely. To replicate that here, however, you needed to be in supreme shape and well rested. The challenge was considerable, facing these defenders. Noel Hickey and Jackie Tyrrell were beasts of men for a young lad to be taking on. If you grabbed the ball, you had to be prepared to ship punishment; walking off the Nowlan Park pitch bruised and battered was commonplace. I joined the squad with a huge reputation and I knew the defenders were dying to take a crack at me. I relished the competition just as much as they did.

There were also other things to figure out, things that bother a player most when they enter a panel and may seem trivial from the outside, but they are important and genuine. Like, where the hell am I going to sit in the dressing room? Who am I going to talk to?

My first night at training I sat between Michael Kavanagh and Henry Shefflin. I had been there early and no one had told me to move so I just togged off. Henry was the reigning Hurler of the Year at the time. From the start his extreme focus was impressive. He struck me as someone who planned every second of his day and adhered strictly to his schedule.

There were two dressing rooms in Nowlan Park for usage: one where most people went into, and the spill over area for the remaining six or seven lads. Conversation was brief in both rooms. Before training lads were too consumed by getting themselves right, while after training they were too wrecked from what they'd endured. There might be some craic in Langtons after, over food, but in general it was strictly business.

There was no welcome mat laid out – for me or for anyone else. You arrived and you got to work. Lads were so desperately trying to make the squad and the starting team that they had no time for anything else. It was sink or swim.

When I started featuring in the starting fifteen, Eddie Brennan was a valuable source of information to tap into. His advice was practical, and his messages were crafted to instil confidence. I played in the same position as Eddie and while I was his teammate, I was also his rival. He could have easily seen me as unwanted competition and kept his distance but he was more motivated by ensuring that everyone in the forward line were working together regardless of who fell in and out of the team at certain times. He was 10 years older than me and had a world of hurling knowledge to impart.

* * *

2007 felt like a lost year in a way, what with the little game time I had with the Seniors, as well as the early exit with the U-21s. It had also shown me that I needed to develop physically.

In the winter before the 2008 season started, I got to work. I enjoyed training. My effort levels were beyond reproach; however, my strategy was more questionable.

I was a young and new player to the squad and so was terrified to ring the Kilkenny trainer Mick Dempsey and get an individual programme before collective training resumed. So I trawled the internet for advice, digging through YouTube videos of tutorials from soccer, rugby, AFL and NFL. I also relied on my memory of the sessions we had done with Kilkenny. The aim was to get faster and stronger; the process to achieve that transpired to be a wild, varying mix of stuff. Looking back, it was an area that the management should have been sharper on. I'm positive that they would have loved a player to ask for advice. However, that wasn't communicated enough, and an environment developed where lots of players were doing their own work in the background so as to keep their heads down.

2008 was also my first taste of pre-season work. The older lads had built it up into a death zone, where you were going to get flogged relentlessly, in the most horrendous weather. The reality was more bearable.

I got a text to turn up for the first Walsh Cup game, playing Antrim in Freshford. We lost by a point, a major shock on a debut. But my personal training schedule stood to me and I got in for the first couple of league matches. In my league debut against Dublin I scored 1-2 and felt I had made a good start to my first full year with the team.

For the next round against Wexford, I assumed I would be retained but was selected on the bench. We were in the middle of teaching practice, which was a really stressful time in college. Cha would tell Brian he was unavailable, but he was more established, I was a novice. Heading down for training midweek evenings, tearing back up the road to Dublin and getting ready to teach the following morning out in Darndale – all the pressure inside me was building up.

And it soon erupted.

Everyone was asleep in the house one night, when I started roaring in bed around 2 a.m. That wouldn't be unusual in itself: shouting in my sleep was a quirk I had.

Pa was sharing a room with me and he woke up with the commotion. I was having a full-blown panic attack. The rest of the lads woke up. They figured they'd ring my home.

Mam picked up the phone but wasn't concerned. 'This happens all the time, throw him into a cold shower and he'll wake up.'

The freezing water gushing down only worsened my state. I was now struggling to breathe. The lads didn't know what to do, so they fired me into the back of a car and drove me down to the Mater Hospital.

TRYING TO MAKE IT

I arrive drowned wet, wearing nothing but a pair of jocks and a jacket thrown over my shoulders. The staff took one look at this scene of chaos – a Thursday night, group of college lads – and assumed I had taken some form of illegal substance. They figured some experiment had gone wrong.

'What's he after taking?'

'No, no, he's a hurler, really fit. He barely drinks, let alone takes drugs.'

They still didn't believe us, so I peed into a cup and they took it away to test for something.

By that time, anyway, I'd calmed down.

The nurses were keen for me to be seen by a doctor, but we grew tired of waiting after a couple of hours and left. We'd teaching practice that morning, after all.

I walked out the hospital door at half past seven in the morning and headed down the North Circular Road, wearing one of those operating gowns with not a stitch of other clothing on. For those in rush-hour traffic, the sight was good entertainment.

The Kilkenny team doctor Tadhg Crowley got a call soon after and discreetly helped me cover up my absence from training on the Friday.

* * *

We lost the league semi-final that April to Tipperary and had a two-month break until the Leinster first round against

Offaly. Space was at a premium in a highly competitive forward line but I was destroying lads in training and knew that I would be included. The number 13 jersey was mine that day in Portlaoise. I was bursting with enthusiasm, marking Michael Verney, a defender I'd faced several times at underage. I couldn't wait to get going.

Then the game proved a personal disaster. I was a mile off the pace. I kept losing possession, struggling to break free, unable to get my strike away. The speed and the noise of the game overwhelmed me; I attempted to problem-solve, but no solutions appeared.

With seven minutes to go, I was whipped off. I had tapped over a point before that when Tommy Walsh fed me a handy ball. I was completely unmarked but still dropped the ball. Fortunately, I had enough time to pick it up at the second attempt and hit it over.

We won by 18 points but I was completely depressed afterwards. I couldn't look at or speak to anyone. I went in the door at home, threw the gear bag in the corner and went to bed. Mam knocked on the door a few times to see if I wanted anything and I couldn't even muster up a response. I was fuming with myself.

Richie Power was on the way back from injury; upon his return, there was now an easy selection decision in the forwards. I had been the best player in training and a shoo-in for a position on the team for that game but I had now blown my chance.

TRYING TO MAKE IT

I didn't get a look in for the rest of the year.

It was a stark lesson in the ruthlessness of the environment. Fail to perform and you will be discarded.

* * *

The one saving grace for me was the progress of the U-21 team that summer. Those games were my place of refuge. I hit full speed throughout the championship, particularly in the All-Ireland semi-final, scoring 2–5 against Galway, and winning man of the match.

Only myself and T.J. were double-jobbing between the Senior and U-21 side. I was partaking in Senior training and going to watch every U-21 session. I needed that sanctuary to ease my mind.

In the Senior championship, we ripped everyone apart that year, cruising to the final. The form of players was incredibly good, and I knew this would mean I wouldn't get a second chance. This amplified my regrets over my performance against Offaly.

Brian had privately given me a few words of recognition for my U-21 form beforehand, but it wasn't sufficient to get time on the pitch.

Before the game Waterford were the storyline that commanded the attention. Davy Fitzgerald had taken over mid-season and there was an aura about him that captivated the hurling public. Brian addressed our group and quashed that talk. 'Look, lads, there's a bit of shit going around here about David Fitzgerald. I want to nail this now. Davy Fitzgerald has zero influence on what happens on the field on Sunday. In the same way that I have zero influence. It's the men on the pitch that will settle this game.'

We went out that Sunday afternoon and obliterated Waterford. The performance the lads served up was awesome, scoring 3–30, which was mind-blowing stuff.

The three in a row was secured. It was a team at the peak of their powers, fuelled by this insatiable appetite for victory.

I was happy that we won, of course I was. But I was so disappointed not to be playing. The team had created history with three in a row, but on a personal level I felt more bitter than sweet about it. I had blown my chance, and it hurt me.

CHAPTER 6

MAKING THE SENIOR TEAM

THE BATTLE TO make the Kilkenny Senior team was the toughest challenge I had experienced up until that point. The climb was not particularly steep physically, but mentally adjusting to starting at the bottom of the food chain was something that took me time to figure out.

In my last year as a Minor I had also played on the U-21 and Intermediate teams that reached their respective All-Ireland finals. I had three years of adult club hurling under my belt and a season of Fitzgibbon hurling with St Pat's by the time the spring of 2007 came around. There was nothing in my apprenticeship up until that point that indicated that I wasn't prepared for a step up. In hindsight, it was more about timing.

Kilkenny had just undergone a rebuild in 2006, backboned by the great U-21-winning teams of 2003 and

2004. Eleven more of the U-21-winning side of '06 had already been part of the Senior panel that year and picked up Senior All-Ireland medals. The harsh truth was that I wasn't needed. The standard was so ridiculously high in the squad and the level of competition so feverishly intense that it meant opportunities were limited.

Not that everyone understood that. As a successful and talented underage player you learn to deal with a lot of barstool bullshit. One of the negative sides of performing well on underage teams is the constant warnings from 'good hurling men' that there have been better players than you in the past who never made the jump to Senior. Stories of players who drank too much, were too soft, got carried away with themselves or simply didn't want it enough to make it are fired at you, largely so that if you ultimately fail, they can say that they were the first to tell you it would happen.

The thought that talented youngsters are born with everything and that nothing has ever been challenging for them was something that I really despised. As human beings, we all love the fairy tale stories of guys who didn't make the grade at Minor level but went on to prove everyone wrong and become greats of the game. I love those stories, too, but that doesn't mean that the path that I travelled was easier. I was more hardworking and determined to succeed than others my age, and so far I had.

My goal once I got the call-up in 2007 was straightforward. I wanted to make the team and win the All-Ireland.

It sounds pretty obvious, and it certainly was not constructed using a SMART goal chart. My impatience and the environment that was the Kilkenny Senior team during that period meant that I could not afford to play the long game.

To my frustration, 2007 had been an introductory year, where I was being exposed to training. The harsh reality for me at that time was that I wasn't in Brian's plans at all. After all, I had not been invited to take part in Mick Dempsey's dreaded winter training sessions after joining the panel shortly before the league final.

2008 was meant to be my breakthrough but it turned out to be a year of hard lessons. I wondered now whether a breakthrough was ever going to happen. Twenty years of age, almost feeling too old at that point to be getting going. Look at my peers around the country all starting for their teams.

There was a theory – likely put together by those 'good hurling men' – that I was trying to do too much on my own, that a life of hurling as the main man for club, school and underage sides had encrypted a specific way of playing into my DNA. When I got my hands on the ball, I was always taking on my man, looking to score or create something.

It was true that, at Senior level, there were more openings to spray the ball around. And feeding off other forwards was not a tactic I was familiar with, precisely because I had always been entrusted with carrying much of the scoring burden on my own. Evolving my game took some time, but

I also needed matches to sharpen that up, rather than relying on training.

A narrative can build up around a player. A label that is difficult to shed. The truth is always more nuanced.

✶ ✶ ✶

I was frustrated and yet determined to rebound for 2009. The flipside of college life was that my hurling responsibilities had stepped up; captaincy in St Pat's meant training the team. I flipped that to my advantage, planning out our training so I could lodge a decent amount of fitness work.

Away from my own journey, it was great to see Paddy earn his Senior call-up papers that winter. It was a deserved inclusion. He had quietened Joe Canning and Seamus Callanan in the U-21 championship, which was the type of form that was impossible to ignore. Paul Murphy got drafted in for training as well. However, when the pre-championship cull took place, only myself and T.J. survived from that team. That winter training season showed just how strong the Kilkenny conveyor belt was. 2008 had finished with Kilkenny as Senior, Intermediate, U-21 and Minor All-Ireland winners. The cull meant there were a raft of 21- and 22-year-olds, most of whom would have walked on to any other team in the country, thrown back to the wilderness of a broken club system that wasn't anything like what it needed to be.

MAKING THE SENIOR TEAM

That January, before the cull, we played a Walsh Cup game against Antrim up in Casement Park. The team bus left Kilkenny and the plan was to pick myself, Paddy and David Herity up at the Louis Fitzgerald Hotel at Newlands Cross. We parked in around the back and waited. When the bus pulled in at the side of the motorway, we got out of the car and walked from the car park over to the bus.

A couple of years later, the Kilkenny management threw that incident at me in a meeting. My body language wasn't right for them, they claimed. I was hammered for it. Strolling onto the bus at my own pace, content for the entire bus to wait on me. They expected us to be standing at the side of the motorway ready to go.

That interpretation rattled me. Was that how I was viewed at the time? After all, I would never draw unnecessary heat on myself and I certainly wasn't arrogant. But it did illustrate how they were always watching your body language, always judging, always guarding against apparent complacency or ego seeping into our camp.

What made it even more bizarre to me was that I took the Antrim defence for 1–10 with 1–8 of that from play that day.

J.J. Delaney was playing full-back and made a speech at half-time: 'Look, lads, Richie Hogan is destroying his man in there. All you have to do is get the ball in. Let him do the rest. On another day someone else will stand up but today we need to make sure that we get the ball to him.'

WHATEVER IT TAKES

Having a quiet word of encouragement in the ear of a young lad is one thing, but singling him out among the group is another. I never knew that I needed an affirmation from a senior member of the team until I actually received it. It was only a Walsh Cup game against Antrim on a wet afternoon in January that no one cared about, but when you are trying with everything you have to make an impression and contribute to the team, you remember every word.

* * *

Sometimes it can be too neat and convenient to single out one game as the turning point of a career. Once a player finally makes the breakthrough from good to great it is easy for us to look back into the past and pinpoint key moments where everything changed. But the 2009 league final was clearly transformative for me.

It was the next real opportunity I had to impress after the 2008 collapse against Offaly. Outside of championship conditions, a league final is the only contest of relevance.

The importance was increased by the fact that Tipperary were lying in wait for us down in Thurles. Our paths hadn't crossed the previous summer after they lost the semi-final to Waterford. In the regulation league game that March, we'd annihilated them, 5–17 to 1–12.

Tipp had home advantage for this final, but I suspect we

MAKING THE SENIOR TEAM

were happier than they were about it. Brian loved this type of challenge, and we fed off his energy.

Every year he'd come out with the same sobering sentence. 'Clare in Ennis, Cork in Páirc Uí Chaoimh, Galway in Salthill – that's how you find out how good we are. That's where we become a real team.'

He was right. The opportunity to send a message to teams on their home patch was invaluable. Now, we were getting the chance to send a message to Tipp in their own back yard on one of the biggest days of the year.

The Tipperary forwards tore us apart during the first half, meaning they were five points up at half-time. I was playing at right-half forward and spent most of the first half chasing the Tipp defence around Semple Stadium. We were read the riot act at half-time, which generally works, but this time Tipp stuck a goal just after half-time and it looked as if they would only push further ahead.

I took a pass on the run from Sheff and broke through the tackle from Brendan Maher before driving it past Brendan Cummins. It gave us a lift, but our momentum was halted when Sheff was sent off. During that league campaign the GAA rules committee were trialling a new rule in the National League where a yellow card now led to a player being sent off for the rest of the game with the team allowed to bring on a sub in his place. Of all of the foolish rules that the GAA rules committee introduced during my time, this was by far the most ridiculous.

WHATEVER IT TAKES

Soon after we were awarded a free. Shefflin's absence created a void. I stepped forward to fill it. I struck over the shot and after that my performance accelerated away. I won possession in the air and on the ground, created scores, got scores, drifting seamlessly between the wing and edge of the square for the rest of the game. Free taking never struck me as a source of pressure; it was simply an avenue into shaping the game.

With the game in injury time and the scores level we got a free on the sideline between the two 65s. With Brian looking on from a few yards away, I struck it as cleanly as I've ever hit a ball in my life. I could hear the roar from the management in my ear as I sprinted back to my position. That was the big moment for me, I knew – the moment that showed the management that I had what it took to deliver for the team when it really mattered.

I thought I had nailed the winner, but Noel McGrath countered to level for Tipperary. No matter, extra time proved a continuation of form. I finished the day with 1–10 and the man-of-the-match award in our victory.

It was the type of performance that convinced people of my hurling worth. Everyone in the dressing room looked at me differently from that moment onwards: with absolute trust. It was the way Brother Damien looked at me when I was a Minor, and Micky Walsh as an U-21, and my teachers in St Kieran's.

MAKING THE SENIOR TEAM

Most importantly of all, it had an influence on Brian's thinking. Seeing someone thrive under pressure – especially when Shefflin was not there – burned an imprint in his mind that would not be easily removed.

I look back now and realise that I was only 20 years old at that point. The burden of expectation that I had felt for the previous two years had been enormous. But now, at least, I felt that I was beginning to meet those expectations.

* * *

The arrival of Galway into the Leinster championship in 2009 sparked renewed interest in the provincial championship. Prior to this, there had been a school of thought that Kilkenny teams were strolling through the province without facing meaningful competition. Galway's relocation from the west was going to change all that, it was felt, providing us with a genuine rival.

Those opinions drove us wild. We were fired up to meet them in Tullamore and remind everyone of the hurling hierarchy that existed in Leinster.

I was counting down the days until that semi-final. In the build-up to it, the only thing I cared about was continuing to play well. My failed championship debut the year before still needed to be put right. This time, though, I felt I was ready for it.

During that long stretch of time before the league final, I was released back to the U-21 side for the Leinster opener against Laois.

Our manager, Micky Walsh, was such a brilliant character and motivator, and nothing stirred his hurling senses at training more than a full-blooded match. A couple of days before the Laois game, we were ambling through a session in the normal way that any team would do before a game when Micky intervened: 'Right, lads, we'll play a match, just 10 minutes.'

We were playing in two days, and this session was meant to be a puck-around, but Micky had completely lost his mind. On we went into a full-scale game without a warm-up. A few moments later, I'm carrying the ball through the defence – and bang. My hamstring snaps. The initial pain subsides and I hobble off the pitch, with Micky on his knees on the sideline, head in hands, the colour drained from his face. The whole game stopped and training was halted; everyone was told to tog in.

That ruled me out of the Laois game and for a further three weeks. I watched on from the sideline as the rest of the Senior team trained hard on the pitch. I could see everything unfolding. My jersey was being ripped off my back by the other forwards on the panel. Gorta and Sheff were hurting from the league final, as both had been sent off with yellow cards. Richie Power was back too. I felt helpless watching on.

MAKING THE SENIOR TEAM

There were seven weeks between the league final and the first championship game and between club games, U-21 games and injury I ended up only training once with the Senior team during that time. The fallacy of team sport hit me. I had worked like a dog for the last year with the memories of that Offaly game stewing in my mind, but still I wasn't going to be given the opportunity to set it right.

The man of the match from the league final was now unable to make the team for the next game, which of course further fed into the narrative of how harsh and uncompromising our training environment was. No one was indispensable.

For any neutral watching on, the night we played Galway was one of those thrilling championship occasions. Joe Canning bagged an early goal for Galway and they led by five at half-time. It didn't look good for us. We came back and took over in the second half, and won by four.

The brilliant comeback, the drama of the evening – all that was largely lost on me. I had been put on for the last 10 minutes, but it was hard to make an impact in that short space of time.

As a sub, you are just consumed by one question while looking on from the sideline at a game: 'when am I going to get on that pitch?' For Kilkenny subs at that time, it wasn't easy to get that opportunity. The 2008 final had demonstrated to me that substitute appearances were carefully rationed – if the starting team were all playing well, then their flow would not be disrupted. This was even more so the case for the forwards. And our attack had class everywhere you looked: Shefflin, Comerford, Larkin, Brennan, Power and Fogarty all started that night against Galway.

Watching on, you wrestle with an internal dilemma. Without question, you want the team to win, and you'd never wish for any of your teammates to have a nightmare performance.

But the natural instinct of any sportsperson is to want to play.

And if there are six forwards shooting the lights out, then you'd better get comfortable in that seat in the stand.

So, you come to settle on an uneasy resolution. Maybe hoping that one of the forwards is off-colour that day. The ball doesn't run for him, meaning the management look to the bench early in the second half. You get the nod to come on and have a good chunk of the game to impress.

The number one goal with Kilkenny was to make the championship team. In those early years, the only way you could do that was by getting game time and proving you could perform. So if I was going to get on that pitch, someone else was going to have to be off-form.

It's human nature to have that mindset. After all, the competitors were not just on the other teams we were facing; it was the lads I was sharing a dressing room with – all of us were fighting for those first 15 Kilkenny jerseys.

MAKING THE SENIOR TEAM

I had waited a year to correct my mistake in the Offaly game but when that opening 2009 championship game came around, I was restricted in the time provided to make an impression.

They stuck with Comerford for the Leinster final – my chances of starting further derailed that day by a back injury – and he rifled 2-4 past Dublin. For all my good form for the U-21s that summer, the Senior side continued to feel like a barrier I couldn't crash through.

I was a sub again for the All-Ireland semi-final against Waterford, though this time I at least made a strong impression coming off the bench. Strong enough, I hoped, that maybe, just maybe, it would get me a starting place in the final against Tipperary.

* * *

Life in Callan represents life on the border.

It is right on the edge of west Kilkenny, located hard up against south Tipperary. It's inescapable, the fact that Callan is the town that serves a large Tipperary hinterland. Travel 10 minutes west and you will reach Mullinahone, while 20 minutes south will take you to Carrick-on-Suir.

By the time of the 2009 All-Ireland final, the Hogan family home was back in Callan. So my family was immersed in a hurling rivalry that bristled with passion. Our home is built on two acres outside the town, looking out onto

Slievenamon. In the 15-plus years since our family home has been in Callan, I have probably only travelled over the border less than 10 times.

The relationships go back further. Both of my dad's grandfathers are from Tipperary. The Hogans are originally Nenagh people. My great-grandfather, Jack Gardner, was a Mullinahone native and a founding member of the John Lockes club in Callan. The old story goes that John Lockes chose their blue and gold colours because of Tipperary influences.

Grandad Jack died aged 95 on my brother's birthday in 1997 and while I was less than nine years old at the time it still feels like he was in our lives a lot longer. His portrait hangs in my parents' 'good room' over the grand piano that no one would dare move yet no one has ever played. His De Valera-type pose, holding his gun from the Irish War of Independence, dominates the room, reminding everyone of where we came from. He was very much a Tipperary man and everyone in Callan knew it. He would travel to Croke Park on championship Sundays for matches with a rosette fastened to his shirt, which was the clothing means of showing county allegiances at the time. His son, Michael, played for Kilkenny in the 1950 All-Ireland Minor final alongside my grandfather Patsy. Kilkenny faced Tipperary in both the Minor and Senior final that day and Jack was happy to wear a Kilkenny rosette in support of his son for the Minor game, but as soon as the whistle blew it was quickly replaced with a Tipp version for the Senior final.

The hatred between Kilkenny and Tipperary is well referenced. Anyone who has attended a cross-border marriage celebration will have had to sit and suffer through the customary Kilkenny-Tipp puns from the father of the bride during his speech. It never appeared to be a hatred of the people themselves, though, but more of the name and the jersey.

In Kilkenny, there is a particular disdain for the Tipperary teams of the fifties and sixties. I was reared on vicious stories about the 'Hell's Kitchen' full-back line of that time and how they bullied and butchered their way through teams on their path to multiple All-Ireland successes. Kilkenny victories during that time were few and far between. In Kilkenny, we are born winners, but we know and accept that we will not win every game we play nor every All-Ireland either. Losing to any county is never nice, but losing to Tipperary – no matter how long it has been since their last victory – was sickening for every Kilkenny person.

Ahead of the All-Ireland in 2009, which was our first against Tipperary in 18 years, the sense of excitement in the county was incredible. It seeped into the dressing room, for sure. It was the game we wanted and the game we needed. Fresh from obliterating Waterford to win our third All-Ireland in a row the year before, there was a real concern that training, playing and winning All-Irelands might become routine for us. It wasn't something that I personally felt during that time, as I was on my own journey – trying to capitalise on my great performances in the league and nail down my place on the team.

Our semi-final against Waterford was the first to be played, a week before Tipp smashed Limerick in the other semi-final by 24 points. During that week we all hoped for a Tipp win but we wouldn't dare mention it in the dressing room. Once it was confirmed, we stepped everything up a level. You could sense from the management that they were trying to make us hate Tipperary more than we actually did. Every post-training meeting was filled with stories of the hatred between the two teams. It all felt like wasted breath. We tried to relate to it but, in reality, we didn't care about the Tipperary dominance over Kilkenny in the past, we only cared about this team. And we wanted to make our own history.

Looking back over our rivalry with Tipperary throughout my time, there was a clear mental hurdle that they needed to overcome when playing Kilkenny. When we played each other, they needed to dictate the terms of the game and be ahead by a considerable margin in order to win. Take their championship wins over us: eight points in 2010, nine points in 2016 and 14 points in 2019. These were clearcut victories.

If we were neck and neck heading down the stretch, the game boiling down to a battle for supremacy in the final moments, we would invariably win. Take the five points in 2009, four points in 2011, three points in 2013 and three points in 2014.

If they had defeated us in the 2009 league final, I'm not sure we would have handed them off in that year's All-Ireland. It was a ferocious game, yet that element of doubt in their heads ultimately counted against them.

Liam Sheedy oversaw huge development in them, but toughness was not a quality we associated with them. They had some fine hurlers – we'd have loved a few of them in our ranks – but when the game descended into a war zone around the middle, we felt that many of them weren't able to compete. We knew that they were mentally weak.

They evolved over time, of course; their range of hurlers expanded and they particularly unlocked us in the 2010 and 2016 finals. Across that phase, they were our undisputed biggest rivals. If we were slightly off our best form, they'd sense it and suddenly everything would flow for them.

But when questions were asked in a tight battle, Tipperary struggled to find the answers.

* * *

In the build-up to that Tipperary game in 2009, I found out that I had finally broken onto the starting team. The impression I'd made as a sub against Waterford in the All-Ireland semi-final did sway Brian's thinking, though the league final display against Tipp was the main reason he put me in. Brian always felt that certain players play better against certain teams, and that I was the man for Tipperary.

They named me at wing-forward, but I was told to start in the corner. My positioning was irrelevant to how I felt; that feeling of being involved was what I'd craved and now I was just trying to keep a lid on the excitement.

The dressing room atmosphere at that time was different to the one that existed later in my career. Brian rarely spoke in those early years on match day. All around us were these dominant players, big characters in command. Brian allowed the leaders to lead in the dressing room. He trusted the team completely. He was still in charge and still ruled with an iron fist throughout the season, of course, but once the team was picked, the players took over. It was the ultimate sign of leadership during that time. He was the alpha male of that dressing room but he had created an environment where he wasn't needed.

Before the 2009 final, Gorta (Martin Comerford) was disappointed at not being picked but arrived on the morning absolutely wired. He wasn't starting but that couldn't stifle the energy he brought to the dressing room. That was a common feature in our team, a sub delivering the rousing speech. With Gorta that day it was clear that if he got on that pitch, he was going to cause damage. True enough, he would lash in the second goal that broke the game apart.

MAKING THE SENIOR TEAM

There isn't any great secret to what is said in those tense dressing room moments before a match starts. Mostly it is people expressing that mix of frustration and nerves as you count down time until you get on the pitch.

But it's also critically important. It demonstrates what this means to people, the core reasoning behind us all being here. It raises the temperature in the room, gets the mood music right before we run out to perform.

I vowed from the start that I would try to bend the game to my will, rather than wait for it to take shape around me. From the first whistle it was chaos out there – a hurling contest resembling a *Game of Thrones* battle scene.

Early on, I grabbed possession and went to strike. As a forward, you stay attuned to the presence of your defensive marker. I dummied to and fro, cut inside to lose my defensive marker, Paul Curran. I knew I'd broken loose and threw the ball up to strike with my left, only to be hooked. In my confusion, I turned around. It was Lar Corbett, a mile from goal, one corner-forward having raced back to stop another.

No one drifted from their attacking post to that extent then; positions were still maintained with some rigidity. Lar's movement and work ethic in that moment captured what Tipperary were prepared to bring to the table. They were trying to be inventive but also showing that they were up for the graft.

A few minutes in and my left ankle got caught under a Tipperary defender, the ligaments torn apart. (The next week was spent on crutches, trying to get it right for the U-21 final against Clare, the ankle covered in an ugly black shade that faded as the days passed.) After waiting so long to get back in to the team, I wasn't about to let a sore ankle ruin my day. I hobbled around for a few minutes, shook it off, and then got up to the pitch of the game, scoring two points.

Tipperary had us up against the wall but we pushed back to break free with two late goals, winning by five points. We were oblivious to the subsequent storm that erupted over the penalty we received in the sixty-third minute for a foul by Paul Curran on Richie Power. It was a soft penalty for sure, and if it was given the other way we would have been up in arms. We didn't often get those fifty-fifty decisions from referees, but we were happy to take it when it came.

There was an exhilarating feeling afterwards. The satisfaction at having contributed to the four in a row, to a final win over Tipperary, was immense. I'd been a young lad on the previous occasions, learning my trade, whereas this had a sense of arrival to it. As I embraced my parents after in the stand, sweat pouring off me, limping with the ankle pain, no one needed reminding of the significance. It was the third time I greeted my parents after an All-Ireland win but this time was completely different. In the previous two years any congratulations directed towards me after the final felt almost tokenistic. An All-Ireland medal is the reward for winning the championship as a whole but when you are not on the field of play in the final itself I found it hard to register that.

This time I had played and this had mattered.

* * *

Seven days later, I played my final underage game as a Kilkenny hurler.

I hobbled around Croke Park, my ankle still roaring with pain, as I tried to win my third All-Ireland U-21 medal against Clare. Being strapped into a boot that week, and aided by a painkilling injection, just about got me to the start line. If it weren't for the significance of the match and the fact that it was my last chance as an underage player, I would have withdrawn and declared myself injured. Instead, I persevered for the entire sixty-odd minutes.

We had a strong, well-balanced side, but Clare arrived surfing a wave of momentum generated by their first ever Munster title win. Clare people have an obsession with hurling. Once they get a scent of success, it sets them off into this crazed state. They brought thousands to Croke Park that day. They carried signs with 'PLAN B' written in black print – a message to stadium director Peter McKenna that they were going to invade the pitch if they won and nothing would stop them. And sure enough they did. My college housemate, Pa, was on to me that week, talking of his hometown of Tulla being emptied that Sunday afternoon.

Is destiny a factor in hurling? I'm dubious but something external was pushing them on that day. Late on, I unleashed a bullet destined for the top corner of the net, but Donal Tuohy made this stunning leap and flicked it away. We came again. I flicked a pass to my cousin, Mark Kelly, who stuck over his third point of the day. On the cusp of victory, they snatched it from us. Cormac O'Donovan hit the winner, four years before his brother Domhnall saved the Clare Seniors on the opposite wing.

My grit yielded four points from play, but we lost by one and the failure to get a third All-Ireland U-21 medal left me shattered. The Clare fans invaded the pitch and we were left with this gut-wrenching defeat, a week after the place had been the scene of such joy.

CHAPTER 7

THE DRIVE FOR FIVE

At the outset of 2010, there was only one theme that dominated the hurling agenda: Kilkenny and 'The Drive for Five'. This was something that had never been achieved before in hurling.

Brian approached it the way he had dealt with a similar situation in 2008. Back then, all the talk revolved around the attempt for the three in a row. Kilkenny had fallen short previously in 2004, and in the aftermath there was a suggestion that they had leaned in too much to the historical significance of the final with Cork.

There was no outright ban on it as a conversation topic in 2008 but it was made clear from the outset that the year would not be framed by three in a row. If it meant something to an individual player, by all means harness it. However, the group focus was all geared towards simply winning that year's All-Ireland.

Brian felt that attitude had paid off and tapped into that mindset once again as we came back from our team holiday to Malaysia in January 2010. 'Talk about it among yourselves,' was the word that filtered down, 'but we won't be sitting in a group for a hurling history lesson.'

For most of the season, I never heard 'five in a row' mentioned inside the dressing room by any player. The three-in-a-row victory over Waterford in 2008 in particular had already given us a taste of what hurling history was like and, in truth, there was a sense of irrelevance around those achievements. As a kid chasing after the ball in St Kieran's, you dreamed of playing in Croke Park, playing for Kilkenny, winning All-Irelands and lifting the MacCarthy Cup. But never during that time were we motivated by records or history. Winning back-to-back or three or four or five All-Irelands in a row was just a by-product of the success of the team. What we really cared about was winning.

We weren't chasing records; we weren't chasing statistics: we were chasing immediate success.

* * *

Snow fell in Thurles in February 2010, coating the Semple Stadium pitch. Every hurling fan was eager to see ourselves and Tipperary lock horns again in what was the opening round of the league, but weather interfered with those plans under the Saturday night lights.

We had no issue with that postponement, but the idea to refix it for the following Tuesday night didn't find a favourable response from the Dublin-based Kilkenny players, myself included. We didn't find the idea of a midweek fixture appealing, particularly having to navigate the rush-hour congestion as we escaped the capital. Still, we had no choice.

Richie Power drove us down, with myself, Paddy, David Herity and Pat Hartley all piled into the car. Richie moaned the whole way down: about the traffic, about being forced to play on a Tuesday and about the weather. It was freezing as we hit the motorway, snow hitting the windscreen.

By the time we turned off at the Horse & Jockey, we were all giving out about this madness and no one seriously thought the game would go ahead. We got to the dressing rooms, togged out and walked out the tunnel. Another white surface greeted us. There was a decent crowd already in, starved of hurling action, but our suspicions were soon confirmed as Barry Kelly called it off.

Brian pulled us into a group to tell us the news. When he finished speaking Richie piped up. 'Ah Jaysus, is there any chance we can even do a training session or something?'

For his passengers in the car, it took a lot of willpower not to burst out laughing. He'd spent two hours whingeing and was now actively leading the campaign to do a training session in the snow.

I don't know if he genuinely hated training or whether he just loved complaining about it. Winter sessions were number one on his list; he despised them. He just wanted to hurl and, when it came to game day on the pitch, he always delivered. Richie was a genius with a hurl in his hand. He had a nonchalant style, which often came under the management team's sceptical microscope. People underestimated his speed, but he was deceiving as his leggy stride would get him clear of defences before his quality striking did the rest. I felt for him, as he was crippled with knee problems, but when required he could still turn it on, like when supplying big goals in the two All-Ireland finals in 2014.

Richie had been an underage star in Kilkenny and in St Kieran's in particular. He was the classic example of a kid who could really have played anything. The first time I saw him play any sport was in Castlecomer when Paddy was playing in a Juvenile Leinster Football final. Richie was playing centre-forward and was magical. We played golf on holidays and Richie had this perfectly crafted swing that would take the average golf enthusiast years of lessons and time on the range to craft. He was just a natural.

It was decided that February night that we would head across to the Tipp training ground, Dr Morris Park, for a few hurling drills and some running. The Tipperary players arrived and soon they started hitting balls on the other side of the pitch. There was a sudden rush of fans in the gates, evidently feeling we were about to break out into a challenge game.

Mick Dempsey surveyed the scene as the crowd wrapped around the pitch, gathered us in and told everyone to go home.

And the whole way up the road to Dublin, we tore Richie apart for the part he played in our delayed return home to the capital.

* * *

A few weeks later and it was third time lucky at the start of March, and we finally got the green light to play Tipperary. Maybe it would have been better for me not to have got that green light.

With 10 minutes to go, I was hunting down Shane McGrath as he sprinted away with the ball on the wing. I was close enough to execute a hook, but Shane had this trait where he checked his stride before delivering the ball. As a result of his sudden check, instead of using my hurl, I ended up hooking him with my hand.

I looked down and it was not good. The ring finger on the right hand looked like it had exploded. The bone had broken upwards from my knuckle and was jutting out through the middle after a compound fracture. The rest of it was a crushed mess; even the nail had been torn off.

While I was assessing the damage to my hand, and with my hurl lost on the grass behind me, another high ball arrived my way. I knew I was heading for the sideline but instinct kicked in and I jumped to contest it, trying to ignore the searing pain charging through my hand.

Afterwards, I was told that I needed an operation to repair the damage. The surgeon did the best he could but the bone was gone from the top of my finger. I've had to watch it ever since. It's the hand I grip my hurl with and, if I get a belt there, it cuts open easily and infection can set in with the inflammation.

That setback knocked me out for the league and set the tone for a year that was stop-start in nature. I'd been trying to sort my ankle from the end of 2009, and now this finger issue cropped up. Even when I got myself right to play in the Leinster championship, I didn't perform. Brian handed me a new role at centre-forward against Dublin in the semi-final. I was excited about it, but never hit my stride. Taken off, I then found myself out of the team for the Leinster final against Galway.

*　*　*

The All-Ireland semi-final paired us against Cork. The backdrop was interesting. The older lads in the panel had history with Cork from previous finals, of course, but the build-up to this game was spiced by stuff going on off the pitch. The player strikes in Cork in recent years hadn't struck a sympathetic tone in Kilkenny. The suggestion they could gather support from colleagues in other counties in their dispute with their county board rankled with us. We weren't colleagues with any other players; anyone outside the Kilkenny border was a rival to be beaten.

Donal Óg Cusack's autobiography had also been released in late 2009. In it, he attached the 'Stepford Wives' tag to Kilkenny players. Most of us laughed it off, this inherent implication that we were boring and robotic. We didn't care, but it was clear that Henry Shefflin took it to heart. He made a point of outlining to us that he had looked up the definition and, as a group, we should be insulted. It was a hurt to be stored up and unleashed the next time we faced Cork. I never understood why Donal Óg released his book while he was still playing. We were the kind of team who only needed a critical article in the paper to drive us on. He provided us with a manuscript of motivation.

There was an element of rancour to the Kilkenny–Cork rivalry then; in time, it faded away, as leading players retired and new ones came to the fore. But in the build-up to that 2010 semi-final, I could see the mood blazing in our dressing room. The older players thought they had finished Cork a few years previously and were determined not to let them rise again.

I didn't possess the same hatred for Cork as the older players did. When the rivalry was at its highest, I was still a

Minor and while it carried on a little into my first couple of years, it was clear that Cork were not the same force at that time as they once had been. My motivation was purely intrinsic. I wanted to get my place back on the team and didn't care who we were playing. There was plenty of time to worry about Cork when my name was on the team sheet. For now my enemy was the player I was marking in training, he was the immediate challenge.

Brian came to me after the Leinster final and said he wanted to put me back out centre-forward for a few weeks of training in the lead-up to the game. Unlike my debut in 2008, this time I had built up enough credit in the bank with Brian and the management to be given another chance to get my place back. The 20 minutes I played in the Leinster final against Galway put me back on track and I knew that if I continued playing well, I would be lining out in the number 11 position on All-Ireland semi-final day.

My concern soon shifted during training one night in the run-up to the game. I was marking Noel Hickey when I heard a distinct cracking sound as I chased a ball. Next thing I know I'm being shipped off the pitch, my ankle screaming in agony.

The retinaculum was torn. *What the fuck is a retinaculum*, I thought. Our physio, Robbie Lodge, explained the damage to me. 'It's like a little velcro strap that wraps around your ankle. It's what keeps your tendons strapped in behind your ankle. You've torn it, and it's not good.'

That snap spelled bad news. Derek Lyng had done the same thing earlier in the league season, so the physios knew the severity of it, and the sheer pain I was in meant I wasn't going to disagree. A scan confirmed the tear and the recommendation was three months out. I was gone for the Cork game, but we figured that, if we overcame that game, a plan could be devised to get me in shape for the final.

We won at our ease against Cork, but during this period waves of bad injury news kept crashing down on top of us. John Tennyson's cruciate went in the same training session that I damaged my ankle. Henry ruptured his ACL in the Cork game. Brian Hogan went through the wars, busting his shoulder in the semi-final and then smashing a finger in training. Hogie was out.

Tenno and Henry were sent down to Gerard Hartmann in Limerick, seeking a miracle. We were unsure what they were doing, but whispers reached us of this intensive regime to strengthen their knees. It was all a bit unsettling. We had a shot at hurling immortality, to claim the five in a row, but our minds were cluttered by disruptions.

Back then there were no training secrets kept in-house. We wore it like a badge of honour, open the gates and let anyone connected with any team in to watch us. You'd see lads in county gear scribbling down notes but it didn't undermine our confidence. Our actions said: *here's the team, here's how we play. We'll still go out on Sunday and beat ye.* It was a different time. It seems crazy upon reflection but it was accepted practice.

It culminated in the end of August in 2010, a Wednesday night when they were hanging off the rafters in Nowlan Park, watching us train. Everyone was training but all anyone cared about was watching Henry. There's a band of Kilkenny supporters who are not directly linked to clubs but were fanatical about the county team, and they were cranking up the hype machine – namely, that he would make a miraculous comeback for the final. As players, we were just trying to stay out of Henry's way. No one wanted to put in the heavy tackle that might derail his recovery.

The circus was in town, but could anyone really be blamed? It was Henry Shefflin. How could you not try to play him? Having Tenno in the same position complicated things, as the risk was increased in having two lads coping with troublesome knees.

It was a learning process. Brian never took the same gamble again with an injured player.

As for the All-Ireland final against Tipperary, Henry went pedal to the floor on the Sunday, but the first time his knee came under pressure, he was forced to succumb. Michael Rice came on and played well, while Tenno hurled solidly at centre-back.

As we were preparing to exit the dressing room for the second half, Henry spoke passionately about the opportunity to win five in a row. He couldn't hold it in any longer. You always got the sense that Henry had a greater appreciation for the history of hurling and Kilkenny. By the time I arrived in the Kilkenny dressing room Henry was already hugely experienced and had begun his career during a time when Kilkenny were going through somewhat of a drought in terms of All-Ireland wins. The younger generation in the dressing room were so used to winning, it was what we had always done throughout our underage careers, but Henry was very aware of the fact that he was part of a special team who were capable of greatness and he was determined to squeeze every drop from it. Myself and Henry are very similar people and we share many of the same values. This is probably what heightens the respect that I have for him above most others I've played with.

Ultimately, on the day, his words were all immaterial.

Tipperary blew us away. When Noel McGrath glided through from outfield to get his goal early in the second half, you could see they were a team that weren't going to be beaten.

A makeshift bandage on my ankle enabled me to be named on the subs list, and capable of being thrown on with 15 minutes left. It was the last throw of the dice, but I wasn't going to influence the outcome like that.

I was 22, in my fourth year of Senior hurling, and this was my first Senior championship loss with Kilkenny.

WHATEVER IT TAKES

I played in the first round of the club the week after and got beaten there as well. My ankle was in a bad state by now – reconstructing it was the only focus that winter.

I was honestly relieved when it was time to close the book on a desperate hurling year.

CHAPTER 8

BACK INJURIES

As I lay on the floor of the showers in our dressing room in the Hogan Stand, willing the cold tiles to ease the discomfort in my back, one overwhelming thought rushed through my mind: *This isn't worth it any more. I can't keep enduring this, being reduced to such a helpless, demoralised state.*

Outside, on the pitch, the 2023 All-Ireland semi-final had started between Kilkenny and Clare, and I was staring at the ceiling. During the warm-up, a sharp, searing pain had shot through my back as I struck the ball. That piercing dart of agony was a harbinger, the red warning light flashing in my mind. I knew that a crippling back spasm was mere seconds away. If that happened, it was game over for me. Not only would I be unable to play, but I wouldn't even be able to walk off the pitch.

I managed to retreat to the dressing room and asked

our team doctor, Tadhg Crowley, for a couple of painkillers. With a back spasm, your muscles completely lock up because they believe you have seriously damaged your back. The aim of the painkillers was to get my muscles to relax. Getting down on the floor was an effort to decompress my spine and aid me into a more relaxed state. Calmness was required. Small controlled movements while lying down would avoid me tensing up completely.

When a back spasm hits me, my body undergoes an abrupt shift to one side. One glance and it appears I have scoliosis, as one side has tightened up and is pulling the rest of my body towards that side. I am not hunched over, but my spine has been bent into a C-curved shape and it is difficult to flex out of that fixed position.

The game has started. I should be sitting amongst the Kilkenny substitutes, watching on, but it wouldn't be unusual for a fella to disappear from the bench, head into the dressing room for some foam rolling or get the eye in with some rapid striking. There's a television in the dressing room; I ask the steward there to crank up the volume so I can listen to the commentary and monitor the flow of the game.

Throughout all the injury setbacks over the years, I managed to maintain my resilience. I never allowed myself to feel any form of self-pity. My body may have been breaking down for several years, piece by piece, but mentally I had always been too strong for it to affect me.

I would talk myself through it.

BACK INJURIES

'Get up. Stop being soft.'

'Why shouldn't this happen to you? What made you so special? 99.9% of players would give anything for the talent you have.'

'Your body will do what your mind tells it to do.'

More often than not, I was right.

But this time was different. This time it really was over. Whether we won or not today, whether I played any part or even managed to get off this greasy shower floor, I knew that I was done.

In general, on match day, I am a really cold individual. No laughing. No joking. No major interactions with Anne or my family. I'm never tense, never emotional.

Just calm.

This time, however, I realised the bleak situation that I was in and for once I indulged in a little self-pity. God knows, I deserved it. For a second, my eyes started to well up. It seemed a long time since I was one of the best athletes in the game. *Look at me now, lying powerless on the ground, pretending I can keep doing this.*

Outside, 48,360 people were in the stadium, and another half a million were tuned in on the TV at home, all watching some of the best athletes in the world competing against each other. Underneath the Hogan Stand, however, I was crumpled on the ground like an old man, hoping to scrape myself off the floor just to sit on the subs bench, never mind take part in the action.

I kept my back nailed to the ground and tried to move my legs from side to side, hoping to hear a pretty decent crack in my spine to give me some sort of relief. After a few minutes, I rolled around and got up on one knee, being careful not to move too quickly. I walked over to my bag, stuck my hand in the side pocket and pulled out a bottle of anti-inflammatory tablets, Vimovo. At this point in my career, having a stash of Vimovo in my gear bag was more important than having my own hurl. If push came to shove, I could play without any hurl, but I couldn't get through a game without these tablets. I took one to add to the paracetamol that Tadhg had given me earlier.

I shuffled back out to my seat. Our S&C coach Mickey Comerford took a look at me and asked if I was alright. 'I am,' I said, 'I'm just trying to stay moving in case I get stiff.'

I moved over towards John Kearns, one of the Kilkenny physios, often a confidant in these scenarios. He would know when I was in trouble but always kept it under wraps. John knew I could play through the pain barrier but, more importantly, he understood what playing for Kilkenny means to every player in that dressing room. If there was a one per cent chance that the player could play, then John would do his best not to be the one to rule him out to management.

I invoked client confidentiality on him straight away. 'John, I felt a little bit of a shot in my back, you might have a quick look at half-time. But if anyone asks, I'm good to go.'

BACK INJURIES

It wasn't an attempt to deceive the management. They had enough occupying their minds with those who were playing; the last thing they wanted to be bothered with was news that Richie Hogan was injured. This was more a strategy to keep going, hoping that, if called upon, adrenaline would sustain me for whatever time I was needed.

The previous four weeks of uninterrupted training had provided me with a ray of hope as to my involvement. If the management got word that I couldn't even get through the warm-up, however, then I knew that I would never play another minute in a Kilkenny jersey, regardless of whether we reached the final.

The choice for me was pretty straightforward.

I can go on, risk that I play badly and never play for Kilkenny again.

Or I can tell them I can't play and never play for Kilkenny again anyway.

The benchmark among forwards in our squad at that time was Eoin Cody. He was in outstanding form that summer, causing chaos for defences with his ball-winning ability and his elusive running style. He was blitzing defenders in training, too, but I hadn't been too far behind.

And then on game day, my body had collapsed. Coping with that tension, that uncertainty, made it difficult to keep going. Yet I couldn't bring myself to let go either. So I took my seat in the Hogan Stand and kept my mouth shut.

And somehow in the sixtieth minute I found myself standing upright, preparing to enter the action, replacing Tom Phelan.

I could feel my feet sinking in the ground as I went on; I wasn't sure if I could function even while lightly jogging. But I got involved in the play and made a couple of contributions. A ball was played between me and Rory Hayes and he beat me to it. I managed to use my body to break it through, losing my hurl in the process. I side-footed the ball to Wally, who was fouled. T.J. pointed the free.

The next high ball was delivered to the Cusack Stand side. I sprinted across and tapped it down. John Conlon was close enough to hook if I shot, so I soloed away, flicked it over Diarmuid Ryan's head as he came near and was fouled. T.J. pointed the free.

In the last minute, Mark Rodgers sized up a 25-yard free for Clare. He lashed a shot towards goal and I blocked it. It broke onto the ground and I kicked it away.

The full-time whistle blew.

We were through to the final. I had done my bit for the Kilkenny cause. My body was falling apart, but my mentality was iron-clad and that prevented it from tearing me down.

* * *

My capacity to play through pain had not always been as great. Over time, I grew accustomed to it. That comes from

BACK INJURIES

living with it every day. Most people complain of back pain in their daily lives, but that level of discomfort, to me, is a good day. Still, the only times I am left crippled are the extreme flare-ups.

My flare-up against Clare was familiar and while I got through the game I knew I needed to get some injections as soon as possible. Tadhg Lynch is one of the country's top injection specialists and by pure coincidence he is married to Anne's cousin Liz. He runs a clinic in UPMC with whom the county board have a relationship through a sponsorship. While we speak often at our in-laws' family events, he knows that when I ring out of the blue I need something urgently. This time round he couldn't treat me until the Friday but called his friend in UPMC's other facility, Sports Surgery Clinic in Santry, where I could be seen the following day.

The injections had become far too regular at this point. I was conscious of this in my final few seasons and opted against getting them unless the situation was absolutely critical. I'd undergone epidurals and PRP injections but the most reliable for me was an anti-inflammatory steroid injection, cortisone. The purpose of this injection is to flush out any inflammation in my lower back. It's a much higher concentration than anti-inflammatory tablets which I had come to treat like vitamins by this stage.

When I get an injection, I'm more or less powerless for 48 hours. The ideal scenario is to lie largely in a resting state for two days, moving gently around, a small bit of stretching and then perhaps a light bit of running by day five. The target is a training session going full-throttle at seven-to-ten days.

My tendency was always to give it seven days and then review. The more time afforded to rest, I figured, the greater the likelihood was that the injection would last for a significant period of time.

The procedure is typically administered under general anaesthetic, but I quickly realised that opting for local anaesthetic would get me out of the hospital faster. Before heading to surgery, I often had to battle with the nurses, convincing them that I didn't need sedation. I always made sure to mention that I had eaten beforehand to ensure sedation was ruled out.

My main reason for this was to be awake during the ultrasound, so I could pinpoint exactly where the injection was needed, as I knew the precise source of the pain. The downside was that it hurt significantly more this way. To distract myself, I focused on the screen of the heartrate monitor that was strapped to my finger. My resting heart rate was generally in the mid-forties, and my goal was to slow my breathing enough to lower it even further.

Despite the pain and subsequent bruising, I preferred this method. Another advantage was that it often meant I didn't have to spend the entire day in the hospital. I could work in the morning and be in and out of the hospital within two hours.

BACK INJURIES

Anne was my chief chauffeur on those occasions. She would sacrifice her week to drive me around to wherever I needed to be in order take some pressure off my back. On the weekends of games I rarely drove. I also rarely travelled on the team bus to games in my final few years. Anne would drive me from Kilkenny to Dublin on the day of the game so I could sleep in my own bed the night before rather than pitching up in my parents' house as I had done in previous years. She'd drop me down to the Crowne Plaza in Santry to meet the bus as they arrived for pre-match meals, and she would be on hand to collect me later after the game. I was completely dependent on her and my routine became her routine without question.

*　*　*

My first back injury flared up in the moments before the 2009 Leinster final. Warming up before we played Dublin, engaged in a routine drill where you race over and back, I bowed to rise the ball and felt a sharp dart of pain, as if I'd been stabbed in the back. I fell to the ground, then attempted to get up but with no success. My back had tightened into a spasm and I was left rolling on the grass.

The Kilkenny physio at the time, Robbie Lodge, rushed over to help but, despite his assistance, I still couldn't straighten out. I got back to the dressing room and was nudged onto the physio bed.

WHATEVER IT TAKES

They had seen this before, Robbie and John Kearns, and so started into a few body manoeuvres, the whole idea being to crack my back and provide me with some relief to enable my muscles to relax. Despite their best efforts, no one had any success. They contacted Martin Fogarty on his headset to inform him that I needed to be ruled out of the match. It took the arrival of Robbie's wife, Clare – another of our lead physios – to perform the move that cracked it and freed things up. My muscles shot with soreness but I was able to stand again.

Within a week I was back hurling and the problem went away. The diagnosis was a couple of bulging discs, one of which had tripped a nerve and spread alarm around my back. I dismissed it from my mind as something inconsequential and returned to channelling my efforts into my hurling.

And I got it away with it for the bones of six years, until we were deep into the middle of the 2015 championship.

We'd gone to Kilcullen for a training weekend, staying in Killashee Hotel. When we went on weekend training camps, we would sometimes rent out a club pitch. Word would always get out and spread like wildfire. 'The Kilkenny hurlers are in town; everybody come down for a look!' We always liked meeting kids and signing autographs, but trying to train when the pitch was surrounded by curious locals could be difficult.

BACK INJURIES

We were a week out from playing Waterford in the All-Ireland semi-final. In the midst of an in-house game, I was travelling through the defence with the ball, sidestepping Mick Walsh only to collapse in a heap. Mick was from Young Irelands, and was a tough-as-nails defender. He didn't spare lads in training when it came to inflicting hits, but on this occasion he protested his innocence.

He was correct.

Writhing on the ground in agony, I immediately knew that I was in trouble. My first back flare-up was a distant memory at this point so it frightened the life out of me. Brian was in the middle of the pitch shouting at our physio Kevin, 'Get him off'. His only concern was that the game would continue. Every time the physios tried to move me I got this searing pain right up my spine and at this stage I was completely frozen. The team medics had to carry me off the pitch. Encircled by onlookers, they bundled me into a car to lie across the backseat and got me back to the hotel. When we arrived, I was still togged out in my gear. Usually, the physio would start manipulating my back, but I wouldn't let anyone close as I was in such horrendous pain every time someone touched me.

There was nothing for it but to help me into the swimming pool where the buoyancy of the water helped a little and I was able to float somewhat upright. I just needed anything to ease that pressure. I was left to my own devices until an old woman came over to me in the pool. Well-meaning but with the wrong timing, she said, 'Hi, there, have you a sore back? I know exactly what you need now, I'm an acupuncturist and I could do it for you.'

Deeply frustrated and worried about how I was going to get right for Waterford in Croke Park, I was not in the mood for random medical opinions. I wasn't physically able to move away from her either so I struggled to smile and listen away, all the while hoping she would leave me be. It was a relief when the physios returned to save me from the awkward conversation and carried me up to bed.

I was left there until the following morning. They had horsed Valium, paracetamol and some anti-inflammatories into me the night before hoping I would wake up a little better, but my gait still resembled that of a crooked old man. By Monday, I could barely walk and by Wednesday's session was unable to swing a hurl.

Tadhg Crowley organised for me to see Tadhg Lynch, who was on annual leave but still met me in Aut Even to give me the first injection into my back. His professional advice was to rest for a week, but in reality he likely suspected that I was trying to engineer a recovery for Sunday.

By 4.30 p.m. on Friday I was undergoing a fitness test. Myself, Brian, Mick Dempsey and our physio Kevin Curran had gathered in Nowlan Park, the afternoon time chosen to avoid the eyes of anyone gathered to watch us train that evening. We began with a few gentle runs to the top of the pitch and back, and I was running like a lame calf. I was a good deal better than I had been a few days before, but I couldn't run much faster than a jog. The plan was to get into ball drills, but Mick interrupted that as I jogged back down. 'Yeah, that looks pretty good, Richie; I think we'll leave it at that.'

They asked me how I felt. I admitted it was painful but was hopeful of improvement with a couple more days' rest. They didn't want any other answer anyway. I was always going to be worth the gamble of starting. The only evidence they needed was my ability to run. Brian had seen me play through punctured lungs, broken ribs and ankle damage by this point and I had managed it. I was the reigning hurler of the year so he was going to give me every chance to make it.

Despite my stretching, I still wasn't comfortable by Sunday and yet when the first whistle was blown, I switched into game mode. I had asked Eoin Murphy to hit his first puckout straight down the middle. I was playing centre-forward but had retreated towards the full-forward line, timing my charging outward run so that I jumped to outfield Tadhg de Búrca. Landing, I swivelled to stick a shot over the bar. That was the first of five points I scored. We won by six. I sat in the dressing room afterwards as happy as I had ever been after a game. My feet were ripped to shreds from new boots that I had worn that day and I sat on the physio bed with two ice packs around them, soaking it all in. I knew that I really shouldn't have been there given what I had gone through that week, but fortune favoured me that day and I was grateful for it. An All-Ireland final beckoned once more.

* * *

I was not the only player struggling with injury. Michael Fennelly was a player who constantly battled his own ones. Typically, his schedule was curtailed, an allowance that was permitted so long as he could partake fully in a training match a week out.

Before that 2015 semi-final, he couldn't even feature to that extent beforehand. We knew Mick's critical importance to our prospects, so his lack of involvement in the training match was concerning. We feared he would be ruled out. When we fired questions at the physios, they batted them away with word that Brian was happy.

We couldn't wrap our heads around it. This lad hadn't pucked a ball since we had beaten Wexford in the Leinster semi-final. That was eight weeks before and he hadn't taken part in a training session since. He just could not be right.

And then he went out against Waterford and his performance level didn't drop. Mick had an extraordinary ability to perform when it mattered and despite having minimal training done.

He was given extra room to prove himself by management but he deserved it. He was an amazing player, to have stood up like he did repeatedly.

BACK INJURIES

My repeated injury worries came later, from 2018 on. Brian and the management were patient but I still generally trained. If you were an injury concern, it was all about the Friday before the game, when you were assessed properly.

In Brian's head, if he wanted you to play, it didn't matter what you or the physios said. He would ask the injured party directly.

'What's the story with the injury, Richie?'

It was absolutely vital that you judged that question for what it was and answered carefully. He doesn't care how you are. He only wants to know if you are going to produce the goods on Sunday or not. So answer accordingly. Tell the whole truth as to how you're feeling and there would be a line through your name on the team sheet. It's a balancing act. For many, it became a case of speaking positively regardless of the situation in order to avoid any questions lingering in his mind.

Tommy Walsh was never injured in his life and then he did his AC joint in a club game in 2011, between the league final and the first round of the championship.

Afterwards, he'd come in to training and someone would ask him how he was.

'Yeah, unbelievable. I've the strapping on now and it's great.'

Tommy wasn't even able to lift his arm, but he was just mentally programmed to make sure that no doubt circulated about his prospects of playing.

There was an element of convincing Brian and the selectors. You couldn't allow doubt to creep into people's minds about your ability to perform. A click of the fingers and you'd be removed. There were too many lads there, all beating down the door to get a chance.

One guy who never figured out the real meaning behind Brian's questions was Shane Prendergast. Shane was a brilliant teammate and always gave his all for Kilkenny. He was far better at reading the play on the field then he was at reading the situation in a dressing room. He suffered a little with hamstring injuries, and when Brian would quiz him on how he was, Shane would mistake this for a genuine interest in how he was doing in life in general. He would try to engage Brian in a friendly chat and return the question, asking about how Brian was himself. Witnessing it always gave me a good laugh.

Shane was the captain of our team in 2016. After the Leinster final we had a weekend in Carton House and Paul Murphy had organised a penalty shoot-out competition where everyone was to contribute €10, with the winner taking all.

In the dressing room before the All-Ireland semi-final replay, the atmosphere was incredibly tense as we hadn't played well in the drawn game. We were all togged out, helmets on, and hurls were being broken off the table in anticipation.

About 30 seconds before we went out onto the pitch, Shane reached into his gear bag and pulled out a tenner.

BACK INJURIES

He walked across to the dressing room and handed it to Paul.

'There you go Murph, that's for the penalty shoot-out a few weeks ago'.

Paul didn't know where to look, and just fired it into his bag as fast as he could before Brian saw anything.

Shane went out and hurled the game of his life at corner-back moments later.

As I grew older and more assured of my status, I felt I could be more honest in conversations with Brian about my physical condition. He knew I would be honest with him about major injuries but that I was also likely to be carrying knocks that he didn't need to know about.

I broke my hand in a club game in 2016, four weeks before we played Dublin. My initial thinking was: *this won't be too bad; I'll manage it*.

But I was struggling. I took off the cast and then hurled with a splint on my hand. But it was my right hand, with which I hold my hurl, and I was in trouble.

On the Wednesday before training I was trying to puck against a wall in a gym, when I had to accept defeat when he asked how I was. The team needed to be picked by Thursday so I didn't have the luxury of the extra few days.

'Yeah, I probably can't play, Brian.'

I hated missing games. All the training and hardship and obsession with recovery was done with the mindset that this would all be worthwhile when getting to play in a match. It never got easier to not be involved.

What kept me going? Sheer stubbornness maybe, that refusal to quit.

And after all the injury ordeals I had faced, I was able to take my mind to a place where nothing else existed and pain did not matter.

Those situations reveal a lot about your character. You learn that your limits are only what you perceive them to be.

CHAPTER 9

2011 REVENGE

After 2010, it was pretty clear that Brian was going to start cutting up the script and penning a new one. Change was coming.

You could always see when Brian had something different in his head to implement for the following season. This was very evident during early season training sessions and the initial rounds of the league. This change would never relate to systems or structures or specifics from the previous year that we could work on. That's not to say that we never sat down in front of a screen to watch specific clips – in fact, we did this quite regularly – but it was always an information-gathering exercise for the players. And once the players had the information, they were expected to come up with the answers themselves.

The changes that were made from season to season only ever related to positional switches for specific players or the introduction of new blood and phasing out of the old. At that time, it was all we really needed because quality players were popping up in Kilkenny like hairs in an old man's nose. The churn of players through the system during that period was phenomenal. (This would ultimately come back to damage us in later years where it became obvious that the newer generation of players were not coming through in the same numbers.)

Derek Lyng had retired following the 2010 season and it was also obvious that Cha didn't fit in the plans. He finished out the year, but was not given a real chance at midfield, where Michael Fennelly and Michael Rice were the preferred partnership. Paddy had joined the panel the previous year and Paul Murphy also broke through, having completed his apprenticeship at U-21 level. Our Danesfort representation had grown.

I was in a perfect headspace leading into that 2011 season and needed it to be a major year. I was now 22 years of age, having made my breakthrough in 2009, only to be hit by injury in 2010. Into my fifth season as a Kilkenny Senior, I didn't want to end up as some cautionary future tale about the young star who never quite pushed on.

I deliberately skipped the November team holiday to Florida to get my ankle operation done. I could easily have waited until late November and spent the Christmas in recovery, targeting a return for the early stages of the league, but I felt that I needed to be fitter, stronger and sharper than the others when we got back to training in January. I knew things would be shaken up and it was my time to stand up as a leader within the team. For me, that started with doing the things that I knew others would not see.

A further MRI on my ankle revealed that the stubbornness to play 15 minutes of the All-Ireland final, as well as a championship first round with my club, had done significant damage. I now needed a tendon reconstruction to add to the retinaculum repair that I had been needing since before the semi-final. Fastened into a boot for eight weeks, post-op, I would remove it in the morning, cycle the 20 minutes from my house in Beresford Lawns to Belgrove Boys' School where I'd been teaching since graduating from St Pat's, put it back on for the day, and repeat the trip home later. That was all part of my exercise plan, and a psychological ploy. The lads were sunning themselves in Orlando, while I was battling the wind along the promenade in Clontarf. There was nothing gained in terms of fitness, that's for sure. Forty minutes a day would barely keep the legs ticking over, but it was the willingness to do it and leave no room for any form of excuse – that was my aim. Once I got the boot removed, I was further along the road to recovery than the surgeon had expected. That was all I needed to hear. Even if I was a week, a day or even just an hour further down that road, it was worth it.

* * *

When we reached the 2011 National Hurling League final, Dublin were lying in wait.

There was nothing in our form that spring to suggest that we wouldn't be competitive – the month before, in the second last round of the league, we had drawn with them. We'd topped the Division 1 table and so, if anything, we felt good about ourselves as we arrived at Croke Park.

Then we went out and got absolutely destroyed.

Dublin went to town on us. They were in year three of the Anthony Daly era at this stage, and you could see that having an effect on their confidence and their drive. They won 0–22 to 1–7. It was a real shock to our system.

I set Eddie Brennan up for an early goal, but we went to pieces after that. The harder we tried that day, the worse we got. How bad did things get? We only scored a single point from play – just one! That was unthinkable for Kilkenny. No one played well, and I wasn't exempt from that. I started on the frees that day and it didn't go well. T.J. took over from me and he also began to miss a few. Things were so bad in our forward line that Paddy was summoned from the half-back line to take the frees that should have been bread and butter for me and T.J.

At the time, I felt there was a perception about me among the older Kilkenny players. This guy could come in, he could score, but could he take any hardship? Was he going to fight for the team?

No one said anything directly – and maybe it was just an idea I concocted in my mind – but it was a sense I was conscious of at the time.

I mostly marked Jackie Tyrrell in training. Jackie took no prisoners. He tempered his approach in matches, but he was a savage in training, knowing he'd get away with it. The line was an irrelevance, he was playing so far over it. This helped place training on a war setting.

No matter the punishment he handed out, however, I resisted reacting, even if I felt like I was being assaulted. The family value instilled in me was never to retaliate in hurling. I remembered D.J. Carey talking to us at a children's summer camp about always being ultra-focused and never reacting to defenders. D.J. felt that if you reacted to a defender then they had you right where they wanted you. I adopted this as my mantra from early on.

We were at one of our regular training camps in 2011 down in Wexford, at the Buffers Alley pitch.

Our training camps were lunacy. We'd go down on a Friday to the Seafield Hotel for a gym session, then we'd hurl a full-blown match on the Saturday, and we'd play another intense game on the Sunday.

Brian would referee. There was never a whistle around his neck. He wanted forwards to get battered by defenders, so as to steel them for what lay ahead.

This day in Buffers Alley was roasting hot. The grass had turned yellow with the blazing sun the previous week and the place was swarmed with flies. The heat had us all on edge. A delivery came in and I held off Jackie with my right hand, caught with my left, and banged over a point. Next ball that came in, I was out in front when Jackie swung the bas of his hurl across, straight into my face, catching me right on the cheekbone. The blood gushed out; it was a scandalous strike.

I rose from the ground, furious. Displays of previous composure under that sort of pressure were parked and D.J.'s advice was thrown out the window.

As the next passage of play developed, I hung back a little and let Jackie rise for the ball uncontested. As he caught it I swung as hard as I could across his chest. He turned, a ball of rage, preparing to floor me with a punch, when I repeated the strike. We started wrestling, even as the game dragged on. When the ball came into our vicinity moments later we were still just flaking away.

Taking belts? No problem. Bully me around the pitch so I sink into the background and fail to make this team? Not a chance.

After training we headed to the ice baths, these huge mortar tubs, typically used on building sites for transporting materials, that were set up in the dressing room. When I got in the door, Jackie was already in the freezing water, these red marks burned across his chest. I just hopped into the tub next to him, my face split open. The whole squad stared silently at us, waiting for the eruption.

It never came. I showered, took my gear bag over, and sat down next to Jackie, showing him that he wasn't going to get rid of me that easily. I remained in that spot for years after. We never spoke about it. There was no need. My respect for Jackie was always huge; I grew in his estimation after that day.

And everyone else witnessed it as well. I had demonstrated that I wouldn't be pushed around. That show of defiance was needed to prove something to everyone. It said: 'I'm in the trenches with ye lads, fighting to stay alive.'

Brian soaked it all in. All he wanted to know was that, when push came to shove, did a player have that desperation to do anything to win? He didn't want players to be reckless, just to have a hard-nosed attitude.

His greatest strength was creating that environment on the training ground. Brian just loved the contest in hurling. If he had his way, we'd just hurl a match in training three days a week and go home.

You could see when he was hyped up before training and demanding a session of intensity. He had that capacity to set the mood in a dressing room, a brilliant motivator. He's a huge man, too, with an imposing presence and a real commanding voice. Very often in a meeting, when you would be waiting for someone to address a particular area, Brian would come in, cut to the chase and strike the right tone.

We rarely heard him during the league. Even at training he was almost invisible, wrapped up against the cold, standing on the sideline, observing.

WHATEVER IT TAKES

When we turned the corner for summer, though, when the sun started shining and training shifted into Nowlan Park, that was when he came alive.

That was his domain.

*　*　*

In my early years with Kilkenny, we trained under the cover of darkness. Pre-season took place out of sight.

We were initially sent down the back of St Kieran's College on a patch of ground to trudge and sweat our way around. Then we moved across to Kilkenny College to one of their rugby pitches, only illuminated by the glow of the street lights from a walkway through the college.

Mick Dempsey would put us through some indoor physical work first and then march us out for these 100-metre runs. You never knew how many were in store. Mick refused to divulge that information, to prevent anyone from pacing themselves. He wanted lads to be emptied.

Martin Fogarty was sent down to the far end of the pitch and told to turn on the light on his phone. We were informed that Murt would be standing beside a cone, and that we wouldn't see him for the first 60–70 yards of the run, but to keep going. Watch for the light; that was the target. Murt would be timing us and as we got to the finish line we would hear him count the seconds. It had nothing to do with times for us; it was all about effort. It didn't occur to us at the time but Murt had the same issue that we had. He couldn't see us start our run until we got to within 40 metres of him, so he just guessed the time himself.

I always aimed to be in the first two groups, a sign that my fitness was operating at a high level. Conor Fogarty and his brother Damien were fliers at this, while Cillian Buckley proved to be a Rolls Royce athlete when he came in a few years later.

Then there was Pat Hartley. A man made of granite and with the capacity to run like nothing I had ever witnessed.

We joined the Kilkenny squad around the same time. Pat was two years older and was in college in Dublin IT, which meant he'd be part of our crew in the car heading home for training.

We had a Friday night session in January during the time of the Fitzgibbon Cup one year. The day before Pat had played a Fitz match, lost it, gone on the beer and his night ended when efforts to skip the queue into Coppers were impeded by falling on the railing outside the club, the spikes impaling his leg. He still turned up for the lift on the Friday, wolfing down a box of Pringles on the way for pre-training fuel. The leg wound was hidden – he got the physios to strap it heavily for him – and he blamed his limp on the belt of a hurl in the college game.

Then he went out and left us all trailing in his wake, destroying the field in every run. I couldn't comprehend the energy of the man. My head was fried watching him sprint clear and with the knowledge of what his body had gone through in the previous 24 hours. He was a machine.

He was also a brilliant fella to have around a squad. It just didn't really happen for him in terms of making a breakthrough. He was a half-back and would have been a star in any other county team at that time, but that was a golden generation of defenders he was attempting to move aside. Once he wasn't able to shift them after two years, his chance was deemed to be over. That was the decision-making process at the time and it would prove costly once J.J., Tommy and Brian Hogan moved on in 2014. We could have done with Pat and Paddy during that period: both of them in their mid-twenties and dominating club hurling in Kilkenny.

That first summer in 2007, Pat got the opportunity to go to America and asked Martin Fogarty what he should do.

'Jesus, you'd be crazy not to go.'

Murt was great for those situations; he'd be approachable for a young player, and pragmatic enough to gauge someone's standing in the panel. If young lads on the fringes of the squad got the chance to travel, they were encouraged; it was never held against them.

Mick Grace was in for a few training sessions in the same year as squad cover, and it clashed with a weekend he'd booked to Barcelona. Murt was in charge of logistics and when he heard Mick was going to cancel his trip, he told him to head away, enjoy himself, and they'd see him next week.

I was wired differently and often thought they were testing players. My college gang booked a trip for us all to Warsaw one November. Pa was chief organiser and had managed to swindle a weekend's accommodation and return flights for €80 a head. I was in – until I got the text informing me that it coincided with an early Saturday morning pre-season testing for Kilkenny. I was experienced and well trusted at this stage and it would have been no issue if I had missed the session given the time of year. But in my mind there was no debate. I never raised it with anyone, I didn't fly to Poland, and I turned up that Saturday to complete the testing with everyone else.

* * *

Later, when my work situation changed, and different hours and exam commitments entered the equation, both Brian and Derek gave me good leeway. There was a level of trust that had been built up and I was always upfront about my personal ambitions off the field and they never made any situation unnecessarily awkward for me.

The attitude was similar when it came to drinking. Brian didn't impose bans, but everyone knew what needed to be adhered to in order to perform. I could go months without alcohol passing my lips, but if I was at an event or a wedding during the season I never hesitated to have a few bottles of beer if I wanted to.

Sometimes, the ordeal around trying to make appearances at social events such as weddings, stags, birthdays and Confirmations just wasn't worth it. The older I got, the more I tended to avoid them, as, if it wasn't clashing with training, I would likely be in need of the recovery. Anne has had to adjust her social expectations of me over the years. When wedding invitations come through the door there is always a sense of 'wait and see'. If the invitation is from a friend of mine, and it falls in championship season, I make every effort to attend some part of it if I can, but if it's one of Anne's friends or family, she generally ends up going on her own. My groomsman, Michael Cunningham, got married on a Saturday in February and both Paul Murphy and I thought we would be good to make it, with training likely to take place on the Friday and Sunday. A last-minute switch meant we only got a chance to wolf down some soup at the wedding before departing for training, leaving Anne there to represent me on her own.

Our arrangements for wedding attendance are often bizarre and when my college friend Declan McKiernan got married in 2021 I managed to catch the early part of the ceremony before hitting the road to get back to Kilkenny for training. Anne needed to teach in Dublin until 3 p.m. and made her way separately, arriving in time for reception drinks and the meal. We never crossed paths and she spent the rest of the night with my friends, celebrating on behalf of the two of us. As a result she has become a better friend to my friends than I am myself.

Family occasions didn't really garner any exemptions from our commitment. My sisters Rachel and Niamh are six years and fourteen years younger than me. Paddy and I were in high-performance mode for much of their early and teenage years and hence missed almost all of their special occasions. Confirmations, communions, birthdays and graduations were below training and matches on our list of priorities. We have all travelled the world individually at different times, but we have never been on a family holiday with all six of us present.

Paddy's stag was one event that I did manage to attend, which was on in Galway in May 2019, during a break week for us in the Leinster round-robin. As best man, I was chief organiser. I was very aware of the opportunity cost so I outsourced the responsibilities to Anne. She piled thirty lads into two large dorms in a hostel in Galway for €40 a head. Being in the middle of championship meant that I couldn't stay in that set-up and have my sleep ruined. It also meant that drinking wasn't really on the agenda for me either. It never crossed my mind to run my weekend plans by Brian as it wasn't disrupting my Kilkenny commitments.

The bus of 30 went to Galway early on the Friday but I had training the following morning. Driving from Dublin to Kilkenny and then jumping back into the car to drive to Galway after training was exactly the kind of behaviour that would bring on a back spasm for me so I coaxed Anne into driving me. She booked a separate hotel for us to stay where I could get a proper night's sleep and a decent recovery. At about 11 p.m., and after I had drunk no more than two pints over a number of hours, she came in to collect me around Eyre Square.

Heading back home on the Sunday afternoon, we noticed traffic building up around Salthill, with Galway and Wexford hurling fans walking around the prom after exiting Pearse Stadium.

Next thing, a man and woman suddenly walked out in front of us at a street crossing. We nearly cleaned them out of it. I took a closer look at them.

It was Brian Cody and his wife, Elsie. He half looked up but didn't recognise Anne in the driver's seat and neither of them copped me either.

Myself and Anne just looked at each other after they'd passed, then burst out laughing.

Brian trusted players. A few lads were pulled after an All-Ireland semi-final one year as they'd gone to a house party and word had got back to the county board. They were reminded that keeping the head down was best, though the real issue was that a call had been made in the first place by some randomer. For a few years the behaviour of these randomers was scandalous, where these anonymous calls were made to the Kilkenny board, outlining what different players were spotted out at night.

The going out was harmless stuff, just a fella going for a few pints after a game, but there was undoubtedly a group in the county trying to undermine us and blow everything up into an issue.

I avoided getting spotted because I was rarely out. I was always on a mission to try and get better as a hurler and drinking and socialising were hindrances to that. I never really drank much at home, not even having a glass of wine when friends came over. We all enjoyed ourselves for a few nights at Christmas, of course, but I'd usually shut everything down then until St Patrick's Day.

After championship games, spirits were always high as we hit the town. In the aftermath of a Leinster final win, the mood would be electric when we'd gather in Kilkenny on a Monday morning to go at it for the day.

In the GAA, drinking bans can be a divisive issue and some managers take it to a foolish level which only serves to cause them unwanted hassle.

I'd often have run into Leinster rugby players in Dublin over the years, out on a Saturday night the week before a game. The critical difference being they were spending the following day in recovery, physio treatment or ice baths.

But we were heading back to work on a Monday morning.

* * *

My confidence spiked after the performance against Wexford in the Leinster semi-final; it set the tone for my strong performance through the remainder of the 2011 championship. Brian singling me out at half-time as a shining example – 'Richie Hogan, that's how you fucking play hurling!' – left me floating on air. The next day against Dublin was a decent showing, then I stepped it up again against Waterford, clipping in two goals in the first half of that All-Ireland semi-final.

That was how we found ourselves back in a final, back facing Tipperary.

Two key figures commanded our attention in the run-up to that game: Lar Corbett and Padraic Maher.

Lar was a natural target after his 2010 hat-trick. Muller (John Mulhall), a wild, eccentric forward we had from St Martin's, fitted that roaming brief that Lar performed in training, as Jackie was detailed to mark him. We kept discussing Lar in meetings, as we put in place the first defined man-marking plan we had ever executed. Wherever Lar went, Jackie was to follow. You could see that Brian and the players were still slightly uncomfortable about it; after all, we never singled out individual players for specific man-marking jobs. We also never named a dummy team in the lead-up to a match. Our attitude during the previous years had been that we invited everything that opposing teams wanted to throw at us. We craved new challenges; the tougher it was, the more we loved it.

Our training sessions had also always been open every night for all to see. If you wanted to know what our team would be, who was playing well, who was injured or what the environment was like in the camp then all you needed to do was arrive in Nowlan Park on a Tuesday or Friday. Now, ahead of the final, we closed our training to the public.

After Lar had stung us in the 2010 final we needed to react, but it did feel a little unnatural. Muller was running around Carton House and a now empty Nowlan Park, doing his best Lar Corbett impression while Jackie hunted him down holding the hurl in his hand like an axe.

Despite this preparation, there remained a wariness of Lar, which I tried to shut down in a team meeting a few days before the final. We had been overthinking situations and asking stupid questions, trying to cover every possible scenario. I ran out of patience, and interjected. 'Lads, Jackie Tyrrell is marking Lar Corbett. Is there anybody here who doesn't have confidence in Jackie to be able to sort that?'

Silence filled the room. I continued: 'There's no need to worry about every scenario in the game as it is impossible to predict how a game of hurling is going to unfold. Since I've been in here I've heard the media predict that Andrew O'Shaughnessy was going to roast him in 2007 and John Mullane in 2008 and he never gave them an inch. We decided Jackie was marking Lar, because we know Jackie will deliver.'

I was on the top tier of the open-top bus the following Monday, Liam Mac in hand as we went down Rose Inn Street. Jackie's father, Dermot, was standing on a bin outside Syd Harkin's pub. I gave him a salute and he was beaming with pride. I ran into him later on that night. He pulled me aside and said, 'Jackie told me what you said about him last week. Thanks for that.'

Jackie didn't say anything to me, nor did I say anything to him. Instead, we picked up the following season the same way we left off: fighting with each other up and down Nowlan Park.

Marking Padraic Maher was another challenge. His domination needed to be curbed. When winning the ball he was launching long clearances by retreating backwards to strike over his shoulder or if in trouble he was very clever at engineering a free. We needed to stop Maher sourcing possession, as we knew he was an inspirational figure who would act as the launchpad for that Tipperary team.

There were a couple of lads in consideration for that task, before they ultimately went with Eddie Brennan. The plan was to exploit Eddie's pace and put Padraic into chase mode. I was to supplement Eddie by drifting out from the corner. Once he inevitably got the ball in hand, I knew he would invariably go backwards to clear from the back foot and my job was to come from behind to get a hook in as often as I could.

2011 REVENGE

The team was well drilled this time around. We had prepared more for that final than we had ever done before. The sting from 2010 had sharpened the minds of the players and management and that fear of losing translated into a willingness to do things that we had never done before. This time, the gates were closed. Eddie Brennan's suggestion that we name our forwards in different positions than they were going to start was given the green light for once. Eddie felt that other teams had been targeting our players based on the team sheet, knowing that we would always line out as selected.

From an attacking point of view we were doing well, but we could have been doing better. In one post-training meeting I spoke to the group about the importance of being clever with the ball in hand. In the semi-final I had lined out at corner-forward and hit Waterford with two goals in the first half. You would think that my marker Noel Connors would be most concerned with not being taken for a hat-trick on one of the biggest sporting days of the year. Instead, he stood well inside me and before the ball was delivered from our half-back line, he sprinted towards the goal knowing that every ball would be pumped down the centre on top of our full-forward. Having been in the team for a few years at this stage I knew well that I would need to be careful in suggesting that the defence get their heads up and use the ball a bit better, as most of the time this suggestion would be trampled on with the suspicion that I was looking for a handy ball. At this point, however, it was getting ridiculous. So I took the chance of explaining to the group that we could still drive the ball down the field without looking but that we could try to open the play up a bit more. Tommy Walsh was sitting right next to me and it obviously sank in as he delivered almost every ball that came his way across the field. Henry and I thrived with the increased possession.

*　*　*

Playing such a critical role in the team that day meant that the final holds a special significance for me. My decision-making, work rate and overall influence on the game had markedly improved from my first final two years before.

Finals are never remembered by players and supporters in the same way. My contribution to that final will always be recognised by the general public for my involvement in the two important goals for our team. For the first, Shefflin sized up a sideline. Having played with Sheff for a few years now I knew that one of the few skills he never had in his locker was a half-decent sideline cut. Even in training he never attempted to hit a sideline in the traditional manner, he always stood over the ball and went short to the closest man he could find and made himself available for the return pass. Before he struck that ball I knew exactly what was going to happen so I turned my back at the start pretending not to have any interest in what was going on. He played a quick one-two with Larks and then I made the dart for the next 30-yard pass.

I turned my man and lined up a point before I heard a shout from Mick Fennelly who was thundering through the middle like a battering ram. I popped a quick handpass in front of him so as not to break his stride and he cut the Tipp defence apart and fired home the first goal of the day.

The decision was easy for me. Mick was an unstoppable force when he got up a head of steam. Both of the Fennellys filled out in their late twenties, having started out as skinny, leggy and athletic players. There is a picture of Mick lifting the U-21 All-Ireland cup in 2006 and he looks like a teenager, with skinny arms and braces. But the Mick Fennelly who thundered through the Tipp defence that day was a different animal. He had transformed himself into a tank.

On a team holiday in Jamaica one year, in a resort where we were treated to 10 days of all-inclusive drinking, our boredom was getting the better of us. We created a game one afternoon where the goal was to lift everyone in the swimming pool and dunk them under the water. Everyone was submerged easily enough, except Mick. Toppling him required three lads. Jackie grabbed him from behind, two of us swam under the water and grabbed a leg each. It took a monumental effort to get him under. He had these big rangy arms, which made for an enormous wingspan that swatted opponents aside. He was a colossal figure to take on.

The second goal has been played back to me countless times over the years. Every time a great goal has been scored in an All-Ireland since, I get tagged in a raft of posts on Twitter about how my goal was the greatest people had ever seen.

Tommy initially won the ball in the corner and would almost always clear it 60 yards down the wing, but his instinct now was to look down the wing and pick out Michael Rice. Michael too delivered down the same wing to Colin who handed it inside to Eddie Brennan, who was in mid-stride at that point. It was much like the first goal. I knew straight away that Eddie would scorch through the defence, and I knew that the ball would come to me. The angle of Eddie's run and definite increase in pace once he received the ball signalled to me that he was going to head directly for goal and was not settling for a point.

I'd seen the end of this move hundreds of times and I'd played the role of the carrier and the receiver, so I knew exactly what to do. My marker Paddy Stapleton had seen it too and he knew he was in trouble as long as Eddie and I stuck to plan. My job was to peel off and maintain the distance between Eddie and myself so that the pass would be long enough to give me time to catch and finish. Initially I moved towards the goal and then began to back off, waiting for Eddie to give the handpass once Paddy went to

2011 REVENGE

meet him. Instead of handpassing it directly from the hurl, Eddie paused slightly and took the ball into his hand before sending it my way. At this point I was already in position. Paddy got the chance to double back, and I knew if I caught it he would have time to bottle me up.

I improvised and took two more steps back, waiting for the ball to drop down a little lower. I took a touch and sent the ball to the top corner. Brendan Cummins just stared despondently, watching the ball and Tipp's chances of a second All-Ireland in a row fly out of reach.

The goals set us up for the victory, but we'd difficulty putting Tipperary away that day. The end result flattered them, with only four in it. Pa Bourke stole a goal back and they hung in there until the end.

But we weren't going to be overturned. There was an anger running through our squad from the previous year. They had not only beaten us, but ripped us apart – that famous image of Tenno throwing a hurl as Lar ran through for a goal a sign that summed up our collective desperation on the day.

The talk that Tipperary were on the cusp of domination annoyed us. They had beaten us convincingly the year before and were a good team, but we were high achievers. Our response in 2011 reminded everyone of the pedestal we were on.

Some moved on after that game with the sweet taste of redemption rather than revenge in their mouths. Eddie signed off on the perfect note and Cha, at 26 years of age, had had enough at this point too. He has always been his own man and he was smart enough to know what way things were likely to go. Brian tried to convince him to stay or at least take some time to think about it but Cha was adamant with his decision.

We had pushed on with a new core of young players and the signs looked good. A handful of my group of U-21s from that '08 win had finally been given an opportunity to show how good they were and it couldn't have gone any better. Paul Murphy and Colin Fennelly had now joined me as regulars. Paddy, T.J. and Muller (John Mulhall) had made good contributions from the bench all year and it looked like their time would come soon. Most importantly our high standards as a group had been met. I captained Danesfort to win the county Intermediate title that autumn, replicating Dad's achievement of lifting the same cup 18 years before. We were promoted to the Senior grade for the first time since the 1930s. Three All-Ireland Senior medals and two All Stars were also brought home to the parish.

* * *

As Kilkenny hurlers playing at such a remarkable era for the county, we enjoyed immense success and, as a result, got to experience fantastic trips around the world.

2011 REVENGE

We had amazing times on Kilkenny team holidays. It's a concept that seems alien to other sports. Professional athletes go together to training camps but it's not like the Kansas City Chiefs, after winning the Super Bowl, were all going to go on holidays together with their coaching and backroom staff.

It's not just about the destination; it's about the spirit it creates in a squad, especially when you're in the middle of your career. If you're in the early years, you don't really know the older guys and there can be vast age gaps to contend with. When I started playing for Kilkenny, James McGarry was 17 years older than me. When I finished up, I was that elder statesman to a player like Billy Drennan, fresh out of the U-20 ranks.

It's an opportune time away from hurling to build relationships with teammates, particularly as the in-season pressures are removed. Lads who got on well on team holidays were able to better integrate into the group; it contributed greatly to the whole spirit. The Kilkenny County Board always made sure we were well looked after. Our partners were also integral to the experience. Anne travelled on most of them with me, making her own close friends.

When I started travelling with Kilkenny, I tended to hang out with Richie Power and Cha Fitzpatrick.

Cha was a serious character. In 2011, when we headed to Cancun, it was Cha's farewell trip. We shared a house in college before we both went on to work as teachers in

Dublin. He had officially retired at the age of 26 that November, a month before we flew to Mexico.

The holiday was delayed a bit that year as Tommy Walsh was getting married just after Christmas. The revised holiday was due to run into the return to school in January, which didn't suit our teaching group, i.e. myself, Cha, Paddy and David Herity. So we rang up Killester Travel, changed our flights and flew out on 26 December, before everyone else joined later. Brian Cody and Martin Fogarty, also teachers, were on the same flight with their wives. However, the management did their own thing when we were abroad. We'd rarely see them; everyone was given their space, which was an arrangement that suited all parties.

The four of us had unreal craic those first few days. There was a wildness to Cha. We were rooming together that year and I was not surprised when he landed with virtually no luggage. All he brought was his Kilkenny gear bag from that year's All-Ireland, some of the gear from the day still covered in the O'Neills plastic. A standard pair of snakeskin shoes and jeans were the only clothing additions.

We both knew Cha's plan here. So I made it very clear from the start that dipping in and out of my bag for clothes for the whole week was off limits. He protested and eventually said he would go buy some of his own gear.

Cancun was this long strip of hotels and resorts and beaches. We did a bit of sightseeing during the day and went drinking at night. One night, we went to a place called Señor Frogs. We paid $40 to get in which entitled us to free drink for the night as long as we kept tipping the barmaid. This bothered Cha as he wasn't one who liked to part with his money for tips. Herro and I got separated from Paddy and Cha and we eventually left for home at about four in the morning but there were no taxis to be found. We decided that we'd run the two miles back to the hotel.

We were running home, tops off, in shorts and runners when a siren went off around us. We didn't realise it but the cops were onto us. They had a speaker mounted on the roof of the car, but we couldn't make out a word of what they were saying in Spanish.

Next thing this cop came from behind the bushes and gave me a whack with a baton across the head and then gave me another whack across the knee as I lay on the ground. I sobered up pretty quickly and began to wonder what the hell I had done wrong. Herro bailed and escaped. I was shoved into the police car where they took my wallet and were left disappointed with only the few dollars inside.

I was driven to an ATM along the strip and instructed to take out $300 and hand it over or else I was going to spend the night in a cell. No reason was given, it was just a shakedown.

They pointed me in the direction of an ATM which was connected to one of the hotels on the strip. An American was at the machine and sussed out the situation.

'Don't go back to them, they'll just keep coming for more money. Walk through this hotel and onto the beach at the other side, they won't follow you. From now on just walk away and ignore the police here, never run. If they see tourists that are drunk, they will try take advantage of it.'

I tore through the sand for five miles and got back to my hotel for sunrise. Tommy and his wife, Marlis, were enjoying a morning walk on the beach as newly-weds when they saw this figure stagger up, sweat pouring off me, limping, as blood dripped from my knee. A beautiful sight, no doubt.

I wasn't the only lad to get a belt when we were there – Conor Fogarty got a particular hiding.

But we all learned.

Don't run on the street at night in Cancun.

Cha never arrived home on that night out. There was no sign of him in bed the next morning, though that would not be unusual. We went off that day for a planned trip on quads through the jungle where we went cave diving in some Mexican cenotes. There was no sign of Cha when we arrived home but we weren't too worried.

We went out that night again, and the next morning Cha still hadn't turned up. We spent the day on the beach and eventually decided that it was best for us to venture down the strip and see if we could find him. We came to this small hut called the Surfing Burrito, a streetside bar across from Señor Frogs that had no more than 10 seats outside.

As we approached we heard from the corner of the bar that familiar south Kilkenny accent floating across the warm air: 'Ah, it's like a mix between hockey and lacrosse.'

Cha was sitting there with a sombrero on his head. He had a woman under each arm and was trying to tell them how good he was at hurling and how famous he was back home in Ireland. He had been back to the hotel at some stage over the previous 24 hours because everything he was wearing was belonging to me.

After a while, he took one look up, saw us breaking up laughing at him, and his heart sank. He knew the game was up.

We called the place Cha's Bar for the rest of the trip.

This was 2011, pre-smartphone era; it was always a roll of the dice as to whether you'd get a signal on whatever basic device you had. Cha's phone didn't work and being such a scattered individual, he'd never told the bank he was heading abroad, so they froze his cards. He ended up whipping whatever cash he needed from my stash in the safe in our hotel room. Never hesitated, but he did reimburse in mini-instalments over the course of a few months.

We lost him again towards the end of our trip. The next afternoon, as I returned to the room, I spotted a message he had left for me. Not scribbled down with pen and paper, but instead written through pebbles that had been emptied from a vase and neatly arranged on the table to shape the outline of four words.

I'M IN CHA'S BAR.

WHATEVER IT TAKES

* * *

Herro had pushed his way to the top of the goalkeeping queue that year. He added extra length to his puckouts and his athleticism meant that he could double up as a sweeper behind the full-back line when needed. The concession of a soft goal in the All-Ireland annoyed him though. He had won his first All-Ireland on the field of play having watched on in 2008 and 2009 from the bench. But getting onto the pitch wasn't enough for him. I journeyed up and down with him from Dublin, always aware of his determination to improve and succeed. He pushed himself to the limit.

Specialised goalkeeping coaching was not a concept in our squad until Herro introduced it. The goalkeepers were falling into our drills and long-distance running, but Herro started rounding them up, pushing for their group to arrive earlier for training, and devising specific drills tailored for their position.

Every other team in the country had a dedicated goalkeeping coach but that was not something that was of interest in our camp, so Herro just took it upon himself to get it done. It epitomised the attitude in our group. There was no time for complaining and no room for excuses. We didn't sit and wait until something went wrong and an All-Ireland was lost and then run to Brian or the chairman to whinge about something that we should have done. We just improvised. This was the attitude that we felt distinguished us from the other teams. No high-profile strikes, no outbursts in the media, just pure honesty and humility

In subsequent years, his competition for game time with Eoin Murphy was fierce. In the league against Cork in 2012, myself and Eoin were the two starting corner-forwards, but Eoin headed back downfield after that game. In time he became established as number one for Kilkenny and the greatest goalkeeper to ever play the game.

There's only a couple of times in my career that a piece of play on the pitch has blown my mind and left me awestruck. Eoin achieved this more times than anyone else. His save in a Leinster game in 2022 against Wexford was one example. Conor McDonald smashed the ball towards the goal from a couple of yards out, but Eoin managed to flick his hurl the other way to block the shot. The ferocity of the strike was so great that he fell back over the line, but the ball didn't cross and we cleared. It was extraordinary, and it was as if the entire stadium took a breath to process the fact the inevitable goal had not been scored.

He has done some incredible things in goal – 2016 against Tipperary, 2018 against Limerick, the 2023 save from Peter Duggan – but that block from McDonald was the standout.

Still, I suspect that it was the standards that Herity set before him that helped drive Eoin on to such heights.

WHATEVER IT TAKES

* * *

I was a 23-year-old multiple All-Ireland winner, finally established at the very top of the game. Four All-Ireland medals in my back pocket and at the absolute peak of physical fitness. If I had been a professional athlete, then I would have been perfectly happy, but the reality of life had begun to filter into my head.

I was teaching in Belgrove Senior Boys' School in Clontarf for three years by this time, and as the novelty wore off so too did my motivation for being there. In the few moments that I allowed myself to stop thinking about hurling I began to think, *what the hell am I doing still working in a classroom?*

I liked teaching for a while, but the reality was that nothing about it really fit with my character. I thrived in a high-performance environment where standards were being pushed constantly and every day I was improving as a person. Teaching put money in my pocket and gave me the flexibility to train and practise as high-performance athletes should. I knew that when my day as a player was done I would need to be content in the classroom for the rest of my working life and this scared the shit out of me. I felt I myself still had so much scope for learning. What was I doing at this age teaching children? Was this helping me develop and get the maximum out of myself?

The issues were all mine. The environment I was teaching in at Belgrove was great; the people I was working with couldn't have been better. The kids were all brilliant to engage with – eager to learn, personable to deal with, even the parents were supportive.

My boss Frankie Byrne was a GAA head and the ultimate leader. The kids and staff loved him. He'd enter the class in the middle of a lesson to deliver an important message in person to the class. First, however, he'd be sure to interact with the kids, picking out some poor young lad who he knew struggled with a bit of confidence.

'You!' he'd say, pointing at some poor innocent in the corner. 'I hear you are a great man to do press-ups?'

Before you knew it the kid would be up on the table with his peers cheering him on as he struggled to do 10 press-ups for the class. The kid would jump off the table arms aloft as the latest hero in his class. Frankie would shuffle off to the next class with his dodgy hip, from years of playing football with Clontarf, having forgotten to deliver the important message that brought him to our door in the first place.

As a teacher, I had a high novelty factor – playing hurling for Kilkenny, appearing on TV, winning All-Irelands in Croke Park. Kids and their parents loved me.

That side of the experience was great, but my enthusiasm for the job was dwindling. A school working day is short, but still I'd be in the classroom, glancing at my watch and wishing the hours away. *How is this day going so slow?* The work just wasn't capturing my imagination.

I also struggled with the reality of teaching lessons from September to June and that the kids were then shipped onto someone else; then you would get another crew, and go through the same cycle of lessons with them.

At the time, the Irish economy was in a bad recession, trying to clamber out of the hole created by the crash in 2008. I was conscious of my fortune in having steady employment, the security that came with teaching, and the comfort of a few quid in the bank account every fortnight.

As I look back, I can see I never had any interest in teaching. My mind wasn't stimulated enough with the content of the work. I had been a diligent student in St Kieran's and left the place with 535 points, mainly through maths-based subjects. Sitting in St Pat's lecture halls having to suffer through an hour of music, drama and early education made my skin crawl. By the time the first year was over I decided to pick and choose between what I needed to go to and what I felt was a waste of my time. My tactics caught up with me, However, and I woke up one morning to a St Patrick's College-branded envelope on the floor that had been slid under the door earlier that morning. I was to present myself to the Head of Education's Office in St Pat's at 1 p.m. I had missed a few too many lectures and I was about to get my official warning.

I presented myself and took a seat in the office. To my surprise, the Head of Education walked in and led with, 'So, I hear you are a good hurler.'

I relaxed a little, thinking that I was off the hook and responded, 'Yeah, I'm okay.'

He looked back at me through his thick black glasses and delivered a harsh message.

'Well, I can tell you what you're not going to be. A teacher!'

I smiled a little, nervously assuming that his message was a little tongue in cheek.

'Now I'm not saying that you won't qualify as a teacher. You might even teach for a few years, but you will never be a real teacher.'

When I realised he was serious I ended up blocking out the rest of the lecture. My head was clouded with the anger, so I decided to nod my way through the rest of the conversation.

Once dismissed I left the office and made my way back out into the waiting room. In a seat, tucking into a bottle of Club Orange, was Paddy.

'What the fuck are you doing here?' I laughed, knowing full well that he hadn't heard about my misfortune and arrived for some moral support.

'Ah, I'm here to see this fella. I missed a few Teaching Studies lectures.'

'Well, he's not in a good mood anyway.'

WHATEVER IT TAKES

And I made my way back to my room on campus thinking about how proudly Liz Hogan parades around Kilkenny telling everyone about how her two sons were training to be teachers. If she could see the appointment list that day she would have died with embarrassment at the fact that her two sons were blocking out the afternoon calendar of the Head of Education for all the wrong reasons.

The Head of Education was right. I may have taught for a few years but I was never a real teacher. I could see how others loved the job, but it just didn't suit my personality and my ambition for myself made me start to look at some other path.

It took me a while to decide but eventually I booked a session in with Brother Damien and he knew there was something bothering me. I told him that I couldn't face going into a classroom again and he wasn't in the slightest bit surprised. He told me that I was wasted in the classroom. We sat down and discussed it and we came to the conclusion that I wasn't suited to a generic job no matter how good that job might be. I was driven by success and achievement, so working in the same role without the possibility to build a career step-by-step would not cut it.

The brother decided I should contact Niall Moyna in DCU and see if there was someone he could introduce me to who could point me in the right direction within the Business School. I met Niall Moyna and Michael Kennedy in the sports centre and they informed me that the GPA had just launched a Master's scholarship with DCU Business School and that I would be an ideal candidate to apply.

I never told my parents. The idea of their son leaving a full-time permanent job in the midst of an economic crisis would not have been something that they would have concurred with.

It took another year before I confirmed everything and hit the books again, enrolling in DCU in September 2013 for a Master's in Business Management and Strategy with the help of the GPA.

My parents were still unaware at this point until one Thursday afternoon in October, I landed in the door at home in Callan enquiring what was in the pot for dinner. My mother was staring at the clock, trying to figure out why I wasn't in school.

'Oh I left school at the end of June. I'm back in college now.'

She looked at me in disbelief not knowing whether to engage in a response or not.

And that's how I started out on a different professional path.

CHAPTER 10

SETBACKS AND SUCCESSES

After the 2012 Leinster final, myself and Noel Hickey were the two Kilkenny players selected for drug testing in Croke Park. We were in a foul mood. The game had been a disaster as Galway obliterated us, a defeat just as much of a shock to our collective system as the Dublin league final the year before. Trying to restore order to the mess of thoughts in our frazzled minds had been the priority, until the news came that we had been chosen from our squad by the Sport Ireland officials.

You are summoned immediately to provide a urine sample, but trying to piss into a cup instantly after a game like that is so hard. You're battling severe dehydration and so end up guzzling water in an effort to produce a sample. It was monsoon-like weather in Croke Park that afternoon, meaning we were soaked to the skin and wanted to shower first. That was something as players we were adamant about after games: we comply with the testing regulations, but only after getting cleaned up. If the tester insisted on coming in to watch us in the shower, so be it. Backed by Dr Tadhg, we'd get our way and the Sport Ireland tester would stand at the door of the communal shower watching as if one of us was going to quickly trade places with another on the team.

Myself and Noel eventually made our way down, a couple of Galway lads there as well in jubilant form after their win. The day couldn't really have got any worse for us so it was no big deal, but I felt sorry for the two Galway lads who missed out on a chunk of the post-game celebrations to piss into a plastic cup. It never ceases to amaze me how closely they watch you during this process. The designated room has two toilets and they stand next to you checking to see if you have smuggled in a fake penis to pull the wool over their eyes and produce a clean sample. This wasn't Russia however and after several bottles of Club Energise and water we got the job done.

By the time we returned to our dressing room, it was empty. We'd missed Brian Cody's speech addressing the squad after. They'd all togged out, got tired of waiting for us on the bus to the point that the driver was ordered to take them back to the Crowne Plaza in Santry.

Our team doctor, Tadhg Crowley, was with us and he

SETBACKS AND SUCCESSES

organised for Tom Ryan, one of the Croke Park stadium staff, to spin us up to the hotel.

When we got there, we found that we'd missed the next bus as well. Their patience was wearing thin after the defeat and so they'd already headed home to Kilkenny. John Kearns was still hanging around – he'd driven up with his physio gear separately – and had been instructed to get us home.

So myself and Noel piled into the car in Northwood with empty stomachs and full bladders with John and Tadhg. We stopped at McDonald's; one of us went in for Big Macs and chips, the other across the road to a petrol station to get a crate of Miller.

And despite the misery of the hurling day, we'd the best craic eating burgers and sipping on bottles on the way home. The sugar and beer had us in good form by the time we got onto the M9 and the misery of the hurling day was pushed aside for the night. When the fun would die down a little we reignited it by piping up, 'I wonder is there any craic on the bus?'

***

We had felt in a good place before that Leinster final. Dublin had arrived in Portlaoise for the Leinster semi-final high on life, all hyped up after pummelling us in the 2011 league final. We killed their good vibes, swatting them aside by 18 points.

The emergence of any talk that a team was fancied to take us down would infuriate our squad. Particularly if we felt it was unnecessary and lacked substance. Dublin were an emerging team, but we wanted to put the concept of hurling out of their head for a few years. We walloped them – though, to give them credit, they came back the following year to beat us. Their squad was filled with some tough, hard units like Tomás Brady, Niall Corcoran and Stephen Hiney.

They weren't a team we had reason to have a grievance with, necessarily, as the only win of consequence they had against us was that previous year's league final. But I always felt they would develop. Dublin had ended my Minor hurling dream in 2005; they were consistently competitive at underage level. I'd often warn the older lads about these Dublin youngsters, saying they were going to come good.

Beating Dublin earned us that final date with Galway. We had beaten them by 25 points on 1 April in the league. The only sour note from that game had been a new entry for my personal injury notebook. It was the only time that I actually felt in real danger on the hurling field.

In the final few minutes, Mick Fennelly mis-hit a shot and I could see the ball set to drop harmlessly in the square. We were 21 points up at the time and there was no need to go after the ball at all. I was playing in the half-forward line and it wasn't even my job to chase it down, but I was outrageously determined to beat these lads by as much as was possible. I raced inside and leaped through the air to

Never too young! Me and Paddy ready for action. I'm wearing my dad's black cooper helmet, which I wore right throughout my career.

New arrival in the snow. Welcoming Mam and baby Rachel home from hospital in 1994 with Dad, Paddy (centre) and my cousin Denise.

Up the Bridge! Me (on the left), Paddy and Rachel ready to support my uncle Richie in the 1996 Kilkenny Intermediate final.

With my nanny, Eileen, having the sandwiches before the 1999 Leinster final. I brought my gear just in case.

Myself and Paddy with our grandads after a county Minor final. Mick McCarthy (left) won six Senior county championships with Bennettsbridge and Patsy Hogan (right) won an All-Ireland Minor title with Kilkenny. Those are the only two honours that I never won in my career.

Champion of the World! Beating Suhn Lee in the 2003 World Handball Championship final was one of the greatest achievements of my career. My coach and great friend Jimmy Holden is in the centre.

Big brother! With my baby sister Niamh after winning the Croke Cup with St Kieran's College in 2003.

So close … Taking on Paul O'Donovan in the All-Ireland Minor final in 2004. Not winning that All-Ireland medal in my three years playing was devastating. (© Brian Lawless/SPORTSFILE)

Eyes on the ball. Hitting a free for St Kieran's College in the 2005 All-Ireland Colleges final. (© Ray McManus/SPORTSFILE)

What a feeling! Celebrating scoring a last-minute goal to snatch a draw against Tipp in the All-Ireland U-21 final in 2006. We would win the replay – my first All-Ireland with Kilkenny. (© David Maher/SPORTSFILE)

Old friends. (Left to right) me with Shane, Michael and Robbie after the 2007 All-Ireland Junior Club final. Shane's loss a year later was hard for us all.

One touch and bang! That goal against Tipp in the 2011 All-Ireland final was one of the best I've ever scored. (© Dáire Brennan/SPORTSFILE)

I'm fine, I'll walk it off. Injuries were always heartbreaking. Walking off the field with Dr Tadhg Crowley and physio Kevin Curran after breaking my ribs and puncturing a lung against Galway in 2012. (© Brian Lawless/SPORTSFILE)

Size doesn't matter! I always prided myself on winning possession in the air. Out-jumping T.J. Reid and Galway's Conor Cooney in the 2012 All-Ireland final. (© Lorraine O'Sullivan/INPHO)

The sweetest feeling. Celebrating with my dad (left) and my sisters Rachel and Niamh in the immediate aftermath of the 2012 All-Ireland final. (© Cathal Noonan/INPHO)

Yes Sir! Giving some instructions to the Belgrove Hurling team in the Dublin Primary Schools final in Croke Park with fellow teachers Noel Joy (left) and Ronán Colreavy (right). (© SPORTSFILE)

Rising high. The 2014 All-Ireland final against Tipp was one of the greatest games of all time and one of my best games in a Kilkenny jersey. (© Dáire Brennan/ SPORTSFILE)

Smiles all round. Picking up the 2014 Hurler of the Year Award capped off the perfect year. (© SPORTSFILE)

Now that's how you play hurling! A few words of praise from Brian after the 2015 Leinster final. (© Ray McManus/SPORTSFILE)

Looking sharp! With Anne at the 2016 All Star Awards. I think she enjoyed those occasions more than I did! (© Ramsey Cardy/ SPORTSFILE)

One at a time lads! Signing autographs for kids was always a pleasure.

The perfect day. On Howth cliff walk overlooking Dublin Bay with Anne after our engagement in 2018.

Spreading the Gospel! With Paddy Deegan on *CNN News* promoting the 2019 Super 11s in New York.

Where are you going?! Being shown a red card in the 2019 All-Ireland final was one of the worst moments of my life! (© Dáire Brennan/SPORTSFILE)

Home for Christmas! With Mam, Dad, Paddy, Rachel and Niamh, enjoying Rachel's return home from Australia.

No need to look! My goal against Galway in the 2020 Leinster final turned the game for us. (© Harry Murphy/Getty Images)

The love of the club … Playing for Danesfort during the 2020 Covid pandemic was a welcome return to reality. (© Seb Daly/SPORTSFILE)

Good days with good friends. From left to right: Paul Murphy, Eoin Murphy, me, Conor Fogarty and Mickey Comerford celebrating on day two of my wedding.

Three generations of Hogans. With Dad, Paddy and my nephew Páidí after the 2022 Intermediate county final win! Dad lifted the same trophy in 1993 and 1999 for his club, John Lockes.

Graduating with an MBA from Trinity College with my godmother, Prof. Linda Hogan.

try to flick it to the net, as the Galway keeper Jamie Ryan came charging out. The impact upon collision floored us, and we landed in a heap on the ground.

I rolled up onto my hands and knees in panic as I couldn't breathe. This wasn't some situation where I was severely winded and gasping to swallow some air – it was serious. I felt like my throat had been cut and I didn't have the physical capacity to attempt to breathe. I was severely panicked and raised my hand to the line to let them know that I wasn't okay. Jamie Ryan had got to his feet at this point and both he and Matt Ruth took one look at me and started waving to the sideline for medical assistance. Matt informed me later that evening that my face had turned blue which in turn caused him to panic too.

By the time the Kilkenny medics got in, I had felt the sweet release of some air going down my windpipe. My chest was sore but once I got that first breath, I was more concerned about my body language than my body itself. Somewhat calmed, I staggered to my feet, refused the stretcher provided and prepared to head off as a substitute came on.

After a few yards, my head was light from the lack of oxygen of the previous few minutes and seconds later I flopped towards the ground. Laid out on the stretcher, I was carted off in an ambulance to St Luke's General Hospital in Kilkenny.

I was hooked up to the oxygen machine in the ambulance

and my head came around pretty quickly. I went to St Luke's still fully togged out and was carted past a full waiting room and straight in to ER. I knew this wasn't good news. I spent many a night in that waiting room after a match fully togged out and knew that the Kilkenny jersey didn't allow anyone to skip the queue. My ribs were broken but more worryingly my lung was punctured.

Much to the dismay of our kitman Rackard, the doctor cut open my jersey and took a scalpel to the muscle at the side of my chest. He stuck his two hands in to prise apart two ribs and this sudden rush of pain coursed through me. He inserted a chest drain to suck out any excess blood and fluid in order to allow the lung to reinflate. That was me for the next week, stuck in the men's ward of St Luke's hooked up to this machine trying to recover.

The way my mind worked, there was only one pressing question: *when will I get back hurling?* I had been in this situation two years before, and although I'd since become one of the team leaders, no one's position was secure.

Tadhg Crowley said the official line was six to eight weeks out, but the compromise was four weeks to let the lung heal and then the situation could be reviewed. My chest was still extremely sore and movement felt restricted. The ache in my ribs remained until deep into 2012, a constant reminder of that collision. Still, I ploughed on for fear of giving someone else the opportunity to take my place.

SETBACKS AND SUCCESSES

The Galway win had put us in top position, and we made light work of Clare in the league semi-final as I watched on. On the four-week mark I lined out for Danesfort in our first Senior championship game in the group stages against Ballyhale Shamrocks. It was a game that I should not have played but there was no chance that I was going to miss this occasion. I was also keen to prove my fitness to start in the league final against a Cork team, surfing a wave of hype generated by Jimmy Barry-Murphy's return as manager. The Ballyhale game was the ideal opportunity to make a statement. We were beaten narrowly, and I played well so this was enough to demand my restoration to the team for the league final.

I knew Brian was pretty sceptical about my rapid recovery, but he was always a man to judge things from what he sees in front of him. A few minutes into the game and I got the opportunity to leave no doubts. Seán Óg Ó hAilpín gathered the ball at wing-back for Cork and I came charging across from the other side, lined him up and prepared to drive him into the stand with a shoulder. The impact forced nothing more than a stumble from Seán Óg over the sideline. It was like I had smashed my body against a tree trunk. The hardest man I ever hit in my life. He was 35, with years of conditioning built up. I trotted away putting on a brave face, not allowing anyone to know that I had come off a clear second best.

WHATEVER IT TAKES

I met Seán Óg a few years later when both he and I were invited to a DCU event in Mallow before their first appearance in a Fitzgibbon Cup final in 2018. Seán Óg had gone to DCU to complete his course through Irish. He confirmed local myths that he would walk seven kilometres from DCU to Heuston Station on a Friday to catch the train home to Cork where he would line out later that evening to train with the Cork team.

He had turned 40 by this stage and his physique would still have put most of our lads to shame. The Cork–Kilkenny hatred had fizzled out a few years by now, so I was comfortably able to relax and ask him some genuine questions about himself. To my surprise, Seán Óg was far more interested in praising me than in engaging in any form of self-laudatory conversation.

* * *

When we played Galway in the Leinster final, we met a team that had bottled up hurt and anger from previous meetings. They uncorked it to blow us away. In the space of three months, they had performed a 35-point swing to win comfortably.

Everything went wrong for us in that game: down 1–6 to 0–0 after eighteen minutes, losing 2–12 to 0–4 at half-time. We'd a brief fightback in the second half – I scored an early goal and set Henry up for a second – but they pushed back and won by 10.

SETBACKS AND SUCCESSES

It felt like the first time we'd been tactically ripped apart throughout the entirety of a game. Tipperary had pulled clear near the end in 2010, but this time Galway were streets ahead of us from early on.

A year later, we were in Chicago on the Super 11s trip. Myself and Tommy Walsh sat down for a few pints with Kilkenny selector Martin Fogarty and Galway coach Mattie Kenny.

Tommy finally got something off his chest.

'Mattie, can you tell us what you were doing with Galway last year? We couldn't understand it, ye completely messed with our heads as defenders.'

We generally regarded Mattie as Galway's tactical mastermind with Anthony Cunningham providing the drive and motivation for the team. He explained it simply. Every time Galway got a score, their forward line rotated, everyone moved around to a new position in sequence. It was a volleyball-style reconfiguration.

Myself, Tommy and Murt looked at each other and burst out laughing. Mattie was very tactically astute, and he proved this with Cuala and Dublin in later years, but it hadn't taken much to outsmart us at that time. We might have been winning All-Irelands, but it was an indication of what might be down the track if we kept refusing to embrace any form of tactics.

Two weeks after hammering Dublin, we had found ourselves destroyed by Galway.

WHATEVER IT TAKES

But in the overall context of the year, the show of defiance in that 20-minute period after half-time was crucial.

It proved we still had some resolve.

* * *

No one was spared after the Galway defeat. Paddy and T.J. were both dropped for the quarter-final. Both were hard done by as, in truth, all of us could have found ourselves sitting on the bench for the Limerick game. T.J. would get another chance later in the championship to redeem himself, but Paddy suffered the same penalty that I had suffered a few years earlier. He would need to wait until 2013 before seeing any more action.

I felt for him, as did most others on the team. Before the Cork game Brian had called out Paddy in the pre-match meeting on the Friday night. He challenged Paddy in front of everyone.

'Paddy, you are midfield on Sunday and it's either going to work or it's not. Okay, you did well last year and made good contributions from the bench, but this is your chance now. Now I'm not putting pressure on ya, but maybe I am. Take it whatever way you want.'

New guys on the panel would be bamboozled by the mixed messages at times but Paddy knew how to read between the lines by now. He went out against Cork and played really well, cementing his place in midfield for the first round of the championship against Dublin, where he played even better. He didn't have a Richie Hogan 2009 league final performance behind him yet, however, which meant that one small slip would push him down Brian's pecking order.

We all headed to play Limerick in Thurles, expecting a response. It took a while for that to materialise, though. Limerick got stuck into us and we were a little disjointed in our play. At half-time, we were only a point up, and not going particularly well.

Having been one of our few good performers in the Leinster final I was doing well without being fantastic. Richie Power had taken over the frees that day from Henry and had missed a few before making way with concussion halfway through the first half. Some poor mistakes from the Limerick defence presented us with two goals which we probably didn't deserve. We made our way down the tunnel and into the dressing room.

We were sitting in the dressing room and everyone's head was down. After five All-Irelands in six years we looked like a group that couldn't figure out where things were going wrong. It felt like we were going to just fizzle away in the second half and watch on as some other team walked their way to an All-Ireland title. I stood up to get lads going rather than sit there and wallow in self-pity.

Brian was so angry outside the dressing room that day in Semple Stadium. That fury built up inside him and when he came in to address us, he unleashed the full force of it.

I was standing up trying to rally lads and get things going. Brian marched in, took one look at me and roared at the top of his voice.

'You shut the fuck up and sit the fuck down.'

I completely froze and stood there silently. It could have been anyone that got that initial burst; it wasn't planned. I was just the one in view when he entered the room.

He turned around and I was still standing.

'I said sit the fuck down!

'When the fuck are you going to start living up to the potential that you have?'

Everyone put their heads down in disbelief for fear that they would be next. He proceeded to abuse a few more before turning around to look for someone.

'Where the fuck is Richie Power?'

A trembling voice came from the physio room to inform Brian that Richie had been taken away in an ambulance.

'Well, he's lucky he's not here or he'd be getting it as well!'

He pointed over to T.J.

'T.J., you are coming in. You've been crying all week to Martin Fogarty about how you're not in the team. Well, you're in now, so do something.'

I went out in the second half, completely pumped up, playing with this furious energy. And 12 minutes in I was walking towards the sideline after being shown a red card.

I'd won a ball transferred down the wing and ended up being shoved over the sideline. I went to shrug a Limerick fella off, but used my hurl swinging back to do so, hitting Seanie Tobin. Seanie jumped to the ground holding his arm. The referee Michael Wadding waved play on, reading it as just a stray swing in the midst of a tackle.

Linesman James Owens started waving the flag and brought over the referee. After consulting, Michael Wadding came up and sent me off.

We won the game, and there had been definite improvement in the second half, but I was raging coming back into the dressing room. Colin Fennelly and Aidan Fogarty had both started, scoring 1–2 apiece. Lads were hitting good form up front and now I was facing suspension.

Brian wasn't finished and he waited until everyone had togged in before lining every member of the panel up on the bench around the dressing room. He tore into us again one by one this time, victory didn't mean we were immune to post-match criticism. There was no solace for those who didn't feature on the pitch either, they too were challenged and warned in equal measure. He came down the line and reached me before pausing, perhaps sensing my anger over the day's chain of events and that I was on the brink of a volcanic eruption. 'Richie … we'll have to see what happens the next day now. Red card, don't know what we're gonna do.'

We made our way across to the Anner Hotel in Thurles for our post-match meal and the players headed out into the lobby while the backroom staff and county board officers, who were served last, finished their food. I was sitting down by myself when the troops were eventually being rounded up and Brian, sensing that I had calmed a little, came over to talk.

We discussed the red card incident; he didn't feel it was justified. He would never come down too hard on fellas sent off, he viewed it the same as injured players: focus on the collective, push on with who is there.

It had been an old-school approach from Brian in the dressing room, but it worked. It was the approach that we reacted best to and the approach that was most effective. The fury he created in the dressing room had influenced our second-half performance. I happened to be collateral damage on this occasion, but I wasn't about to take it personally.

Three weeks later I paid the price for that decision, confined to a seat in the Hogan Stand for our total destruction of Tipperary. We expected that Tipp would bring everything they had but the theme of close-fought matches between us was eradicated. Tipp managed to go in at half-time a point up; by the end we were 18 clear having trampled them into the ground. The whole day was extremely difficult for me. Having played hundreds of games in all forms of team sport I had never been sent off before and hence never had to endure a suspension. Paddy and I had a few pucks in the back garden that morning as we generally would before leaving Callan to catch the team bus in Kilkenny city. We'd never talk about the match or anything at all for that matter. There would just be the sound of the ball whizzing across the garden as we sharpened our touch while simultaneously killing time. I always struck the ball at Paddy a lot harder than I would at anyone else. I always wanted to turn it into a competition, hoping he'd get thick and belt it back at me with more venom. It was the perfect way to shake off any sort of casualness before a game.

When it came time to throw the hurls into the car and head into Kilkenny it hit me hard. Here I was heading into the team bus fully decked out in my black and amber tracksuit but with nothing in my hands, no gear bag, no hurls. I felt a little lost for the rest of the day not knowing what to do with myself. Even as a substitute you are still in the zone as you know that anything could happen, and you might be sprung into action after a minute. Today however, it didn't matter if the whole team cried off ill before the game. I was fit and ready to go but I couldn't play.

Before the game Murt Fogarty came over to me as he was doing his rounds.

'If you see anything during the game make sure to come down and give me a shout.'

I looked at him with a puzzled face as we both knew that I would be keeping my mouth shut after the way the Limerick game had gone.

For most of the game I couldn't relax because I was terrified that this could be the last game of the championship. As the game went on and we stretched further and further ahead of Tipp my worry was starting to shift from being blamed for Kilkenny's championship exit to the security of my place for the final. My suspension created a gap in the forwards for T.J. to get another chance to redeem himself and he took it, grabbing two goals. The rest of the forwards also played pretty well with Henry being the least impressive for once.

After being the team's best forward for the Leinster Championship I was now in danger of finding myself on the bench for the All-Ireland final. How do you get back into a forward line that's scored 4-24 in an All-Ireland semi-final? I knew Brian wouldn't want to juggle his attacking options; starting me on the bench would have been a sign of our strength, the type of message he would love to send out.

Towards the end of the game Michael Rice fell victim to a wild stroke from Padraig Maher near the sideline. Ricey's hand was badly damaged, and this ruled him out for our rematch with Galway.

Brian came to me before the final to discuss how I felt about playing midfield and operating a deeper role than I usually played for the team. Because of my fitness and ability on the ball he felt that I would thrive in the middle third of the field with a little more freedom. We had tried it earlier in the season when he wanted to turn me into a Paul Galvin type character snatching onto breaks around the middle and working back into the midfield area. A few broken ribs and a punctured lung put an end to that experiment but now Ricey's injury had forced his hand. I was just happy to be on the team sheet and willing to do whatever it took to be there.

The demolition job we did on Tipperary was only the second most talked about aspect of that game. The sideshow involving Lar and Jackie as well as Tommy and Pa Bourke was top of everyone's mind after that game. Jackie, as per the year before, was instructed to follow Lar everywhere he went with our other defenders picking up whoever else came their way. Their plan to counteract this was for Lar to run around after Tommy in the hope that we would just give in and tell Jackie to revert to marking Pa Bourke for the day.

When it became clear that we weren't going to let the Tipp forwards dictate who was going to mark them, instead of getting on with it, Pa and Lar turned the game into a farce. At one stage in the second half when we were at least ten points ahead, the four of them were running around in a circle in the Cusack-Davin corner while the game unfolded at the other end. My reaction was part disgust, part ridicule. It summed up some of the bullshit around Tipperary in between the Liam Sheedy eras, epitomising a mindset of seeking uncontested play and avoiding contact.

WHATEVER IT TAKES

* * *

Collectively we were conscious that Galway had blown us away in July, and in this September game, they started sharper. Joe Canning surged through our defence to lash home an early goal, the type of score that had an ominous feel to it. Having lined out at midfield I found myself closer to our goal than I would normally have been in the past. As Joe got the ball outside the 21 he walked through five of our defenders as if they weren't there. Deep down we would have believed that Galway were not capable of winning an All-Ireland. Almost every time we played them the same warning rang out in our dressing room.

'Galway are deadly dangerous. If we give them space, they will skin us. They can fuck up our year but they don't have the balls to finish off the job and win the All-Ireland.'

For the first half it looked like this time was going to be different. We were five down at the break, but we wiped away any element of doubt that existed by taking charge in the second half.

Near the end, gripping a one-point advantage, I saw David Burke jump to gather the ball near me. I was aware of the need for discipline as I tackled him, but he still hit the ground and Barry Kelly awarded them a soft free. I was freaking out that I'd cost us the chance to win the All-Ireland when Canning missed the free. Then, moments later, Galway got another lifeline, this time with an even more dubious free when Jackie was adjudged to have fouled Davy Glennon. Canning made no mistake with the second chance and so we were going to a replay.

Henry had been instrumental in our recovery in the second half. Brian Hogan and Paul Murphy gave performances that stood out, but Henry's leadership that day was outstanding. You could see how much the possibility of winning a ninth All-Ireland meant to him. One of his greatest attributes was to constantly demand more from others and stay organising the team. He put a lot of emphasis on motivating those around him to get better and better.

We were disgusted at not winning but needed to change our mindset. We hadn't been defeated either, but for the first time in 53 years there was an All-Ireland final replay required. It was a new scenario for everyone to embrace.

We seized our second chance. I was restored to the forwards, in at 14 with two giants either side in Walter Walsh and Richie Power. We scored 2–8 between us and, as a trio, we were just all on song.

The whole balance of our team worked and Galway had no answers.

At that time we felt Galway were talented enough to beat us in an isolated game, but lacked the consistency to string together the performances that would land them an All-Ireland.

And we didn't want to see them win one.

That would have sickened us. We really didn't want Galway players to have All-Ireland medals in their pockets.

Saying that, when they did achieve it five years later, it was deserved.

They'd become huge rivals by virtue of their entry into Leinster. The increased frequency of meetings spiced up our games. When they beat us, they were capable of inflicting a hiding. We always felt that if we allowed them the freedom to hurl, they had the talent to destroy teams. Reduce the game to a battle, however, and it was a different story.

* * *

A few days after the drawn game, Joe Canning had given an interview at a press event. He mentioned how Henry's behaviour had been a bit unsportsmanlike and we were a bit cuter with the referee. It was a harmless comment, but it got brought up at a team meeting and we twisted it into something that it wasn't. That would have been common; we were told to avoid the media, but if it was beneficial to let a comment filter through, it would happen. We'd find something that could be useful in firing us up, stirring up a little bit of anger.

Pundits are asked at the start of every year who's going to win the All-Ireland. They can only pick one side but if we weren't chosen, we'd feast on that comment, reference it and ensure it spiralled into this sense of a conspiracy against us.

Anything to generate motivation and prevent staleness. In a high-performing group, you'll do whatever it takes to maintain your edge and ensure softness does not creep in.

Media coverage never bothered me. When I first entered the Kilkenny squad, there was almost a disdain for the media. Brian felt that if you were going well, no good could come from doing an interview. He hated seeing young players in situations where they were talking at commercial launches or chatting to TV reporters when accepting man-of-the-match presentations. In his eyes, it was a sign that people were getting carried away with themselves, and players needed to remain grounded.

In my first season with the team in 2007, Cha had come off the back of one of the most successful seasons that any player had put in. He won a league, Leinster and All-Ireland medal with the Seniors, an U-21 Leinster and All-Ireland medal. With his club Ballyhale Shamrocks he won the Kilkenny Senior and U-21 county titles and finished the year as the Kilkenny Club Player of the Year and the GAA Young Hurler of the Year. Naturally, commercial opportunities were following Cha around the following year and being Dublin-based and in college he found it easier to take up the offers.

Brian was determined that no player would get carried away during the period and Cha got his warning at a team meeting.

'Cha! I hear you are going around with a scissors in your pocket.'

That comment was enough to quieten Cha and others once the business end of the championship came around.

Different methods were tried to control access. At times, requests had to go through Martin Fogarty or the county board, or, at other times, there was a blanket ban on talking altogether.

The primary focus was on shielding us from external distractions. During video analysis sessions, when we reviewed past games, there were even instances where we were asked to mute the commentary. The rationale was that listening to Marty Morrissey and Michael Duignan extolling the virtues of Kilkenny players offered us no tangible benefit.

Navigating what was permissible in terms of media could be both awkward and stressful. As a younger player, these situations could be particularly nerve-wracking. However, I was more mature than others my age. I adopted a pragmatic approach: if someone requested something of me, I would comply, engage in the conversation, and move on, assured that it would not impact my performance in subsequent games. My general demeanour in these settings was one of confidence. Living in Drumcondra, I was frequently invited to participate in GAA promotional events, such as those for the Fitzgibbon Cup or various initiatives launched by the GPA.

SETBACKS AND SUCCESSES

The message I was getting in Kilkenny was crystal clear, however: 'A player like you should never speak to the media.'

I wasn't passionate enough about it to protest. So I went along with it, the party line.

* * *

Ultimately, 2012 was a hugely satisfying All-Ireland to win. We'd absorbed the setbacks and still come through. The narrative out there was that we'd picked up some handy All-Irelands, going the direct route through Leinster. But now we'd shown that heading through the back door couldn't stop us either.

We consistently demonstrated our resilience. We were never truly defeated; our determination kept us moving forward. When we were at our best, we overwhelmed our opponents. Even on our off days, we remained in games until the bitter end.

Beyond being great hurlers, we were the ultimate survivors.

CHAPTER 11

STRANGE TIMES

On the night that Clare beat Cork in the 2013 All-Ireland final replay, Paul Murphy and I were out for a few pints and eventually found ourselves in Coppers. We were part of a Leinster team that played against a Munster selection in an GPA Super 11s exhibition match as part of the curtain-raiser to the game. I was 25 and this was the first time since I started playing Senior hurling that I wasn't involved in the All-Ireland final, having featured in the previous six.

I watched the drawn game at home on the TV and it was an unsettling experience but our cameo before the replay made me sick to the pit of my stomach. We felt like the punchline to a joke, playing a curtain-raiser that meant nothing before the serious hurlers took centre stage later on under floodlights and played out their epic contest. Whatever about being on the pitch and tasting defeat, watching on in a passive state felt way worse.

All-Ireland final day had always been a special occasion in our house. As a kid if Kilkenny were playing, we would travel in support. If we didn't feature in the final then we would sit down as a family and enjoy the spectacle from the couch. When half-time arrived, I would skip the punditry and go out to the garden and get 15 minutes of banging the ball off the wall, emulating the great skills that I had just seen on the TV.

Now an All-Ireland that didn't feature Kilkenny represented a lost opportunity and a reminder of our failures in that given year. Once you are knocked out of the championship you want its conclusion to arrive as soon as possible so you can mentally look towards the next year.

As we sipped our pints sorrowfully in the side bar of Coppers the Clare team arrived in. Having been fed a diet of hotel banquets on the nights of our All-Ireland finals, we were surprised by the fact that they had ventured into town rather than staying at their own after-party.

Their All Star full-back David McInerney spotted me and came over to say hello. David is from Tulla and his family and Pa Minogue's family are friends. When he finished his Leaving Cert he lived on our couch in Dublin for the best part of three months, trekking across to Froebel College where he had started teaching college but was a little unsure as to whether he wanted to do it. We lived in a large house in Beresford Lawns, right across the road from

Bertie Ahern who had 24-hour Garda protection on the property. We converted the ground floor into a pad for our entertainment. We had a gym with the best of equipment, a games room filled with consoles and a table tennis table. I would arrive home from school at about 3 p.m. and dish out some ping pong lessons to him before I headed off down the road to training. If he was unsure about teaching life before then, we had made up his mind for him. We sold him the dream.

More of the Clare players came over and asked us to stand in for a photo. It would be a memento from the night they were crowned All-Ireland champions, a photo with the Kilkenny lads, Richie and Paul.

We were getting slightly uncomfortable as we felt like gatecrashers even though we were there first, so we left. Halfway down Harcourt Street, I grabbed Paul and put him against the wall. Half in jest, half in seriousness, I said, 'That's it now. We're not spending All-Ireland final night like this again. We will remember this night when we win the 2014 All-Ireland.'

Sometimes when you don't reach the All-Ireland final, it can be a deeply regretful experience. But we had been so far off the pace in 2013 that we had no reason to feel hard done by.

* * *

We dismissed Offaly in the first round that year and played well against Dublin, before allowing them a route back into contention. It was unlike them to make a comeback against us, and unlike us to let that happen. We scraped a draw in the end, and everyone assumed we'd come back to Portlaoise and make amends, preserving our strong replay record.

Except we couldn't quite locate our best form then either. Danny Sutcliffe scored the only goal of a game which saw Dublin beat Kilkenny for the first time in the championship in 71 years.

It set the tone for a summer where we stumbled through games, scrambling to find the flow in our performances.

After we lost to Dublin in the Leinster semi-final replay we got hit with a serious dose of reality. Our three-in-a-row bid couldn't have been further from our minds as we were dumped into the qualifiers. Usually we would be angry after a defeat, but this time we were more embarrassed than anything.

The qualifier first round draw was made the following Monday morning and it transformed our mood. We were paired against Tipperary, the game fixed for the following Saturday night. Suddenly our minds sharpened. Even though it was the first round of the qualifiers, we felt the prize couldn't be greater. The fear of losing was always a great motivator for us and this time the consequences of coming second best were enormous. On the flip side the prize for winning was equally motivating. An opportunity to bury Tipperary, sending them out of the championship at the earliest possible stage of the competition. In many ways this game meant more than an All-Ireland to us – we hated Tipperary even more than we loved winning.

Every year we compete for an All-Ireland and regardless of the result the cycle begins again a few short months after the conclusion of the season. But opportunities like this are rare and this elevates their significance to us as well as the tension in the lead-up. In my career we were presented with this kind of opportunity only twice. The other was in my last year when we went down to Wexford Park to face a Wexford team that had slipped up against Westmeath in the Leinster round-robin stages. A Kilkenny win that day would have relegated Wexford to the Joe McDonagh Championship for 2024. We really didn't like that Wexford team and nothing would have been more satisfying than sitting down on a Saturday evening the following summer, pulling out the phone and swiping through Buff Egan's Snapchat stories, seeing them tour the country playing Kerry, Kildare and Meath. We weren't ruthless enough to take advantage of it on that occasion, and I firmly believe that the lack of killer instinct that day festered in the group and was a huge contributing factor to us not putting Limerick away in the last 20 minutes of the All-Ireland.

During the week leading up to the game, Brian approached me and asked if I would speak to the team on

WHATEVER IT TAKES

Friday after training. Players would often be called out for their views during meetings but he rarely lined up players a few days in advance. It was clear that he wanted me to think about what I was going to say. When we sat down for our final meeting in preparation for the game Brian addressed the team, letting them know that the only members of the group that would speak tonight were Henry Shefflin, Richie Hogan and Richie Power.

Giving speeches in the lead-up to games would weigh heavily on me, so I generally avoided it. It heaps additional and unneeded pressure on the player who speaks. The environment was one where players were expected to walk the walk first before talking the talk. Adding a few words before a big game amidst the intensity of the dressing room was different because it served mainly to show your teammates that you were up for it and most players were not listening to the actual words anyway. Tactical contributions in the lead-up to the game were also fine as this was providing us with an advantage and there was a general understanding that no player was expected to be a tactical genius. When Brian asked me to speak, a small part of me was thinking, 'Jesus, this is the last thing I need now' but the larger part of me took it as a serious vote of confidence in me from him so I agreed and got on with it.

When the time came, we burst out the dressing room door and onto the field. We felt like we were going to war. Tommy Walsh was in front of me and in reaction to the roaring crowd he broke into a fit of jumping into the air, landing to take a few steps before jumping again as if he had just scored the winning goal in an All-Ireland. I didn't really know what to do so I just copied him until someone threw a ball my way which I drove over the bar and into the stand.

Myself and Wally tore the Tipperary defence apart in the first half that night. I sprinted across the field to pick up the first ball and pivoted back, delivering a cross field pass to Wally who rifled it over the bar for our first score. The next ball was driven high down my wing, and I leaped above Conor O'Brien to catch it. I fell straight to the ground, ball still in hand but bounced back up, shrugged off O'Brien and drove the ball, high and over the bar. I was on the sideline close to the crowd and the roar inspired me to raise my fist into the air. I felt it was going to be a special day.

It wasn't a high-scoring game but the pace was relentless and the intensity of the contest sent jolts of energy racing around the pitch. We won All-Ireland finals in various brilliant ways, but that Saturday night in the early July sunshine, playing in our home city, was the greatest encounter I've ever been involved in.

We raised the stakes more for ourselves all week in the build-up. We felt a loss to Tipperary would have erased all of the great work we had completed before. Victory was essential. It wouldn't secure a trophy, only your name in the drum for the following week's draw, but it would reinforce our status. That game epitomised the difference between us and Tipperary. As hurlers there wasn't a huge amount between us. But as survivors we were always superior.

The choice of venue really added to it. We had only ever played in championship against Tipperary in Croke Park. Winning home advantage gave it an extra dimension, we were determined not to let them arrive in our backyard and take us down. We had rarely played championship matches in Nowlan Park, certainly not on a similar scale.

It was the most incredible hurling occasion I've played in. Whenever the question is asked of anyone who played on that day to name their favourite ever game, this one is cited. Tipperary players think likewise. While in an Irish Bar on an All-Star tour to Singapore in 2017, Padraic Maher cornered me.

'Remember that game in Nowlan Park. That was unbelievable.'

We reminisced about the game for a while with Austin Gleeson and Noel Connors while also abusing them for ruining the game of hurling with their mass defence and short passing which was beginning to set a tactical trend.

Though we won that day, 0–20 to 1–14, our overall performances remained patchy. Take the qualifier against Waterford. We were five points up near the end of full-time, but then Kevin Moran produced this one-man point-scoring show that helped them claw their way back into it.

We were under ferocious pressure but we were surviving. Then, in the last play of the game, with the game level, the ball fell out to Matt Ruth. He gathered and swung a shot that sent the ball travelling over the bar to ensure a narrow Kilkenny win.

As the ball was sailing over the bar James Owens quickly put his whistle to his mouth and blew for full-time. We went berserk. Matt was a millisecond away from breaking into a celebration having won the game for us and when he heard the sound of the whistle snatching away his moment from him, he couldn't believe it.

We've all seen situations where a referee gives a team a couple of extra seconds to get an equaliser in an evenly contested game and in general anyone who plays or watches sport accepts it. Had he decided to give Waterford another chance following the score it wouldn't have bothered us too badly. But deciding to take away a score in order to call a draw was as infuriating as it was baffling.

We ran over to him awaiting his explanation. He didn't say anything. Never answered back, never mentioned why he'd blown at that moment. He just turned away with a blank face. It wasn't the last time he'd make a game-defining decision against us.

As he left the pitch, our county board officials and management vented their frustration.

We tried to regain some calm because extra time was going to be thrown at us a few minutes later. We managed to channel our grievance into getting over the line by three points.

There would have been uproar if we'd lost but that full-time drama was largely forgotten about because we were moving forward to a quarter-final with Cork.

Coming off the back of my best league campaign and two of my best championship performances in a Kilkenny jersey against Tipperary and Waterford my confidence was sky high. By the time we got to the All-Ireland quarter-final against Cork we already had five championship games played. We weren't used to this at all, we barely trained from week to week, instead prioritising recovery for the next game.

Shane O'Neill was detailed to mark me in the quarter-final. Later Shane and I would work together for PwC on the same consulting team. Shane was an incredible athlete with blistering pace. He was a similar defender to Paul Murphy, he loved to attack the ball from the front knowing that he could rely on his pace and agility if he made a mistake. I was playing so well that I wasn't thinking about Shane for a second. I didn't care who I was marking. I was playing full-forward and I was going to dominate that area no matter who came my way.

Before the match I was going through my usual routine at Semple Stadium and using the time in the dressing room to chat with a few players about how we were going to play. Brian would always encourage forwards and defenders to get amongst themselves in the dressing room beforehand.

As forwards we were instinctive, and we understood each other on the pitch. I preferred to speak to the midfielders and defenders. I would spend some time letting them know where I would be when they got the ball. The goal was that they would deliver the ball quicker without needing to pause and see what options were available. In an instinctive forward line like ours, speed was everything.

Brian came over as he always did to give me a few words as we were about to head out the tunnel.

'Now, Richie! O'Neill is lightning quick. When you get the ball don't try to take him on. You are not going to beat him for pace.

'So the minute you get the ball, take a few steps and hand it off or stick it over the bar!'

I could feel my shoulders just sinking. It was one of the few times in my life where I've been hit with the most incredible sense of self-doubt. I had often gone through phases in my career where I was lacking confidence or when my form wasn't good, but I'd never lacked self-belief.

I was reeling going out onto the pitch, wrestling with a bout of anxiety that I couldn't shake off.

Because of Brian's status in the game his words, no matter how meaningless, carry incredible weight. The words that come out of his mouth are never framed as his opinion, to us it is reality. This was different to the lashing from last year's Limerick game, this was an expression of his lack of belief in an aspect of my game. At least that's how I took it. He was trying to deliver a very clear and simple instruction that he felt would help me in the game. But instead, it floored me.

The game started and Shane absolutely destroyed me from the first moment to the last. When I got the ball, I didn't know what to do.

I turned and threw it up, but got blocked so many times. I was running in a sort of trance, trying to hook and block lads, and then I was panicking as nothing was going right. I failed to put a score on the board and with seven minutes from the end, my number was up and I was taken off. In the immediate instant I was semi-relieved that the embarrassment was over. I capitulated, we had lost by five and our year was over.

In the weeks after, thoughts about that game kept rolling around my mind. It was the most disappointed I had ever been with myself. I was 24 years old, no longer the new kid trying to break in. I was an experienced, multiple All-Ireland winner who had performed on the big stage and won everything there was to win. How could I have been so mentally weak?

I couldn't discuss it with anyone, not even Brother Damien. A conversation with him wouldn't fix anything, it would only serve to make me feel better about myself in the short term. It was something that I needed to take ownership of myself. Figuring this one out on my own would benefit me more. I came to the realisation that Brian's words, good or bad, could not have any effect on me whatsoever.

STRANGE TIMES

How could I dedicate so much of my life to this sport, train so intensely and be so brilliant at times, only to fall apart at the first sign of a lack of belief in me from my manager?

I made a decision during that off-season to never again give him, or anyone else, that amount of control over my levels of self-belief. My self-belief was about me, it was intrinsic and thus it needed to be immune to any noise from the outside. I extended this attitude to everyone else whose opinions I respected, and it gave me the most incredible sense of freedom.

I didn't need to prove anyone right or wrong because doubters didn't matter to me anymore. Even those who I knew believed in me unconditionally became irrelevant. I was grateful for their trust but I was not beholden to them either. I filtered everything that was said to me from then on.

* * *

At this point I had gone back to college to study Business Management and Strategy. I was terrified of telling my principal, Frankie Byrne, that I was leaving teaching. I planned the right moment for ages, rehearsing what I would say. Frankie had been very understanding towards my hurling commitments, and helped facilitate my playing for Kilkenny, being particularly supportive when we had big upcoming games.

I tried knocking on his office door a couple of times but bailed. Eventually, we were chatting in the school yard on break one day. I talked about having an interest in business and he could relate, having a similar outlook. I mentioned that I was considering doing a course in some business area, a proposal he backed with plenty of enthusiasm.

Then I pointed out the full-time nature of it and that I would need to go on career break. He was taken aback a little, but also full of encouragement for my decision.

I enrolled in DCU in late 2013 for a Master's in Business Management and Strategy.

I did end up returning to teaching for another year once I finished my course to properly settle the decision in my mind. But it had essentially already been made. The taste of another career I'd had during the Master's meant I knew teaching was no longer for me.

In one sense, teaching was the greatest job in the world for a county hurler. I was finished at half two in the afternoon, and if I needed to leave for training, I could go home and have a nap before hitting the road for Kilkenny.

I would also use the alternate midweek days without squad training effectively. I would bring my gear with me to school, tidy up a few things after classes finished, and if I wasn't going coaching young lads, I would head to the closest hurling pitch I can find, whether it was Clontarf pitch in St Anne's Park, St Vincent's, Na Fianna, or the sportsground in DCU.

STRANGE TIMES

I've been kicked off them all during an afternoon puck-around.

I persevered, discovering various spots of grass with goalposts. Equipped with just my hurley and a bag of balls, I would set off, ready to practice.

During my time at DCU, I reached out to the sports department, and they began to support me. Fergal Smyth was particularly helpful. I explained that I wasn't conducting a running session that would damage the pitch; I simply needed a place to practise my striking. They gave me the green light to work away and I did for a few years.

Near the main DCU campus, adjacent to St Clare's Nursing Home in Glasnevin, there was a collection of high-quality pitches. At the back, there was a private field where the Dublin footballers often trained. I could drive into the nursing home, park, slip onto the field, and practise.

In the summer of 2015, I started practising around 3.30 p.m. If I wasn't satisfied with my rhythm and standard by 5.00 p.m., I would continue until I was. One afternoon, with about fifty balls scattered across the pitch, the St Clare's car park was suddenly filled with cars. More vehicles parked on the grass at the edge of the pitch. Players began tumbling out, fully geared up, and I recognized them immediately: Diarmuid Connolly, Stephen Cluxton, and others. The Dublin footballers were clearly about to start an in-house game. It appeared as if they'd had a meeting somewhere else in advance and as a result they all arrived here together.

Their pristine surface was covered in sliotars. Cluxton and his goalkeeping coaches headed to the opposite goal. I grew concerned when I saw a man walking towards me. As he approached, I recognised him: Jim Gavin. Before I could explain, he extended his hand and spoke first. 'Hi Richie. Nice to meet you. How are you? Take your time here. Finish whenever you're done, and we'll work around you.'

I wasn't sure if he was being serious, but I decided to take him at his word. I finished my session, continued practicing my frees, and ensured my accuracy. Shortly after, I gathered the sliotars, nodded at a few familiar faces, and headed to my car.

The following Monday, one of my preferred practise days, I returned to find a nine-foot-high fence erected around the pitch. It had become a fortress. Whether this was a coincidence or a reaction to a Kilkenny hurler disrupting the Dublin footballers' training, I wasn't sure. I hopped the fence that day, but soon began searching for another venue in North Dublin.

CHAPTER 12

WHY IS HURLING SO EASY?

CHANGE WAS ALWAYS going to come before the start of the 2014 season. There needed to be a reaction to how the previous year had panned out.

That winter, there was a big shake-up of the management team. James McGarry and Derek Lyng came in as selectors while Martin Fogarty stepped away and Mick Dempsey moved to focusing solely on strength and conditioning. As players we were excited by this. Even though we had won six of the previous eight All-Irelands you could see that Clare had brought something new to the table and we needed to freshen things up in order to react.

The routine before this year was to start training in the first week of January. We were sometimes given running programmes to follow in pre-season but there was never any collective training until the turn of the new year. Our superior hurling talent allowed us to focus on our mental and physical conditioning in the early part of the season. No hurl had been brought to training for years, except for Sunday morning sessions, until nearly March. Mostly, we focused on running, weight training and plyometrics, with hurling reserved for Walsh Cup and National League games as they came up. But when we got the text to present ourselves in November for training it was clear there would be a definite move towards incorporating more hurling into the early part of the season.

Prior to that year, we had also rarely used a proper floodlit ground for the pre-season slog. We could have gone to Carlow IT or somewhere outside the county to use their facilities, of course, but the preference was always to just go running in some pitch in semi-darkness. That year, though, we started training down in Mooncoin, a south Kilkenny parish that skirts the boundary with Waterford city.

It was a serious trek from Dublin but I was back in college by then, studying in DCU. My timetable was more flexible, which meant I was able to plan for the extra travel time required. In Mooncoin, the club had a full floodlit pitch and gym to cater for lads working their way back from injury. It was clear that we weren't being asked to travel down that far south for nothing.

There was an influx of new players to the panel to freshen the place up; about 15 were added to the extended panel in total.

WHY IS HURLING SO EASY?

But only one person was axed in the wake of our 2013 struggles.

And that was Paddy.

In the previous three championship seasons Paddy had played his fair share of games in multiple positions. The half-back line was well established with Tommy, J.J. and Brian Hogan all in their peak years as Paddy was trying to break in. Paddy's versatility meant that he was often thrown into positions that were not familiar to him, nor had he ever trained much in those positions. In 2013, Paddy was thrown in corner-back for some league games and while he coped pretty well, he was never going to dislodge full-back experts like Jackie or Paul Murphy.

After we lost the first round of club championship to St Martin's, Liam Dowling, our manager, gave me a call for a debrief on the year. I had played terribly in the game but amidst the disappointment of defeat, Liam reached for a positive. 'Wasn't it great, though, to see Paddy playing so well at centre-back? That will give him a big boost next year with Kilkenny.'

And it was a big boost for him. He was training hard in that winter up in Dublin in anticipation for the following year. All three of the famous half-back line were over 30 now and a poor year usually meant that a clean slate would be likely for everyone.

Then in November a message came in on my phone from Paddy. Two words.

'Got dropped.'

It was as brutal and sudden as that. The text shook me and I needed about an hour before I could ring him back.

Getting cut from a Kilkenny panel was generally after a short conversation with Brian. You got informed of the decision, told you were no longer required, then the call ended. It was pointless asking for reasons. There'd be some reference to form or moving in a new direction, but no explanation would prove satisfactory.

When we landed down for our first training night in Mooncoin, I scanned the room, seeing plenty of familiar faces and some new ones. There was no WhatsApp group then, so you'd no way of knowing who was involved for the new year until the panel gathered. Looking around, I realised that Paddy was the only one not there; everyone else had been invited back.

I knew that Paddy wasn't indispensable. He had been there for four seasons and the management were entitled to have formed an opinion of him by then. But to single him out as the only one discarded after 2013 was, I felt, a horrible way to treat him. We had been very poor as a team in the 2013 season but Paddy didn't play in those games so it was hard to see the logic in why he would be the only one discarded.

Paddy and T.J. were similar players at the time, very talented with a history of underage success. Both were struggling to fully nail down a guaranteed place in a team that was laced with once-in-a-lifetime players who were at the peak of their powers. It was clear that those great players were coming to the end. All three members of our great half-back line retired at the end of 2014. Paddy, T.J. and others from our 2008 U-21 winning side would take over and thrive once given a vote of confidence.

We knew it was a ruthless environment which was a product of our exceptional conveyor belt of talent up to that point. But that conveyor belt was drying up as the next generation of underage players was not as good, or as successful.

Fifteen new players had been introduced and the entire panel from the previous year were retained, bar one. There would be a culling of the panel at the end of the league anyway, so I could never figure out why Paddy was the only one singled out before then. Except for the fact that Paddy was a big name in Kilkenny hurling and sacrificing him would send a message to everyone else. It was sickening.

We didn't talk it through as a family – that wasn't really our style – but I know it hurt my parents, particularly the manner in which it happened.

I kept my thoughts to myself, but the anger over that decision stayed in the pit of my stomach for a while.

* * *

Life back in college suited me in early 2014. I slipped seamlessly into my routine. I used my time efficiently to train and get a head start before the new season. My college schedule was ideal, meaning I could fit in a weights session in the morning in DCU or do some running. Every facility I needed was around me with access to the gym, pitches, pool, sauna and ice baths.

My energy levels were notably higher. When you're teaching, you're always engaged, standing to perform at the top of the classroom. Now I was doing something I was interested in. Studying again suited me. After training, I'd grab a shower and head to a lecture. I was learning, reading up on performance leadership and management. I found it all so rewarding and interesting.

The schedule helped me nurse my knee back to full health as well. On the last training session in December 2013, about 10 days before Christmas, I had jumped for a ball and landed on my knee, hyper-extending it. I'd damaged some cartilage and was sent down to Tadhg O'Sullivan in Waterford to get it assessed. There was relief in learning that I didn't need an operation, but it was going to take eight weeks before I got back to full-contact training. It could have derailed my momentum, but I was hyper-focused at the time. Our training sessions had moved to Carlow IT by this point and while the rest of the squad were training on the pitch, I was in the gym with John Power, both of us building up our fitness through bike sessions.

WHY IS HURLING SO EASY?

I squeezed in two Fitzgibbon Cup games with DCU in early February but was not chosen as part of the panel to travel to Ennis to take on the All-Ireland champions in the first round of the league. I sat at home watching from the couch in anger as we lost. Brian tended to stick with a winning team until they were overturned, so I knew I would be back in contention for the next game against Tipperary in Nowlan Park. To my frustration I was amongst the subs that day as Tipperary ripped through us in the first half. Brian came over at half-time and told me that I was being introduced at midfield for the second half.

We had been training now since November and I didn't play one minute of training sessions at midfield. Deep down I was still angry with him at the way Paddy was discarded and I immediately thought the same was being planned for me. I thought back to the 2011 league campaign when Cha was thrown in corner-forward for a few games having played at midfield for the previous half decade. I was completely paranoid. These fuckers are trying to get rid of me, I thought, just like they got rid of Paddy! I will show them.

I went out in the second half and played as if I'd been playing there all my life. As the league progressed, I rotated between midfield and centre-forward and I was playing the best hurling of my career to date. Man-of-the-match awards against Waterford, Wexford and Tipperary in the league final followed. Hurling suddenly became so easy. I was named Player of the League and I could do very little wrong.

*　*　*

After a few successful games out there, my paranoia waned and I thought back to a conversation that I had with Brian a few years before where he likened me to Paul Galvin for the Kerry footballers. He felt I could play a similar role for Kilkenny, bringing the same levels of dynamism, vision, positioning under breaks and aggression that Galvin brought to Kerry. Maybe now Brian and I were on the same page.

I had seen Tony Kelly having such a breakout year for Clare in 2013, scooping up all the individual awards on offer. I looked at a youngster like Kelly and strangely found that it infused me with confidence. Observing him, I felt that there was nothing that he could do on the pitch that I couldn't also do in the middle third. If I could just play with the freedom that he did and bring my experience and work rate then I would be very difficult to stop.

I wasn't satisfied with just playing well at midfield, I wanted to redefine the position. I knew that my speed and vision were superior to other midfielders, but it also gave our forward line an advantage that we had never had before. I'd spent the last two years as an inside forward giving out about lads just lofting the ball in high to the square, whereas now I could direct the game from the middle, conducting how we would play.

My teammates began actively seeking me out to deliver possession to the forwards. I became the link between defence and attack. We started to track possessions for the first time in our analysis that season, another sign that our preparation for games was evolving. Our stats were presented to the team after every game and my possession stats were through the roof. I was a magnet to the ball.

I just really loved playing around midfield; it felt so natural and as a result, every day I stepped onto the pitch feeling entirely pressure-free. Yet it wasn't always that straightforward to get selected there. Brian liked to discuss positions for players, but he hated feeling like somebody was dictating where they wanted to play. His philosophy was that you should be delighted to get a Kilkenny jersey, whatever the number.

I agreed with that thinking, but also felt in the latter part of my career that I was needed more around midfield than in the forward line. What I brought to the game around that area was what what we were lacking: somebody to get their hands on the ball and transfer it inside. We had brilliant guys to work up and down and tackle and hassle and chase, but we just weren't getting enough ball through. It was hard to believe that 2014 was the only full season that I played in that position.

My attitude was always to seek improvements for Kilkenny. When we were winning games and had scraped through, Brian would be delighted because we had emerged from a tight game, whereas I'd be concerned and was stressing the improvement that was required.

He'd be looking at me, confused. 'Richie, we've won, we're in the All-Ireland final, what are you on about?'

I was always looking down the road, towards the day when we would be caught. I could see the game changing and while we were hanging in there I knew that brilliance from individuals wouldn't always work.

I looked at the way Limerick were starting to play the game, the way Galway were, the way Wexford were. Teams were better structured, they had plans and puckout strategies and were all on the same page.

We were only ever on the same page from a work-rate point of view.

And I knew that this was going to come back to bite us.

We could not keep surviving.

* * *

There was a definite changing of the guard in the Kilkenny team in 2014. Older guys were starting to be phased out, and younger players were coming in to grab the jersey. There was real ability in some of our emerging players. Cillian Buckley had been an underage star at colleges and Minor level. Joey

Holden was a late developer and brought incredible defensive skills to the team that allowed players like me to attack more. T.J. was given the free-taking responsibilities and this vote of confidence jolted his level of performance and consistency to new heights, allowing him to finally nail down his place.

Conor Fogarty made a surprise breakthrough that year, forcing his way into the midfield conversation. He was regarded as a corner back up until then but was shifted to midfield in the Leinster Championship. Much like me, he had virtually no prior experience there. It turned out to be a genius move from Brian. He saw something in Fog that proved to be invaluable to the team.

We struck up a strong partnership together. It was a potent blend; I had the licence to go forward, knowing he would cover back for me. Mick Fennelly was injured, but when he came back into the team, he was slotted into the forward line. This portrayed the importance of Conor to our team.

There was a lot of outside attention on those who weren't making the starting side at the time. Henry was naturally an iconic figure in our squad. After being sent off against Cork in 2013, he would have put a huge emphasis on bouncing back, but it wasn't easy to force his way back in.

There were countless great players and leaders around us, though, to support him: Derek Lyng, Eddie Brennan, Tommy, J.J., Jackie, Noel Hickey, Brian Hogan. They all brought something different and, when combined, it made us so formidable.

Tommy Walsh, for example, had this deep love for the game of hurling. He would have wanted to play until the age of 50 for Kilkenny if he could get away with it. Tommy was one of the greatest teammates you could ask for. When he went into training, he was more concerned with others on the team, always trying to build them up.

During my first midfield league cameo I had fielded a ball against Padraic Maher in the second half. I'd forgotten all about it until a few months later, when we were on the beer after winning the All-Ireland. Tommy moved over to me with a serious look on his face. 'Tell me now, Richie; how did you catch that ball over Padraic Maher, what did you do?'

And I sat looking at him, thinking: *he's the greatest catcher of all time in hurling. He knows exactly how to catch the ball so what's he asking me advice for?* No one is better than Tommy at fielding. Johnny Glynn was an outstanding catcher, while Austin Gleeson used to amaze me with his leap off the ground, but nothing outstripped Tommy's sense of timing and his assured touch. Still, he asked me that likely knowing that I would leave the conversation elevated by his words.

Tommy was continually amazed with other people's abilities. He was the greatest hurling hype man of all time and that put so much confidence into the people around him. He made players feel a hundred times better than they actually were. A chat about hurling with Tommy and you'd be walking on clouds afterwards.

WHY IS HURLING SO EASY?

He won nine All Stars in a row between 2003 and 2011. Award selections are a subjective business but that is still extraordinary consistency. He won them all over the pitch as well, yet always carried himself with such humility.

* * *

As the 2014 season unfolded, my failures from the previous year seemed a million miles away. Brian was now throwing questions at me about different scenarios unfolding in my area of the pitch which revealed his growing trust in me. I thrived with the added responsibility and was continuously growing as a leader.

In the Leinster final we beat Dublin by 12 points. I was positioned in front of the half-back line for their puckouts, marking Johnny McCaffrey. For the first couple, McCaffrey took off sprinting over to the far wing. I tracked his runs initially before realising that he was acting as a decoy to take me out of the game. He didn't care if he never got the ball. I held my ground to see what would happen and sure enough, it worked. I began to mop up their arrowed puckouts towards Conal Keaney, who was their key possession-winner.

I had the trust from management to make on-field decisions, now being their eyes and ears in the middle third, organising players around me, making sure we were well structured.

At the time, we viewed ourselves as the protectors of hurling as the championship went on after Clare had introduced this defensive running game. Positions were becoming redundant. Dublin had started to play sweepers around that time, a tactic Waterford and Wexford would follow later.

There was an element of disgust in our camp at how the game was being played, that teams would actually go out and actively try not to contest the ball man for man. Drifting around searching for a free pass, that was against the Kilkenny ethos. The traditional attributes of the game – high catching, fifty-fifty contests for the ball – were starting to be phased out, but we were fighting to keep them alive.

If we wanted a battle to test ourselves, we got one in the 2014 All-Ireland semi-final against Limerick. The conditions that day were the worst I ever played in. The clouds formed over Croke Park and fired rain down at us with a ferocity I'd never experienced in hurling. It was a war of attrition from the start. We struggled to adapt and Limerick had the better of the first-half play. They took shots from everywhere, seemingly crazy angles, and yet the white flag was being raised. They had blown up the year before at that stage against Clare, but had the look of a team who were destined to get the job done. Declan Hannon, Shane Dowling, Graeme Mulcahy – all these lads were on fire.

And yet we found a way, stubbornly refusing to yield. Before half-time, I struck a sideline cut up the wing to T.J.

WHY IS HURLING SO EASY?

and raced through the middle to create a passing option. The ball came to Colin and he handpassed it across to me. It was slightly behind me so I reached back, touched it down and swivelled.

Next thing – bang.

Wayne McNamara, a powerhouse for that Limerick team, came out and tried to knock me with a heavy shoulder. He was a tough unit, but I bounced off him.

Usually I would fire across the keeper to his left but with Nickie Quaid there I switched, knowing his right side was weaker. The ball flew past him and nestled in the corner of the net. It gave us a huge lift going in at half-time.

Richie Power made a critical difference when he came on in the second half and we came out on top, having not played well. That was a true sign of the great team that we were becoming.

* * *

Plenty of people elevate the 2014 drawn match between us and Tipperary to a higher plane when they discuss the great All-Ireland finals in the history of hurling. Sign me up for that fan club. It was an amazing game to be involved in, with the score-taking relentless from the start.

We talked a lot before the match about clamping down on the short puckout style that Tipperary liked to employ. The debate was between marking zonally and following our men. Brian preferred our players to be touch tight but was happy for us to judge it for ourselves. At the end of the day he didn't care as long as what we were doing was working. We felt James Woodlock would mark me but Shane McGrath lined up next to me early on. For the first puckout, McGrath retreated towards his own 45m line. I knew this was a tactic to take me away from winning the breaking ball from the longer puckouts, so I allowed him a 10-metre cushion. The decision backfired and Darren Gleeson picked him out with pinpoint accuracy. That was a warning sign of what was to come: they were confident of exploiting any puckout with even the slightest bit of space. Soon after, Woodlock was tagging me everywhere: a fast, energetic presence at midfield.

I did okay in the first half, performing at a similar level to our team as a whole. We were two down at half-time. I gathered myself in the dressing room. I urged myself to stay steady, composed, to go again. After the incredible year I had, I vowed that my form was not going to collapse now on the biggest day of all.

In the second half, I exploded. Midway through I was switched to centre-forward where I pinned Padraic Maher back. I created chances, scored points and was relentlessly hoovering up possession. Kieran Bergin was moved on to me, then later Mickey Cahill was brought in to man-mark me. I loved to see that, when teams shuffled around their defensive options and I faced a succession of markers. I took it as a sign of fear. The ultimate compliment.

WHY IS HURLING SO EASY?

There was nothing in the game, both teams refusing to yield. Near the end, I strained my calf and was hobbling around. In the final play of the game I was hobbling towards the sideline when Brian Hogan strode out from our defence. He ran straight into Padraic Maher and was knocked to the ground. The referee Barry Kelly blew for a free to Tipperary, gesturing towards Brian as if he had taken a dive. We were staggered. We weren't campaigning for a free for Brian but it certainly wasn't a free against him.

Tipperary were presented with a chance to win the game as Bubbles Dwyer lined up the long-range free.

I was silently fuming that he was about to snatch an All-Ireland away from us. But I didn't need the HawkEye announcement to confirm what I'd initially suspected.

It was a wide ball, resulting in a drawn game. We were going into another replay.

After a shattering, emotional epic, we were still alive.

CHAPTER 13

THE LIFE OF AN AMATEUR

After the 2014 drawn All-Ireland final we made our way back to the Citywest Hotel on the Kilkenny team bus. I was well used to All-Ireland occasions at this point. At 26 years old I had just played in my eighth Senior final.

We had our post-match meal there, refuelling after a game that left us all physically and emotionally spent.

All the Sunday night plans were cancelled, no banquet, no overnight hotel stay. We boarded the bus again and headed straight down the road to Kilkenny, where we all dispersed and were told to get our minds right for training again. The season unexpectedly had another three weeks to run.

My life at this stage was still in Dublin. After a year spent in DCU I went back to Belgrove for another year to preserve my career break and gather my thoughts on what I was going to do with my future. September All-Ireland weekends and the subsequent days of celebration or drowning of sorrows had often been a logistical nightmare for me. Usually, I would drive home on the previous Friday night leaving my car in Langton's hotel and collecting it the following Tuesday or Wednesday in order to get back up to Dublin for school.

I had a few course days booked off from school, but a draw meant that I would need to cancel these and hold them for the replay three weeks later. I went with the rest of the team on the bus back to Kilkenny where we arrived at about 11.30 p.m. I then jumped into my car and turned straight around to drive back to my house in Drumcondra, five minutes away from Croke Park, where I had just spent most of my day. I got home in the early hours of Monday morning having gulped down a shaker full of pre-workout caffeine along the way, finally closing my eyes to rest.

I limped into school the following morning, my calf still bothering me from the previous day's exertions. Sitting in the classroom, I considered the sporting showdown I had participated in the day before, an All-Ireland final that instantly has classic status bestowed upon it and was the prime conversation topic around the country after that weekend. I had won the man-of-the-match award in the greatest hurling final ever played. In the greatest sport there is. For one weekend I could legitimately claim to be one of the greatest athletes in the world, yet here I sat in a classroom in Clontarf writing maths questions on a whiteboard while trying to keep myself awake. Not only this, but I needed to jump back into the car after school and drive home to Kilkenny to complete a recovery session in Nowlan Park followed by a team meeting. Our status as amateur players really hit home then. The travelling up and down from Dublin, the time wasted in traffic, the effort to stay alert while driving, it can be wearing.

It was a ridiculous schedule but sometimes you just have to do what is required for the group effort. If that means everyone recovering together in the same place then so be it. The tone needed to be reset early for the replay and this required everyone.

Later in my career there was space afforded to do those sessions in the pool or with a physio in Dublin. Brian knew that my broken body needed all the recovery time it could get. I was allowed to meet the team at the hotel in Santry before matches in Croke Park, it saved my back the ordeal of being stuck on a bus for a couple of hours.

It epitomises the challenge that leading GAA players face in organising their lives to meet the demands at that elite level. A professional athlete is shattered on the Monday after a weekend game but can coax their body and mind back to prime condition once more. They are focused on recovery and getting ready for the next game, not considering lesson plans and handing out homework.

The lack of financial reward for playing hurling never bothered me. Of course I would have loved to have been paid. The financial value we create for the Association and the social value we contribute to the country absolutely merits payment, but we would inevitably lose an irreplaceable part of ourselves in the process as all professional sports have.

The major negative to being an amateur is the reality that you cannot fully dedicate your life to your sport. You do know that you can never reach your full potential as an athlete because you are working 30–40 hours a week. It's completely unreasonable to suggest that you could ever be anything close to your best.

On balance I think that being an amateur athlete in the GAA is net positive. The love of the game, the pride, the passion is not present at the same level in professional sport no matter how other sports try to fabricate it.

We have an unbreakable connection with our homeplace, the players we line out alongside and the people we represent. We're sacrificing everything, inhibiting every other area of our lives just to play and succeed for our team. This is what elevates the status of our sport beyond all others. Money would add an unnecessary level of complexity.

Over the years I have had some approaches from Dublin clubs to join them. Nothing serious, more an initial enquiry as to whether I'd ever consider switching allegiances. It certainly would have eased the travel load, but I always dismissed them within an instant so as to leave no doubt. The GAA community can be a small place at times, so a tongue-in-cheek comment can suddenly turn into a rumour that you were considering a transfer.

I would never consider leaving Danesfort. I transferred club as a child when it was forced upon me and it wasn't an experience that I wanted to relive. The Kilkenny County Championship is the most prestigious and competitive club scene that exists in the game. Travel commitments were always a struggle and it definitely held back my working career but the opportunity cost of changing club was never worth it. Playing for Danesfort in the Kilkenny Championship means too much to me.

* * *

Our mood after that 2014 draw with Tipperary was not too downbeat. Clearly it was not the result we had wanted, but it was preferable to wrestling with the regrets of defeat for months on end.

We went to Carton House for a training camp. It was generally accepted that our defence was destroyed in the first game. The defenders were angry and determined to redeem themselves; you could see that in the training sessions – the siege mentality they had created within their own group.

There were plenty of meetings to thrash things out. Myself, Mick Fennelly and Conor Fogarty were drafted in to the separate conversations for the backs and for the forwards.

That first game had really drained me, and my calf was still niggling at me, so my training load was reduced. My switch to centre-forward in the drawn game proved successful and the plan was that I would start there for the replay.

Tensions were riding high in training and the subs could smell blood. The three-week break provided just enough time for those outside the starting 15 to be dislodged. We watched some footage from the game and sat down on many occasions to discuss how we would get over the line in the replay. Discussions about tactics led to arguments about how to implement them.

We didn't even leave Carton House with any plan; the only thing that we were on the same page about was that what happened to our defence wasn't going to happen again, no matter what it entailed.

We had the most brilliant individual defenders whose skill levels were very high. We defended as a group through minding our own patch or the field and marking our men. We supported each other on the pitch through acts of bravery and teamwork. But we were never playing within a system or a defined structure which made video analysis difficult. When frailties were exposed during games we often focused on the individual players in the team and their effort or mistakes. This approach made it difficult to find the root cause at times.

The team was shaken up for the replay. Brian Hogan and Joey Holden lost out in defence with Kieran Joyce and Padraig Walsh coming in to replace them.

We started sharply, even if it didn't translate to the scoreboard. We trailed 1–7 to 0–8 at half-time, but on the pitch you can always sense in the first 10–15 minutes if you're likely to win a game. The mood of a team can be assessed. It's expressed in body language and little interventions: a block, a run, a hook, a pass, an interception.

So the amount of mistakes we made was almost immaterial. We could sense the difference in our performance level. It was similar to the feeling I would get early on against Limerick in the 2019 All-Ireland semi-final – a defeat felt out of the question.

If there had been any dousing of the fire in us when playing Tipperary, it reignited before that replay. It's hard to keep beating the same team year after year, especially when they're hurling at a really high standard. For that replay, however, the emotion in our play lifted us to victory with a scoreline of 2–17 to 2–14.

* * *

The 2014 season was rounded off with an All Star and a Hurler of the Year award. They were meaningful accolades and it was brilliant to receive them.

But any individual awards were always dismissed within the camp and I had become programmed to think in that way. Instead, it became an internal standard bearer for me. I was 26 and the best player in the game but my focus was to get even better, immediately. Similar to my fear of being a talented Minor left on the hurling scrapheap as an adult, I didn't want to be on a high stool around Kilkenny 20 years later, reminiscing with lads about 2014 and having achieved nothing thereafter.

My mindset was simple: *You were the best player in the game this year. Now you don't drop below that. You go higher than that.*

That award ceremony was on a Friday night in the Convention Centre and we lost to Ballyhale Shamrocks in the quarter-final of the club championship the following day. I had a day of rest on the Sunday and got back training that Monday.

Winning that award gave me a shot in the arm and the hunger for more success. I met Mick Dempsey and Brian for a meeting in early 2015 and they reminded me of what I had said to them the year before. Mick reminded me that I had told him that my ambition for the year was to win the All-Ireland and to be the best player in the country. It was a statement that I didn't remember making but Mick had made a mental note of it. 'You weren't the only one who made that statement. But you were the only one to make it in that order.'

The desire to get my mind and body ready for 2015 kept growing. I practised more than I had ever done before on the field in that off-season. The financial reward for winning the Player of the Year went straight back into improving my game. I bought 250 O'Neills hurling balls to fuel my pitch sessions where I worked on my striking, my first touch, my shooting and my free-taking. I was a member of the DCU gym in Dublin but I signed up to the National Athletic Development Academy in Blanchardstown where I got one to one athletic development training, working on my speed and vertical jump to enhance the advantages that I already had on the pitch. 2014 was the first year that the players were given video analysis clips of ourselves and other teams. Any clips that were shared, I studied them closely. I was looking at my strengths and weaknesses, those of my teammates and those of our opponents. My main asset as a midfielder was that I knew exactly where our full-forward line should be on the field when I got the ball in hand. This understanding gave me an advantage, so I felt it was vital that I continue to study the players that I played with.

I kept going non-stop until the following year's All-Ireland final. Looking back now I was overdoing it and needed to be reined in. But I had this crazed obsession with continuous improvement and I was isolated in Dublin where no one could see me. I would dare myself to get carried away by the praise and tributes that were coming my way, then having to prove to myself that I was staying grounded by undergoing more punishing training sessions.

We lost several key figures to retirement that winter. In a fortnight between Friday 20 November and Friday 5 December, we saw Tommy Walsh, David Herity, Brian

Hogan, Aidan Fogarty and J.J. Delaney all walk away. Henry bowed out a little later once his club season had concluded. Goodbye messages sent into the WhatsApp: *time to leave, lads; thanks for the memories.*

The departures of Tommy and J.J. were a shock to the system. Tommy was only 31. The number 5 jersey was still up for grabs and I felt that Tommy was still capable of getting it back. Tommy was obsessed with winning, but he loved playing even more. You could see that not playing recently had just been having a huge effect on him – I know, as I've been in that position myself. J.J. had been so strong in defence for us that year, so I'd been convinced that he would stay going and try to land a tenth All-Ireland.

They were key players, ones that any panel would desperately miss.

* * *

The dynamic naturally shifted in our dressing room. Suddenly I was an elder statesman, only 26, but with eight years' experience behind me. In the first round of the 2015 league we went to Cork with a shell of a team and I picked up where I left off, winning the man-of-the-match award and captaining the team for the first time. We only won one more game in the league, and barely survived relegation, beating Clare in a play-off by a point in Nowlan Park.

THE LIFE OF AN AMATEUR

Our panel was tight on numbers, stripped of long-serving figures by that wave of retirements, while also missing the Ballyhale contingent who were on a winning club championship run. I remained confident that we'd get back on track when everyone returned but you could see that the panel was not as strong as it had been the year before.

There were murmurings amongst the hurlers on the ditch before the first round of the championship against Wexford that we were susceptible to an ambush. As players, we took that personally. The media were dismissing the ability of our younger players who had come through the year before. And we blew Wexford away. I got 1–06 that day and Ger Aylward scored 3–06. The whole Wexford team only managed to get 0–16 between them.

I was marking Lee Chin. I cast my mind back to that time in 2013 when I had struggled against Shane O'Neill of Cork. Chin was a similar type of hurler – strong, fast and athletic – but I was on fire with my movement and hurling and pace. It cemented the belief that mentally, I was a different animal. We did what was required for the rest of the season.

It only took three more wins after the Wexford game to land another All-Ireland: beating Galway by seven in the Leinster final, Waterford by six in the All-Ireland semi, and it was Galway again in the final in September, this time winning by four.

WHATEVER IT TAKES

My demands on myself for continuous improvement were starting to spill out in my demands for the team to improve. I felt that we weren't getting better as a team, in spite of the fact that we were still winning. We were doing just about enough to get through the Leinster final and All-Ireland semi-final and I believed we were living too close to the edge.

The end result was justifying the means by which we got there. As long as we were winning everything was deemed to be going fine and this was frustrating the life out of me. Clare and Waterford had introduced new ways of playing and we were keeping them at bay for now but we weren't entertaining any form of tactical changes in our own game. We were a group of talented hurlers, who pushed ourselves to the limit physically in every training session and lived every day by the values of Kilkenny hurling and that gave us a chance to win every game. Playing off the cuff was still working for us and the plan was to stick to it. All too often the feeling after games was one of relief rather than satisfaction that we were moving in the right direction. We were on top of the pile for now, but we clearly needed to take the tactical side of the game more seriously if we were going to stay there.

I had my back injury scare before the Waterford game, but shook that off to fire over five points. In the run-up to the final against Galway, Brian pulled me out of training. They were mindful of the back issues prior to the semi-final and so sought to prevent a repeat. It was with my own well-being in mind that I was given extra rest, but I didn't want to miss any collective work.

The physios arranged a short speed and agility session followed by some tempo running to flush my legs out a little while also keeping me fresh for the next session. I was pushing myself hard through the speed and agility when I felt a tear on the front of my leg. It was a quad muscle tear and I immediately pulled up and called a halt to the session. After the form I'd produced that year and the extra work I had put in I was furious but wasn't ruling myself out just yet. My recovery from the crippling back injury a week out from the semi-final taught me not to jump to any conclusions.

I recovered in time for the final and lined out with a strapping on my quad for support. I got off to a good start but didn't manage to glitter that All-Ireland final in the way that I had in previous years. Despite that, I was nominated for the Hurler of the Year Award for the second year in a row.

We had retained the title. It was particularly sweet, given how the whole country had predicted our downfall after all the retirements the year before.

We had struggled in the league, sure, but we never panicked, and the more that journalists predicted our downfall, the more determined we were to shove our success down their throats. Joey Holden had filled the void left by J.J. and quickly became the best full-back in the country, wrapping up the opposition's best forwards. Shane Prendergast took the number 4 jersey from Jackie and Kieran Joyce nailed down the centre-back position that Hogie left vacant. The golden generation of Kilkenny hurlers were replaced within a couple of months.

At regular points in the season Brian reminded us of the hurler on the ditch talk that existed when he first took over as manager in the early 2000s. It was often stated that once Kilkenny lost D.J. Carey they would not win an All-Ireland for years. Yet D.J. retired in the winter of 2005, and Kilkenny won the next four All-Irelands in a row. That was used as his reference point, hammering home the message that that there are many great players in Kilkenny but none are irreplaceable.

It also helped, of course, that we had also retained the core of the team that won the 2014 final. J.J. was the only established starter from that time who'd departed. Those guys leaving actually gave us the impetus that we needed to go again for the following year's championship; otherwise, a small bit of complacency could have set in. The departures just gave us a cause straight away. It proved we were not dependent on any one individual.

We felt we were in a seriously good position after 2015. After all, Kilkenny had also won the Minor All-Ireland in 2014, beating a star-studded Limerick team in the final. The age profile of our team was ideal and there seemed to be a few more players there who would kick on and join our panel for the coming few years.

We knew the whole hurling public was sick of looking at Kilkenny winning. By the end of 2015, maybe a sense of boredom had set in among neutrals, and as a result that particular team didn't get the recognition that it deserved. We were dismissed as only having some average players who worked hard. The dismissal of us as a team was largely due to the traditional hurling that we persisted in playing, but the individual players in that group would have walked onto any other team in the country.

The following year we were one win away from completing the All-Ireland three in a row in the final when we faced Tipperary. How many teams in the history of hurling are successful enough to get that opportunity?

* * *

Galway twice tried to beat us in finals in Croke Park in 2015 and came up short both times. They made a lot of the running in the first half of the All-Ireland, going ahead by three at half-time, but once we took over and raised the temperature in the second half, they melted away.

Galway always posed a serious challenge but we always felt that we had it over them in games of consequence. They beat us in the 2018 Leinster final, but we defeated them in the next three provincial finals where the teams met. Once the Leinster Championship moved to a round-robin format, they sometimes got the upper hand there, but again, we felt that the finals were the games of real significance. They couldn't overturn us in those situations. They would get close and challenge strongly, but when we applied the pressure, they had a tendency to fold. Once we got ahead on the scoreboard in those finals, there was no fight left in them to give.

When they eventually won the All-Ireland in 2017, their team contained tough individuals. In those hard, important games when it came down to generating the right result, they had the right characters – ones they had previously been lacking.

Three players changed the course of their history: Johnny Glynn and Conor Whelan in the forward line and Daithí Burke in defence. Burke and Whelan weren't in their team in 2012, while Glynn was only a teenager coming off the bench. All three were there in 2015 and they'd become hugely important by the 2017 All-Ireland win.

Glynn and Whelan finally gave them proper outlets to win hard ball in attack. Ask any Kilkenny defenders of the time and Conor Whelan was the Galway forward that nobody wanted to mark. Like, how could you stop him? He was strong, fast and direct, while also being so good at snapping the ball on the ground and in the air. Whelan didn't look like the most stylish of players, but he was incredibly accurate and effective.

Meanwhile, Glynn was a monster. He was only 19 in the 2012 final replay when he came on and nearly broke Cillian Buckley in half with a shoulder. The game was over as a contest but he was tearing into lads and rocketed one goal into the top corner.

He came on as a sub in 2014 in the drawn Leinster game that we played with them down in Tullamore, and he dragged them back into the game single-handedly. We rarely made specific plans for individual opposing players, but before the following week's replay we devoted a lot of time to devising a plan to curb Glynn's influence. Joey Holden was ultimately entrusted with one job: stop the ball going cleanly into Glynn's hand. He was their focus for puckouts, and so when he'd stick up his massive paw, we needed to find a way to deprive him of clean possession. I was central to that plan as well. The previous Sunday I had won man of the match and rifled over five points from play but the attacking aspect of my game was to be parked and sacrificed to help Joey with Glynn. When the ball broke I had to be alert and positioned correctly to gather breaks in front, or sweep in behind.

We won that semi-final and kept him scoreless – job done.

Daithí Burke was their defensive cornerstone. He was outstanding in the air and was frequently tasked with the man-marking job on me or T.J. Burke. He consistently delivered strong performances for Galway in big games.

Because they were such consistent players, that fostered huge trust within the team. Galway had people they could depend on now, and that made them more dangerous opponents.

David Burke came really good around that time as a controlling midfielder. He had a great pair of hands and was a great deliverer of the ball. Joe Canning, meanwhile, was always capable of magic and when Galway started to develop strongly in those 2017 and 2018 seasons, he was one of the best hurlers in the country.

We were always confident that our Kilkenny backs could hold Joe when he was alone in the forward line, but the addition of Glynn and Whelan changed the complexion and gave them an extra dimension that changed the Kilkenny-Galway rivalry.

There was great respect for those lads in the Kilkenny camp; the fact that we bothered to make plans for them displayed that. They never would have been anywhere near winning the All-Ireland without those guys. They were so instrumental to their progress.

* * *

I permanently pulled the plug on teaching in early 2016.

I knocked on the door of Frankie's office in Belgrove and told him that I just couldn't do it anymore. Leaving teaching in the middle of the school year was not the done thing, but he knew I wasn't going to change my mind. He asked me to stay until the February mid-term break so that he could line up a replacement.

The plan was to use the Master's degree for something, though I hadn't yet decided in what area or figured out the best route to go down. I just had complete certainty that it was time to get out of teaching.

Making that move was a release of pressure off my mind. I didn't bounce any ideas about the future off anyone, I just remained confident that I would figure out the best strategy for myself going forward. Having mulled over it for long enough, it was time to take action.

The series of injuries were starting to make me really suffer. I wanted the time and space to sort those issues out properly, too, to concentrate on my recovery.

In time, I started working for e-Frontiers, a recruitment consultancy. I used my connections and experience to set up their teacher recruitment business in the Middle East. The experience was incredible and I got exposure to the highest levels of business, which reassured me that I was finally on the right career path. The owners, Brendan Carroll, Paddy Doyle and Vincent Blake, knew the importance of my sport and gave me the flexibility I needed.

Ultimately my focus remained on hurling, though. At a sponsor event in Croke Park in 2017, I went into detail about my life off the pitch. 'I'll sweep streets for 50 years if I can hurl till I'm 35,' was a throwaway remark I gave, which became a quote plastered all over newspapers and websites afterwards.

There was some truth to it. Hurling was my passion and my number one priority. I wanted to just try and reach the maximum level on a consistent basis.

But physically that was beginning to become a huge challenge.

CHAPTER 14

WHY IS HURLING SO HARD?

EVERY DAY WHEN I wake up, there is one question that rushes to the front of my mind.

How does my back feel?

It is a lottery as to what the answer will be and that will dictate how the rest of the day will pan out.

If I sense a familiar discomfort, I know I am in trouble, that trying to get through the day is going to be a serious challenge – particularly if it's a busy one with work followed by training.

I'm not capable of just bolting upright, leaping out of bed and running down the stairs. Instead, I have a certain process when I wake up that must be strictly adhered to. When the alarm goes off at 6 a.m. I stretch my arms out in a T-shape and slide my legs up, bending my knees. I move my bent knees left and right, repeating it 10 or 15 times, listening out for the cracking sounds throughout my back. From my neck all the way down to the base of my spine, I will have completely tightened up during the night. So those moves are necessary to release all the tension that built up while I slept.

People talk about how they start their morning by rolling out of bed. Well, I literally have to roll out of bed in an effort to ensure that my day starts well. On particularly bad days I'll slither off the bed and onto the ground until my feet and knees are on the floor. I gather myself and assess how I'm feeling. If the signs are positive, I'll place my hands on the bed and use it as a support to stand up properly.

And then, once I've manoeuvred my way into a standing position, I breathe a little easier. I will then crack my neck and go through a few minutes of a mobility routine to get me started. Then I can get going and get on with my day. But if I woke up like a normal person and ripped the bed covers off and lifted myself up instantly into a sitting up position I'd likely trigger some form of back spasm and that would be game over for me.

So every day when I wake up it can feel like a lottery.

This has been my routine for a number of years, and it is necessary because of the sport I play and the level I played it at. The same routine may not be needed for an ordinary person with the same issues, but there is nothing ordinary about high-performance sport. We are required to do things physically that are extraordinary.

Regularly at night I would end up sleeping on the ground. Particularly during those times when I was battling hard to stay going with Kilkenny, stuck in the middle of a rehab programme, and sleeping comfortably was becoming difficult.

The ground worked because the timber surface is cold and it's hard. If I was in severe pain, I'd sometimes choose to sleep on the ground because, as I sink into a mattress my body falls into awkward, uncomfortable positions.

Thankfully the one thing I've always been able to do is fall asleep, regardless of where I lay. So I had no problem spending a few hours on the floor if needed. If anything, it eased me into a state of relaxation. Pillow under my head, duvet over my body, and off I'd go.

That ploy would be useful sometimes; on other rare occasions, if sleep was coming in sporadic bursts, I would go downstairs and just try and loosen up the back a bit. Anne has often woken up in the middle of the night to the sound of me rolling around on a foam roller or a hurling ball.

And there would be multiple occasions when she'd have to jump out of bed in the middle of the night to drive her elbow into my back for me to be able to sleep. Anne is nearly like an expert physio now; she knows exactly how to react in these situations.

WHATEVER IT TAKES

We were in China in April 2024, the spring after I had retired, when the two of us went for a run along The Bund – a waterfront area in Shanghai. It was a chance to see a bit of the city while getting some exercise. We got about half a kilometre in when I just looked around and, in that moment, I knew we were going to have to stop because the muscles in my back were too tight to go any further.

So, in the middle of Shanghai, I just had to lie down on a patch of grass at the side of the road. Anne knelt next to me and, with her elbow, just loosened up my back enough so that I was able to get through a few kilometres of a run.

✷ ✷ ✷

2017 was a horrendous year for me from an injury perspective. I needed multiple back injections to keep going from month to month; it was chronically sore. It was the first year where I couldn't even get my body through any sustained block of training.

The problem with a back injury is that you see a specialist and they give you a recovery programme to do over a period of time, but you can find yourself a couple of months in and no further down the line. So you have to go back to another specialist and start all over again. That was incredibly frustrating.

WHY IS HURLING SO HARD?

Within a couple of days of being knocked out of the 2017 championship, S&C coach Mick Dempsey got in contact, arranging to meet me in Nowlan Park. He spelled out his objective.

'You're not playing until you're fully right. We're going to get you to 100 per cent no matter how long it takes.'

He wasn't happy seeing me struggle so much physically and was determined to restore me to peak condition. We set up our WhatsApp group with the medical team: 'R Hogan 2018 Training.' The members were: myself; Mick Dempsey; Kevin Curran, the physio; Tadhg Crowley, the doctor; Noreen Roche, our nutritionist, and Chris Coburn, a S&C intern.

The ambition was to control every aspect of my training programme to ensure I would hit full speed the following summer. They started sending me to various specialists and organised a full physical screening programme to assess where I stood.

That was in September, but Mick was already thinking ahead.

How could we help this player? That was his sole motivation.

Mick was a quiet figure. He was thoughtful and wouldn't often talk individually to players. When you did get him in a one-on-one situation, it always felt useful and benefitted your preparation or outlook.

I was once talking to him about ways to develop my game. He could sense how I was consumed by this and asked me if I knew any older people. I said of course. He suggested taking the time to ring them during a week, have a chat; it would help me switch off from hurling and gain perspective. Rather than continuously obsessing about the game, getting that headspace and distance to think clearly was very helpful.

Mick was very personable, in a quiet, understated way. He genuinely came from a good place, as he was concerned about you as a person.

The screening program confirmed that my back was the main issue. Was it a wear-and-tear injury from playing too much sport as a kid, constantly pushing my body with all that twisting and turning? No one could say for sure. What was certain was that I had significant damage to multiple facet joints causing constant, daily back pain that I couldn't shake off.

Learning this didn't bother me much because, as an athlete, you always expect to have aches and pains. For instance, there was an 18-month period when my wrist was constantly sore, and I couldn't figure out why. But I would warm up, play, and then deal with the pain afterward. I just got on with it.

You deal with strains, inflammation and pain in multiple areas of your body all the time. These issues are likely exacerbated by the fact that we are amateur athletes with limited access to professional physios and doctors. People tend to keep quiet about their pain, heading out to the pitch and playing regardless. I came from an environment where mental toughness meant ignoring anything that could be used as an excuse.

Your leg is hanging off? So what. You've busted your ankle in an All-Ireland final? So what. Grit your teeth and get through it.

I adopted that attitude when my back problems first surfaced. My mindset was to shake it off, thinking it was just a bit of stiffness.

When I called Tipperary's Eoin Kelly in 2017, we traded war stories. He had experienced back issues towards the end of his career and spoke about pains down his leg linked to nerve issues in his back. I managed to avoid that problem, but my facet joints – the connections between the bones of the spine – were wearing away. Sciatic pain such as his wasn't an issue.

My body reacted to this wear and tear. If I twisted in a certain direction and a joint movement was off, my back muscles would lock up as a defence mechanism against causing any damage to the sensitive area. This happened every four or five weeks, setting me back significantly. I needed regular cortisone injections and daily Difene tablets just to get through training sessions.

I worried about the consequences of all this. I was locked into a cycle where these injections sustained me for three or four weeks before the problem flared up again, and their effectiveness was diminishing.

WHATEVER IT TAKES

I couldn't practise any hurling. For example, on the Friday night before a match, we'd have a training session involving striking the ball hundreds of times over a short period of time. It was killing me that I couldn't participate, as this was my favourite thing to do. Working on my touch, striking and sharpness was what I excelled at, and being sidelined was incredibly frustrating.

Running wasn't an issue at this point, but matches were more challenging because of the physical demands – twisting, turning, and changing direction. Then I started to experience hamstring troubles associated with my back issue. It felt like everything was breaking down.

My last appointment with a consultant was in 2019 when I went to Prof. Ciaran Bolger, a Neurosurgeon in the Hermitage Clinic in Dublin. He put the injury into perspective for me. A spinal fusion for three of my facet joints was the only surgical option available to me. He said Tiger Woods had had the same procedure done a few years back, but that his only required one joint to be fused. He confirmed that a few rounds of golf might be possible post-op, but meeting the physical demands of hurling at the highest level was extremely unlikely. He reassured me that I was doing absolutely everything possible from a rehab point of view already and playing through the pain was not going to do any further damage as long as I managed my load. There was actually a certain amount of relief in that news. I knew I'd be limited, but if I was willing to play through the pain, then I could still offer something.

* * *

My physical struggles in 2017 mirrored those that the team were experiencing.

The big theme that season was that Davy Fitzgerald had taken over Wexford and almost overnight instilled a defensive style of play that instantly made them more competitive. They played multiple extra defenders and avoided landing any ball down on top of half-backs who were going to catch it and dominate in the air. Instead, they worked the ball up the field mainly through running and handpassing. It was a gameplan geared specifically towards negating the traditional strength of Kilkenny.

They qualified to meet us in the league quarter-final in Nowlan Park and their style of play caused us huge problems. They dragged most of their forwards back towards their midfield and defence, crowding out our forwards with their extra numbers.

We pushed up the pitch in search of a man-on-man contest which left our full-back line completely exposed. Our game was more traditional with little movement and our forwards were encouraged to keep their own positions at all times.

We had grown to despise modern tactical innovations in hurling over the years. It had begun back in 2004 with the Cork team who introduced a running game littered with short passing. Every few years something new would arrive and it might catch us on the hop once or twice but we'd eventually find a way to win. It fed into our siege mentality as a team.

This was different, however. We were left in a state of utter frustration.

Tipperary and Galway were less old school than we were and made light work of Wexford. Tipp put five goals past them in the league semi-final and Galway beat them by nine in the Leinster final later that year. When going up against this style of play, it felt like trying to break down a door with a sledgehammer when all the time we had the keys resting in our pocket if we'd had the openness to look.

Wexford turned us over in the league quarter-final. We had a few weeks to learn from our defeat but changed little and they repeated the trick in the Leinster Championship a few weeks later down in Wexford Park, even more convincingly this time.

Our traditional Kilkenny way was failing us, and we needed to start asking ourselves some hard questions.

* * *

We stumbled through Limerick in the qualifiers before Waterford applied the knockout punch in the next qualifier game in Thurles. We gave it everything, constantly trying to dig the game out and find something within ourselves. We trailed by eight points with eleven minutes of normal time left and managed to claw it back to a draw at full-time. But it only proved a stay of execution and when extra time ended they were ahead, 4–23 to 2–22.

It was the first time a Kilkenny team had lost to Waterford in the championship since 1959. They had finally caught up to us.

There was a touch of personal embarrassment about how the game ended for me. I got taken off in the sixty-third minute, forced to watch from the sideline as that dramatic finale played out.

Mick Fennelly was taken off during extra time. He came up to me in my seat. 'Richie, are you alright? Are you injured?'

I assured him I was fine.

Fenno marched straight down to Brian on the line and, with a sense of urgency, told him to get me back on the pitch.

Brian deeply trusted Fenno. Brian would always do everything in his power to get him onto the starting team on match day. The investment of faith was always rewarded in Mick's performances.

In this instance, his instruction was heeded. I got summoned down and brought back on in the eighty-fifth minute of the game. It was nice to get the reassurance that my teammates still rated me highly, although the clearly dwindling faith from management was a real worry and to be fair it was justified. I was nowhere near the Richie Hogan of the previous six seasons.

The plan for 2017 was to engage in a complete rebuilding process once more, like Kilkenny had done in the past and why not? It had worked before. After losing in 2005, you could dip into an outrageously talented U-21 team that had won the All-Ireland in 2004 by annihilating Tipperary.

When we were defeated in 2010, the U-21 winners of 2008 were fast-tracked into the Senior set-up and made their mark. But in that phase between 2012 and 2015, the Kilkenny conveyor belt was not operating as effectively in rolling off ready-made Senior players.

Established players got shuffled around the starting side in 2017, while an influx of six or seven new guys kept rotating in and out, while none of them really nailed down a place in the same way that others had done in the past.

Introducing new players was always part of the strategy in Kilkenny, but this time it didn't produce the results. The players were not the issue, we were the best in the country, but we had fallen so far behind the other teams from a tactical point of view that our work rate and our individual brilliance was no longer keeping up in games when it previously had.

✷ ✷ ✷

WHY IS HURLING SO HARD?

I would never have made an appointment to speak with Brian. I never called him up on the phone for a chat or walked over to him at training to ask for a few words. Brian dictated when we talked. Every player would be called in for an individual meeting early in the season. Most players would be dreading the moment when they were summoned. It was often an interrogation.

In spite of what rumours often circulated about myself and Brian's manager–player relationship in later years, there was rarely any significant tension between us right throughout our 16 years soldiering together. All I ever needed from Brian was for him to put me on the pitch, and all he needed from me was to deliver when I was on it.

Following my bad performances in the early part of the 2017 league I was summoned to meet Brian and Mick in Nowlan Park dressing room. By that time, I had reached the stage where my mindset was simple: *I don't care what we have to do, as long as it contributes towards Kilkenny winning.* So, if I disagreed with Brian's opinion on something, I let him know. I felt I would be bluffing no one except myself if I just nodded in approval in every conversation.

We both held strong opinions and we both had the stubbornness to stick by those. Regardless of my opinion I was never under any illusions as to who the buck stopped with. I understood who the manager was and who the player was at all times. I would never undermine him. And if he made a decision, I would absolutely accept it and stick by it.

On plenty of occasions, it would transpire that he was right and that was fine with me. I had no issue with that. The end goal was Kilkenny winning; it was bigger than the two of us, and the only thing that truly mattered.

At the start of my career, my meetings with Brian went fine and I didn't say much. But as I became more obsessed with the performances than the results, those meetings tended not to end so well. I was constantly pushing for more to be done from a coaching and tactical point of view, and that started to piss Brian off.

*　*　*

In the 2016 championship, I had played exceptionally well. A broken wrist cost me the first round against Dublin, but I came on at half-time of the Leinster final against Galway and scored five points. I kept that high level going in the two games against Waterford, scoring four points in each, and then we got to the All-Ireland final against Tipperary.

We were a better team than Tipperary over that period, but that day we just handed it to them on a plate, losing 2–29 to 2–20. A lot of Tipperary's scores in the first half stemmed from our mistakes: a ball mis-controlled, a runner not tracked, a strike mis-hit, a clearance blocked down. At the other end, our efficiency was down in the forward line; we created big chances and just didn't capitalise on them. We'd to work so much harder for our scores and they were getting theirs so easily. All these small things added up, our performance just littered with individual mistakes.

We should have been much closer. Tipperary were well up for it and often they were causing mistakes on our side with their pressure. But we made them look far better than they actually are.

Being on the pitch that day I could sense things going wrong. Tipp, retreated their half-forward line in to the middle of the field and left Seamus Callanan on the square and Joey Holden minding him on his own, with oceans of space in front of them. All Callanan needed was space. We always knew when facing Callanan that if he got the ball into his hand with time to turn and look at the posts, he would score 100 out of 100 shots.

Instead of reacting by holding our defensive shape we doubled down on our traditional man-marking strategy.

It wasn't working.

I had a competitive dual with Ronan Maher that day, both of us influential. He got in behind me for the first high ball between us to catch it. That fired me up and I caught the next one between us. The battle flowed between us all day.

Ronan was dropping back towards the full-back line as a holding centre-back, leaving me with plenty of freedom to drop in to midfield. Any aimless clearances were mopped up by him and he'd fire it cross-field straight into this open space, mainly for Callanan to get onto.

With the Tipp half-forward and our half-back a mile out of position it was a dream for Callanan. And a nightmare for Shane Prendergast and Joey Holden who were tasked with curbing him at different times.

By the end we had lost by nine. Callanan killed us, scoring 13 points.

We got destroyed by Tipperary that day, absolutely destroyed.

* * *

We had a long time to stew on that Tipperary defeat and I watched it over and over for weeks. When I reflected on the game, I thought I played well and was involved in most of the positive things that we did that day.

Having got off to a bad start in 2017 I knew that Brian had an agenda for the conversation and that was fair enough. But I was also thinking about our tactics in that final and that I needed to raise it.

How could I explain it to Brian articulately? I needed him to know it was coming from a good place and with the right intentions. Brian's an intimidating figure and he didn't have huge respect for tactics so when suggesting alternative ways of playing to him I always started with my own core principles:

WHY IS HURLING SO HARD?

I don't care who plays on the team as long as I'm on it.

I don't care what way we play.

I don't care what position I'm playing within the team.

As long as we are winning – that is all that matters, and I think this will help.

I needed to make sure that this attitude was clear and understood from the start. I was not trying to be argumentative because I wanted everyone to play Richie Hogan's way. I was not trying to overstep my role as a player. It was simply, from having been on the pitch, laying out the problem I could see and what I felt was a solution. Please take that into consideration, was what I was hoping to say to him.

But those discussions were always difficult. To change our style of play would have gone against everything that Brian believes about hurling. The game was changing, and it was changing in a direction that Brian didn't like. I didn't like it either but the loss to Tipperary had sickened me and I couldn't live with myself if I kept my mouth shut and let it happen again.

So we sat down in the dressing room of Nowlan Park for our chat. Brian had a great knack of being able to sense if you had something to say. He'd beat you to it and that day after some initial small talk about my injuries he fired a question at me.

'Richie, what did you think of the final last year?'

I felt this was my chance. Time to finally get it all off my chest. I started talking, but Brian interrupted.

'Do you know one of the reason why we lost that match?'

He gave me no time to answer.

'The first puckout that went down the middle and Ronan Maher caught that ball over you. That set the tone for Tipperary for the whole game. And we put you out there a few weeks ago against Tipp down in Thurles and Maher caught two balls over you again.'

I was completely amazed that he said that. I wasn't hurt by it, not in the slightest. I just couldn't get my head around him saying it. But I was on the back foot straight away. Anything I was about to say was gone out the window.

He likes to reduce the game to a handful of key moments and this time I was at the centre of it – he was blaming me for the loss to Tipp.

I accepted what he said and reminded him that I caught the next puckout after that bad start. I tried to present some arguments about our defensive shape, and how we'd needed to push back down the field in the second half. It was all just swatted aside, totally dismissed.

I sounded like I was deflecting and making excuses at that stage.

We argued about it. Not in the sense of a shouting match, but more that I tried to explain my view, and he met it with his disagreement.

At the time, I felt I was the best hurler in the country, when operating in that triangle of 8, 9 and 11. I wasn't hugely precious about where I played, any jersey from 1 to

15 would have sufficed, but it pissed me off that I was being dismissed in that area of the pitch. Brian had now made his mind up; he didn't trust me in that position anymore and even though I did play there again in big championship games it was always the last resort. I was an inside forward in his eyes and that was it.

In the middle of the argument, I moved the conversation on to the way we were playing. I should have left it but I was too headstrong and needed to exit the conversation with some small win.

Tipperary had hammered Waterford in the 2016 Munster final, scoring 5–19. I felt we should have done the same in the All-Ireland semi-final. We had the best hurlers in the country, but we were struggling to put lesser teams away who had created new systems to counteract the way that we played.

We were still just trying to use our sledgehammer approach filled with work rate and intensity. The problem was when your only tool is a hammer, all your problems look like nails. We needed to add more strings to our bow.

Play a small bit different, I argued, use the ball better and it'll change completely. Why were we making it so hard on ourselves?

My frustration often revealed itself in my communication style. Maybe I came off as being too clever. I didn't have all the answers, but I knew that we needed to change what we were doing.

'Look, Brian, we're both on the same team here. If you win, I win. If I win, you win. The difference is I will do anything to win, whereas you just want to win your own way.'

And he didn't like that.

I probably shouldn't have said it and I knew there was a chance that I'd pay the price for it, but at the time it felt like it was true.

Brian created an environment in our dressing room where winning was everything, and I was a product of that. If I needed to step over the line once or twice to ensure it continued, then so be it.

I didn't have another meeting with the management for a couple of years.

* * *

In the off-season after the 2017 championship, I was trying desperately to make progress with my fitness. I was doing some work every day, training at least four times a week and the other days involved getting stuck into rehab work. I was on the programme carefully crafted by Mick Dempsey to my specifications and, in truth, I was obsessed with it.

I was determined to get back playing, to return to the level I knew I could attain. It was breaking my heart not to be playing. When hurling means everything to you and when you have an injury that you feel all of the time, it's a constant reminder of how far you are away from the level where you want to be. It chips away at you all day, every day; that feeling never relents and fades away.

I missed the entire league in 2018. I stayed away, obeying the order from Mick Dempsey: no return until the time was right. I went to Abu Dhabi for a few weeks' work with e-Frontiers while in the middle of rehab. My friend from college, Pa Minogue, was living out there.

Now Pa didn't do a whole lot in college except drink and eat in the Cat & Cage, and play a little bit of hurling. But by the time I'd flown out to him in the Middle East, which was 10 years later, Pa had taken up running and found that he had a natural talent for it. I was delighted, as it meant I had a training companion that I could utilise while abroad.

He lived in this apartment complex called Gate Towers, which was similar in design to the Marina Bay Sands Hotel in Singapore: three large individual tower blocks joined together at the top.

They had an outdoor swimming pool with a little running track wrapped around it in a communal area in the complex. The track was about 250-300 metres long, which we used for our shuttle runs.

But once we started I was trailing in Pa's wake, with no power whatsoever in my lower limbs. They just couldn't move off the ground. I felt stuck.

The lack of physical progress was sobering.

WHATEVER IT TAKES

All the while, Brian was ushering new players into the Kilkenny starting side, forming a group that won the league final.

I still remained completely determined and completely full of self-belief because I knew that, once I got right, I would be back.

* * *

I had known for a long time that I wanted to spend the rest of my life with Anne, but proposing to her was something that I didn't plan in detail until the day before I actually did it. Anne was just 26 so I wanted to propose at a time when she was genuinely not expecting it.

We had gone pretty regularly to the cliff walk in Howth for a walk on summer days and I spotted a tiny little beach below the cliff face near the lighthouse. I drove to Howth under cover of darkness with two deck chairs and a champagne bucket and glasses. The following morning I picked up the ring in a jeweller's in Fairview and ran in to the local Spar to get a bottle of prosecco. I had arrived 15 minutes before the 10.30 curfew on alcohol sales lifted, and had to stand waiting in embarrassment until the ladies behind the counter spotted the jewellery bag and put two and two together. Anne and I made our way to the beach and I popped the question. We sat on the cliff beside the lighthouse in the sun watching the boats sail around Dublin Bay, delighted.

WHY IS HURLING SO HARD?

* * *

In the Leinster final replay that summer in Thurles, I announced my return. At half-time we were nine points down and getting absolutely blitzed by Galway. The emergency glass was smashed – myself and Colin Fennelly were both sent into the attack. T.J. was still there, central to everything. The gang was back together.

Colin kickstarted our revival with a goal, then, after T.J. was surrounded by a swarm of Galway defenders and the ball squirted loose, I cracked a ground shot to the net past James Skehill. We were pumped and only trailing by a point.

Galway got into a flow again with a series of points and ultimately won. But I had proven myself again. My back was feeling much better. I was still able to contribute. Everyone had witnessed that. I was not fully at 100 per cent, but through sheer force of will I had dragged myself to a stage where I was able to perform.

I played for the third Sunday on the spin, we faced Limerick on a day of downpours in Thurles when most of the eyes of the sporting world were turned to the World Cup final in Russia that afternoon.

I knew I was going to be in from the start for that quarter-final. Colin was starting as well. That 11, 12, 14 triangle between the two of us and T.J. was functioning smoothly, and the team was benefitting. We felt we'd got our mojo back by the end of the Galway game, with a proper sense of structure restored.

Our tactics that day against Limerick appeared to be borne out of a sense of panic. We lined up with new plans and new formations that we hadn't seen before. Mossy Keoghan and Pat Lyng came in as wing-forwards and were asked to play as extra midfielders. This left me, at centre-forward, as the only player in the half-forward line. T.J. was sent in to corner-forward with Colin. All puckouts were to be hit short to Paddy Deegan at corner-back who in turn was to drive the ball as far as he could into our full-forward line. It all sounded a little confusing to me but I didn't care, I was back and ready to go. I felt we could figure things out and adjust on the field if needed.

And still we were 0–7 to 0–3 up after the first quarter. We worked our way further into the game well. Limerick responded strongly, as the momentum ebbed and flowed. It always had the look of a game that was going to the wire.

In the second half, my shooting let me down. I finished with 1–03 but I should have scored at least 1–06 considering the changes I created. A few shots dropped short, a few trailed wide; as the rain fell, the sharpness wasn't there in my striking.

Still, the timing of the goal seemed key. John Donnelly had a storming finish. He grabbed a ball from a crowd and escaped, charging towards the Town End in Semple

WHY IS HURLING SO HARD?

Stadium. He fired a stick pass at me, I trapped it with my first touch, swivelled and fired low past Limerick goalkeeper Nickie Quaid.

A couple more phases went against us in a frantic finish. I caught another ball, having been switched inside, tossed it off my shoulder as John ran clear, but James McGrath blew for a throw ball. I went ballistic, as I've never thrown a ball in my life, the handpass striking action being something I've always prided myself on. But it was a free out.

Then John won possession again, made ground and was fired back with a shoulder to the chest. We got no free and Limerick scrambled downfield to get a point. Those little moments went against us and Limerick won by two. Our county board officials went berserk with the referee afterwards, but those frees were only small excuses. We had only ourselves to blame for that defeat.

It was a statement win in the life cycle of that Limerick team. You could see that they had brought their tactical approach to a completely new level.

They had moved Declan Hannon to centre-back. He was very loose, so I got a lot of scores off him and played a lot of hurling in that sector. But it was a deliberate decision to free him up, and to offer more protection to their full-back line; they placed their midfielders in this narrow shape, operating in that small area between the 65-yard lines for puckouts. Their half-forward line would also start their runs from a deep-lying area, then run at angles, the ball delivered into those free spots. You could see their puckouts were so well drilled. Everybody knew what they were doing.

There were no calls coming from the goalkeeper. Everything was driven by their half-forward line. Nickie Quaid had a range of options; he was just picking the best one.

They were all working in sync. They also worked the ball really well through the middle instead of sending long lofted balls in aimlessly. Aaron Gillane made a huge impact as a target inside, while Cian Lynch had come out to midfield, which suited him a little bit better. He was taking short passes and handing them off and connecting things out there.

We didn't think they were going to win the All-Ireland that year. In reality, Cork should have beaten them in the semi-final. Galway looked the best-placed team, as they were the reigning champions and in strong form. But Limerick developed and were powered by serious momentum.

The previous year, I'd gone down with my father to Thurles to watch the All-Ireland U-21 final between Kilkenny and Limerick. Eddie Brennan was the Kilkenny manager and we had what we felt in the county was a relatively strong team. A lot of guys were already on our Senior panel and they had won the equivalent Minor title.

Limerick won by six points, yet the margin felt greater. I remember distinctly thinking to myself that either we were incredibly bad or they were playing incredibly well, because it had always just felt like they were a step ahead.

Underage success can be irrelevant. Clare won three U-21s in a row and only managed to get one Senior title over the next ten years. Limerick reaped a rich dividend in comparison. The Senior defeat to us in the 2017 qualifier had been a blessing in a way for them. It allowed their core group to focus on the U-21 championship, free of interference from Senior commitments. It reminded me of our progress with the Kilkenny U-21s in 2008, bonding together at underage level, being successful, and later all pushing on together in the Senior grade.

That quarter-final win in 2018 was a turning point for them. Would a victory from us have stopped their charge in its tracks? I doubt it. Limerick were a force that was always going to emerge and get stronger.

But claiming that first All-Ireland is so hard; once you make that elusive breakthrough, everything feels more achievable. You could see the confidence rise in the Limerick camp after that day.

That they had beaten Kilkenny in a knockout game; they had beaten one of the best.

CHAPTER 15

THE FINAL RED CARD

As the Kilkenny team bus reached Saggart and slipped off the motorway after the 2019 All-Ireland final, I was hit with this sudden, awful realisation. There was a banquet awaiting us at the Citywest Hotel. A dinner that had to be sat through, speeches that had to be listened to, people that would need to be interacted with. It would be an evening of ceremony, when every fibre of my being wanted to go home, lock the front door, turn off the lights, pull the curtains and sit alone, resting with my tortured thoughts.

A red card for me, a loss for the team – individually and collectively, this day had been a shatteringly low experience.

I'm a hurler who has been sent off in an All-Ireland final, get me out of here.

But I was forced to grit my teeth and brace myself for

what lay ahead, as the bus trundled slowly down Garter Lane and up the tree-lined avenue to the hotel.

The hours since the final whistle blew had already been a test of patience. We spent some time in the Croke Park players' lounge in the Hogan Stand. I am at a loss as to the purpose of putting a defeated team through that miserable experience. We had showered and togged off and sat down on couches in the bar, sinking bottles of beer in a vain attempt to numb the pain of defeat. Tipperary were the ones celebrating, caught up in their own world of singsongs, backslaps and photoshoots. We had 45 minutes to ourselves, a beaten group of Kilkenny players. Some lads tried to make small talk, but I couldn't engage. I didn't take a drink, I just waited to get on the bus and get out of there.

Our partners were all there before us. I walked past a couple of lads' girlfriends at one stage and they had this look of terror on their faces. 'What do I say? Should I say anything?' They knew the score and tended to stay out of our way. Anne generally left me alone in these situations. She knew that a few conciliatory words would make no difference in altering my mood.

At last the call came that our bus was ready to leave. That's when another problem arose – the losers of the All-Ireland final are not granted the privilege of a Garda escort, as there's no urgency to get us back to the hotel in time for the live TV show that night on *The Sunday Game*. This left us stuck in the matchday traffic, the roads around Croke

THE FINAL RED CARD

Park choked with cars after over 80,000 people had spilled out of the stadium.

Eventually, we escaped the jam and got to the Citywest. One of the hotel staff came out and started distributing our room keys. I became aware then of the group of Kilkenny fans that had gathered outside the bus to greet us, while I realised that more would be waiting in the hotel reception.

This cheer erupted when I came down the steps of the bus. But I couldn't deal with it; I was just too devastated. Their intentions were well-meaning, of course. They wanted to show appreciation, but all I could think about was how there were no medals in anyone's pocket, how there'd be no cup coming home to Kilkenny and I was at the centre of the reason why.

Sticking the head down and avoiding eye contact, I just got through the crowd and escaped up the wide staircase in search of my room. Anne was there before me, as she had travelled on a separate bus from Croke Park. She was trying to get ready for the night ahead, while I just threw myself on the bed, still in my Kilkenny tracksuit, unwilling to change clothes and instead frantically scrolling through my phone as it exploded with notifications.

Everyone had an opinion on my tackle on Cathal Barrett. The reactions were split about whether a red card was justified not. That storm would rage on for a few days. Nobody outside Kilkenny and Tipperary cared as much, but inside county borders this was our Saipan moment – controversial and divisive and polarising. Was it a red card or not? Which side were you on?

It was nearly time to go down to the banquet room. I was still silent when Anne came over to the bedside.

'Now I know it's been a bad day for you,' she said. 'But you're going to have to put some tan on my back now.'

She handed me the mitt and we both just burst out laughing.

Thirty seconds of hilarity to break up the days of being trapped in a fog of depression.

* * *

After Limerick beat us in 2018, we were dying for another crack off them. It came in the 2019 semi-final. We hadn't sparked much that year in Leinster, losing a final to Wexford had sunk our spirits, as it felt like another defeat in the same predictable manner.

Brian came to me before the All-Ireland quarter-final against Cork, with news I was set to start. The plan was to take me off after 50 minutes, no matter how I was playing or the way the game was going. They were mindful of injury issues.

I felt great in the victory over Cork, scored 1–2. Our experienced band of forwards were all there and we'd added a real talent as well in Adrian Mullen.

We consciously focused on our set-up. We were letting their corner-backs get the ball and then pushing up as a group, it was so well-structured and we put a lot of time and effort into rehearsing it. The players drove that strategy and the management backed us to implement it. We sat down to discuss our plans, looking at what could be done better. On match day, we moved as a collective unit and clamped down on Anthony Nash's puckouts.

Cork had some serious attacking threats. Patrick Horgan got a lot of plaudits in scoring 3–10. But we were very wary as well of Alan Cadogan and Séamus Harnedy, conscious of the threats they posed. There was a lot to be mindful of when playing Cork.

Thankfully we were in such an organised place that we overwhelmed them in that second half.

And it brought us to a semi-final showdown with Limerick. The backdrop was the hammering they had dished out to Tipperary in the Munster final. All the talk was of a rematch in the All-Ireland final between the pair of them. That talk fuelled our drive; we were like caged animals waiting to be unleashed.

Now we had a structure. Now we had a player-driven system. Now we had extra physicality facing Limerick, with Mullen, John Donnelly and Huw Lawlor all in as big additions. We also had Conor Browne primed to follow Cian Lynch. And we felt we could topple the champions, knock Limerick off the pedestal every team gets put on after winning the All-Ireland.

Our start was explosive. We were dominant everywhere. Colin got a goal that put us nine up. They hit the net from a penalty which we felt was softly given to get back into it, but we maintained the pressure.

We withdrew our half-forwards in order to prevent the pockets of space that had killed us the previous year. Our two corner-forwards retreated to cut off puckouts to their wing-backs.

We wanted the ball to go to their corner-backs for puckouts.

The second the ball went to them, I was in on Sean Finn and others like a shot because we felt they were uncomfortable with it. We knew that they wanted to pinpoint balls left and right, and we weren't going to let them do that again.

That Saturday evening we applied the squeeze.

The game still went the distance. Only a point to spare at the end. A Shane Dowling goal gave them a boost, but even that score came from Paddy Deegan tearing upfield only for us to be turned over. It typified our approach: no standing back, always attacking.

Around the fiftieth minute mark that day, I chased a ball on the right wing as a few players came in to challenge. I went over on my knee and heard the sharp sound of a crack. My lower leg was dangling below the knee. I had never torn an ACL before but it was my instant fear that this was what had happened.

My leg kept buckling and I couldn't shake it off. A consultation with the physios confirmed the game was up for me. They felt my medial ligament was damaged and my prospects of playing in the final suddenly looked uncertain, but that couldn't dampen the satisfaction I felt after the game.

Our group had turned the season around, as we'd gone from a team that fizzled out against Wexford to one that toppled the champions.

It was very much an affirmation that when we give the tactical side of things the respect it deserves, and when we're on our game, then nobody can live with us in terms of the quality of the players that we have.

There was such a sense of contentment in our camp afterwards. I never felt a wild elation after Kilkenny wins, as it wasn't a surprise to come out the right side of the result. Other teams were different. I remember the aftermath of the 2009 All-Ireland U-21 final, getting whacked by a couple of flags as Clare fans lost the plot with the joy they were experiencing.

In Kilkenny, success was what we expected of ourselves. It was the standard that had to be met. That 2019 win over Limerick was about upholding the rich tradition of Kilkenny hurling.

The buzz around Kilkenny in early August was electric. We were back in an All-Ireland final after being marked absent for a couple of years and, in the process, we'd toppled the reigning champions. I couldn't get swept up in that feeling of elation, though, as my knee was pulling me back to that familiar race against time to prove my fitness.

Another injury setback was hard to accept. I had reached my favourite phase of the season – when the knockout games commenced in the All-Ireland series – and I was back in good condition. The road had been long and unforgiving to get to that point, but in my mind the target was crystallised. I had lost interest in the league, while the Leinster championship was no longer a top priority. All that mattered for me now was that end-of-season run. I had watched great Kilkenny players like Henry, Mick Fennelly, Noel Hickey and Derek Lyng achieve this in the past – ridding themselves of injury woes in time for the business end of the year.

That was the crux of the matter. Will you be right for when it matters most? Every player knows that is the key time for a hurler. It's easy being a Munster or Leinster hurler, but are you an All-Ireland hurler? When desperation and jeopardy are dominant emotions, that is when real men stand up and perform.

I had worked tirelessly to get myself into that position in 2019 – and had succeeded for the initial part of it – but I knew limping away from the Limerick semi-final game that I was in real trouble. The physios suspected serious medial ligament damage. I hadn't experienced an injury there before, but the lack of stability in my knee reinforced the severity of the issue.

I was despatched down to Waterford a couple of days later, sitting across from Tadhg O'Sullivan again at his office in Whitfield. Tadhg is an expert knee surgeon. He looked at the results of the MRI scan and didn't mince his words. The medial ligament was torn, and the prognosis was eight weeks out of action.

Tadhg also has a deep understanding of athletes, as his sons have hurled for Ballygunner and Waterford. He's embedded in the game, and so understands that an All-Ireland final changes the dynamic at play. Look, don't completely rule yourself out yet. If you get the knee heavily strapped you could be okay for 10–15 minutes.

With just under three weeks to go that was the chink of light I tried to exploit. Turning up at the next Kilkenny training session, I tried to get the message across that the injury was serious but that I was still capable of playing.

Convincing the physios wasn't easy. They would have seen the medical reports, after all, so they knew the precarious position my knee was in. But no player was ever scrubbed from the equation; everyone was given a chance to prove their fitness. Brian always allowed an injured player that luxury.

For the guts of 10 days, it was hard to discern any improvement. Different strapping techniques didn't work, I was still unable to break out into a run never mind twist or turn. On the Friday week before the final, our physio Kevin Curran tried a heavy duty medical tape on the inside of my leg, which almost acted like a splint for the inside of my knee.

I tested it out and got the first sign of encouragement. Some running and twisting and turning, and I was starting to move more freely. There was enough positivity about it that I was thrown into an in-house training match on the Sunday morning. The gamble was working. I still felt crippled during downtime, but when the strapping went on, my mind was free of fear and I was able to compete.

Seven days out from the All-Ireland final and I knew I was going to make it.

* * *

Every player wants to divorce themselves from the hype in the build-up to an All-Ireland final. Shift the mind to focus on other areas. Avoid talk about the game from people you encounter. Place yourself in a bubble.

That approach was impossible for me to adopt in 2019.

The previous January I had started out as a commercial manager across the GAA and GPA. My working weeks were now spent in Croke Park. As a result, everywhere I turned there were reminders popping up about the final and the magnitude of the occasion.

If we had lost to Limerick, I would have been working on the match day itself. Playing in the game removed me from that roster, but I was still exposed to a notable intensity in the build-up. It is the biggest day of the hurling calendar and there is no end to the amount of boxes that have to be ticked in preparation.

I spent the week surrounded by the commercial team as we liaised with sponsors on their planned activations for the weekend. We fielded ticket queries on a constant basis. The stadium was a hive of activity as we worked to get everything right and I was immersed in it.

It was an unusual dynamic but I wasn't hugely bothered by it all. Walter O'Connor is heavily involved in the handball association. He's a Meath native but has family links to Tipperary. He landed into Croke Park one day that week to collect tickets from the stadium director Peter McKenna, and as he walked through our office, he was fist-pumping and shouting, 'Up Tipp'.

He knew me from my handball days, but he never spotted me in the office. Peter brought my presence to his attention, thinking that he was winding me up on purpose. When Walter realised, he got a little flustered and rang me to apologise. We had a good laugh about it. I used that interaction as an excuse to take the final few days off before the final.

It was a strange week, but nothing could throw me off-kilter. At that stage, I was too streetwise. I knew that small stuff wouldn't influence my performance on the Sunday.

* * *

WHATEVER IT TAKES

By the Sunday morning, I felt confident and assured. My attitude mirrored that of the team. We had momentum after knocking out Cork and Limerick. Tipperary were a little unconvincing after getting walloped in the Munster final. Wexford had let a winning position slip against them in the semi-final.

I stayed in my own house in Dublin the night before and Anne dropped me down to meet the team in the Crowne Plaza in Santry. Cutting down on the travel helped and my pre-match routine kickstarted instantly in the hotel. I hopped up on the physio bed while others were tucking into soup and sandwiches and John Kearns got to work. That extra time in advance of the stadium was a huge benefit. My knee had been consuming my attention over the past couple of weeks, but I couldn't ignore the rest of the ailments that I had been carrying with me. My back, hamstrings and hips all needed work done before I even started my warm-up routine.

Everything was going according to plan. My body was playing ball, showing no signs of breakdown. That knowledge that I was in great shape released this wave of positivity over my mind.

When we got on the bus, I sat down the back next to T.J. We'd started out together as two fresh-faced young lads who knew each other well from St Kieran's and have remained firm friends ever since. When we first joined the Kilkenny Seniors, we sat halfway up the bus on the right-hand side, but over time we'd migrated to the back seat.

I have never been superstitious; there is no ingrained routine that I slavishly follow before a match. When I was younger I tried listening to music once or twice and following a set routine like sitting in the same dressing room seat but it all felt like too much hassle after a few outings. My mindset was that nothing specific had to go right beforehand. Once the ball was thrown in, I always trusted in my ability to perform.

T.J. is the complete opposite. When he was younger, he would get physio treatment on a Saturday before a game and head to Mass that evening. Some things fizzled out, others stuck. By the time of the 2019 final, he had to sit right next to me at the back of the bus; even if there was just the two of us in a five-seater, he'd sit in the one next to me. He also had these little hydration shakes, a mix of glucose and water, that he downed. He has a particular pair of socks, particular colour grips for games and he also insists on missing the first half of the matchday parade to go to the bathroom before big games.

If his routine was interrupted, there needed to be a solution found. One time, he arrived in Croke Park without his ash guard. There was a panic in the dressing room until Conor Fogarty offered his as a replacement. The fingers were too long on Conor's glove so the physios needed to cut it down to size before we could go onto the pitch.

He is particular about his music. There is a unique pre-match playlist that gets flicked on when the bus is approaching Croke Park.

'All The Things She Said', by Russian pop duo t.A.T.u.

'8 Mile', by Eminem.

And it's capped off as we drive under the stand of the stadium by Survivor belting out 'Eye Of The Tiger'.

The volume is cranked up to the last in his cheap set of earphones and so the whole bus is forced to listen; new fellas to the panel often look around curiously for the source of this random concoction of tunes.

Chaos ensued at the back of the bus before one game when his earphones were not pairing up to his phone via Bluetooth. No one else had his playlist, so there was this search for earphones that worked. Michael Rice saved the day.

I couldn't relate to that type of preparation.

But it worked for T.J.; like Rafael Nadal before a tennis game, he was obsessive about it and it relaxed him.

I've had a front-row view for his Kilkenny career, watched him grow from struggling bystander to the dominant presence that is fundamental to our hopes of success.

It was challenging for him to reach that stage and it took time for him to mature. Training in the early years was difficult for him; the management were always on his case in pre-season, demanding more. His hurling talent was unquestioned; it just needed to be married with a greater work ethic.

THE FINAL RED CARD

Things changed off the pitch in his mid-twenties. When he opened his own gym in Kilkenny city, it allowed him to shape his whole life around hurling. His physical shape changed, as he was working harder than ever outside of collective sessions. That's been critical to the longevity of his career and his performances.

Brian was the perfect manager for him. He loved T.J. as a hurler. A lot of that stemmed from his brilliant ability to catch a ball in the air, a skill that was rare and that Brian coveted in a player. Once T.J. got settled and developed consistency in his performances, there was no looking back.

He is a player that I hugely admire. The manner in which he turned his career around from his mid-twenties was just extraordinary.

* * *

We'd landed in Croke Park for the final. It was time to get in the zone and get my warm-up going. I was already togged out from the hotel, so it was straight back up on the physio bed for John to finish off the work we'd started in the hotel. Manipulate my back, work on my hips. Before I applied the strapping to the knee, I needed to feel free and loose, and to ensure the blood was flowing through my hamstrings, because my movement was very restricted once fully strapped.

I had a quick chat to the younger lads, as it was a first final for John Donnelly and Adrian Mullen. Help them fill that dead time before the game started, remind them of the form that got them here in the first place.

Timing your warm-up is key on All-Ireland final day. There are extra formalities to allow for with the presidential handshake and a longer than usual pre-match parade. You need to be mindful not to burn out early. Conserving energy while maintaining focus is vital.

It was a first experience of an August All-Ireland. The air felt thicker and more humid

My mind was at ease and I carried a familiar focus. And when that first whistle blasted, I tore away and got into the game.

I was marking Cathal Barrett and the early signs were good. I held him off with one hand underneath a puckout and caught the ball at hip height. I fed well off Colin Fennelly to take a handpass on his inside and stuck it over the bar. I latched on to another ball, taking it away from Ronan Maher and Noel McGrath, but I skewed my shot wide in the torrential rain that had arrived.

I controlled a cross-field ball from John Donnelly into my hand when Barrett came in to challenge. He swung his hurl across my face, clipping my nose and knocking me to the ground.

A free was awarded but I was left looking quizzically at James Owens. Was that the extent of the punishment?

He's not a referee that interacts or even speaks with players which is very unusual, and highly frustrating. Brian Gavin, Barry Kelly, James McGrath – they would all be more personable. For a player, not getting a decision explained and having to put up with silence can be infuriating. An explanation can help build up some sort of relationship. I jogged off after that foul, as the nose needed to be tidied up to wash away the blood coming from the cut. I returned wearing the number 31 jersey.

After 21 minutes we were in control, ahead 0–8 to 0–3. Tipperary then got some joy in the game, Niall O'Meara darting through our defence for a goal against the run of play. We pushed on, undeterred, looking to close out the half.

Tipperary tried to reorganise their defence, addressing problem areas. Tommy Dunne raced in a couple of times to urge Barrett to lift it. The panic in their faces was obvious and all too familiar. They'd switched their wing-backs. John Donnelly was dragging Padraic Maher around the pitch, so they put Padraic in on top of Wally Walsh, getting Seamus Kennedy to track John.

A long puckout was pumped down on top of Wally and Padraic. They competed but neither won it and the ball broke cleanly straight through. I'd anticipated that it would break to the side and so was caught off guard. Barrett read the break first and he collected the ball near the sideline. His peripheral vision is really good; he's well-equipped at twisting away from a tackle, but as I raced in

I felt that I was timed perfectly to shoulder him over the line.

I leaned in for the challenge but Barrett had applied the brakes as I approached. He took a step back and dodged the challenge but I brushed off him. The cable ties on his faceguard that fasten the chin strap to his helmet were sticking out and I felt them scratch my tricep as we made contact.

My momentum sent me careering towards the crowd; I turned as I heard the whistle and saw him lying on the ground. 'Get up you little weasel!' I roared at him, having felt the extent of the contact myself. I knew exactly what he was at: trying to find an easy way out instead of standing up like a man and getting on with the game.

I looked over at Johnny Murphy, the linesman who was right next to it, and he was shaking his head while looking at Barrett sprawled out on the grass. A free had been awarded to Tipperary. James Owens made his way from the middle of the field across to Murphy.

'Ask the linesman, I didn't really touch him,' I said to Owens.

'Right,' Owens responded.

The linesman then spoke to the ref. 'Right ... I'm not so sure he got hit. Did he say I didn't mean to catch him?'

'No,' Owens said.

Murphy responded, 'Yeah, I'm not so sure that he got hit now; it could be a slight little bit, but I'm not sure. I think he's playing.'

THE FINAL RED CARD

'He's playing it a bit?' Owens asked.

'I think he is,' Murphy said. 'I'm not so sure now but he didn't ... I was right beside it ... I don't think he got hit.'

'Right,' Owens said.

'I think this fella [Barrett] knows what he's doing,' Murphy continued.

Owens made his way off to look at Barrett and the Tipp physio interjected to plead Barrett's case. Then he returned to Murphy.

'What did you think?' Murphy asked.

'There is actually blood there,' Owens said.

'Is there?'

'Yeah, yeah.'

'Okay.'

Owens called me over and I was raging with Murphy because I thought he'd done me with a yellow card. I gave my name when asked for it by Owens and I was visibly unhappy with the booking.

The referee then said, 'I know, Richie, you caught him late, up high, head high.'

'Very little in it,' I said.

And then he reached for the red card in his book. He flashed it and sprinted back down the field before I had time to question him. I was stunned.

'What?! Where are you going?'

My mind was scrambled. I had been half-expecting a yellow card, and so the sight of the red left me shocked.

I walked towards the sideline. Derek Lyng was the first person I met. We were both stunned.

I went up the steps of the stand, threw down my hurl and helmet, and slumped into my seat. My mind was a mess, ablaze with thoughts. *What has just happened?* I was still dazed. I felt I'd been screwed over. Refereeing is not an easy job and fifty-fifty decisions can go either way – but I just couldn't believe that Owens wasn't taking the word of the linesman who was five yards away from the incident.

Half-time came a few minutes later and there was this howl of disgust from Kilkenny fans towards the referee. The boos vibrated throughout the stadium. Later that winter I was sent the video clip of the incident by the GAA, capturing what happened and the subsequent conversation.

We all trooped down the tunnel. I was asked to speak and initially struggled to string the words together, although eventually I did mumble something to the team before they went back out. Padraig Walsh tried to rouse the lads further.

'Look at what that man has done for Kilkenny hurling. How many times has he gone out there and won games for us? How many of us wouldn't have All-Ireland medals in our pockets without him? Are we going to let this happen to him today?

It's our turn now to win this game for him. Or are we going to look at Barrett lifting the cup in 35 minutes' time with a smug fucking head on him?'

THE FINAL RED CARD

Later, I appreciated the sentiment behind the words, but at the time it just washed over me.

* * *

I have a history of red cards with James Owens. After hundreds of games during my career he is the only referee to have sent me off. When I got sent off in 2012 against Limerick, he was the linesman who directed that decision to the referee. He blew the whistle early against Waterford in 2013 when we thought we'd struck the winning point much to my disgust.

Figuring out where you stood with him was tricky because he doesn't speak to the players during games. Off the pitch I had only one interaction with him up to that point.

Tom Fitzpatrick was a great friend of mine. The Games Promotion Officer in St Pat's, he put a lifetime of work into the GAA. He grew up in the Burren in West Clare and moved to Dublin where he invested years into the schools game. He managed the Dublin Minors that beat our Kilkenny team in 2005. He sadly passed away in September 2023, but was a true gentleman.

Tom had a deep interest in refereeing. He was involved in various committees and every year he would ask the referee from the previous year's All-Ireland final, along with an inter-county player, to give a talk to new referees who were training under Leinster GAA.

WHATEVER IT TAKES

Tom asked me if I would come to Portlaoise and speak about a player's expectations of a referee the winter after the 2015 final we played against Galway. James Owens refereed that game and was there to give his talk. He spoke about progressing through his refereeing career, and how he'd learned to use better judgement. It was actually interesting to hear.

He then referenced a first-half incident in that Kilkenny–Galway final as a sign of his maturity. It was a clothesline tackle around the neck by Johnny Coen on Colin Fennelly as he was bearing down on goal. He said that his immediate reaction was that this was a red card offence for a high tackle but, as he walked in, he reasoned to himself that the foul could not have been meant as nobody would want to get sent off in an All-Ireland final. And so, a yellow was shown. That thought process baffled me but what baffled me more was that he said it while I was in the room.

I spoke to Tom afterwards and we laughed about it. He referenced Brian Gavin's advice at the previous year's event when he was asked if he was a referee who liked to stamp his authority on the game. Brian responded by saying that it is not his job to stamp authority on the game. His job is to blow the whistle when he thinks it's a free and to keep it round his neck when it's not.

I am not a player that referees seek to put manners on. During a match I will try to influence their decisions, of course I do – to the same extent that anyone does – but when the game is over I will shake hands and move on.

If I meet a referee in another setting, I will always chat away. On All-Star trips, I would always try to mix with the couple of referees that were there. I felt that there was no need for them to be isolated as most are genuine hurling people.

* * *

When the second half started, I remained convinced that we could win this game. We had hurled so well during the first half and kept their big players out of the game. Noel McGrath was the conductor of their orchestra, Seamus Callanan their biggest attacking asset, but both had been kept quiet.

After five minutes, I could see that we were all over the place. We were going to get blitzed. One point down at half-time, three points down on 37 minutes, we found ourselves eight points down after 42 minutes. Callanan and Bubbles both got goals and their whole team were firing. The pressure was off and the freedom liberated the Tipperary team.

And the contest just fizzled out. Tipperary won at their ease.

Our dressing room after was a scene of devastation.

I was bereft of emotion, scanning the room and surveying my teammates. Over in the corner, T.J. raised his head and attempted to speak. As captain for the year, a victory would have carried great meaning for him. He started thanking everyone linked to our camp, but his voice cracked with emotion and he broke down, incapable of going further. The hurt was glaring.

It was a torturous place to be. Grief wrapped its tentacles around everybody, catching us all in a tight grip.

I wondered: *is this my fault?*

The scratch on my arm was a reminder of the true extent of the contact between us. In my frazzled state, that settled my mind. I knew exactly what happened. There was a contentment in that later, as everyone in the country pored over the footage, dialling it down to slow motion for closer inspection. Everyone is entitled to their opinion, of course, but as a key protagonist, my view carries more weight.

Out on the pitch, moments previously, the Tipperary players had filed past. Padraic Maher marched up to me. 'What the hell happened? What did he say to you?' he asked, referring to the referee.

We know each other relatively well. Padraic is a sincere, straightforward fella. He's not going to indulge in plámásing. So his surprise over the red card decision was genuine.

'I don't know; well done, Padraic', was the only reply I could muster.

He stood there for a few seconds, then we shook hands and he moved off. Noel McGrath was another who sought me out afterwards. They were delighted with the outcome, of course, as they'd won and so the exchanges were brief.

* * *

That Sunday night was a grind to get through.

I could see all night that people were walking on eggshells around me. 'Do we talk it out with him or leave him alone?' I stayed at the table to avoid any awkward conversations at the bar counter, where you're more likely to get interrogated over the day.

Paddy Deegan was with me for a while, Cillian Buckley for another time. Anne was generally nearby.

Brian made his traditional banquet speech. At times during my career, I was unsure if he had a liking for me. And yet, in public engagements, he often made a specific point of praising me. After the 2015 final he singled me out for my recovery to get my body right for that game. And at this night in 2019 he made this passionate defence against the sending-off, saying that he'd watched it back and that he would challenge any man, woman or child who said the red card was justified. 'There's absolutely no way Richie Hogan should have been sent off today,' he declared.

The Kilkenny crowd there burst into applause.

Remembering that now, it was a nice touch. At the time, however, I felt completely empty.

The homecoming on the Monday was horrendous. I didn't bother drinking that day, instead just stumbling on through each passing hour.

Amid the blizzard of incoming text messages, one from Henry Shefflin stood out. He complimented me on the player I had been for Kilkenny and said the people would show their appreciation for me that night at home.

I rang him a couple of days later and did the same to Jackie Tyrrell. They had both fought my corner on the different *Sunday Game* shows, pushing back against any pile-on.

Usually when we get back to Kilkenny on the Monday night after an All-Ireland final, they introduce the players individually, but there was a relief that they changed course that night. They brought us all on together and there was a cheer from the crowd, then we got straight off and scattered into the night.

* * *

I didn't bother staying in Kilkenny that night. There was a bed for all of us in Langton's Hotel but I just drove straight back to Dublin and was sitting in the Croke Park office by eight o'clock the next morning.

I had no interest in dwelling on it at home. Getting back to work was preferrable, even if that meant returning to the site of my hurling heartbreak.

As the office began to fill up that Tuesday, people had no idea how to react around me. I'm sure they felt I was a ticking timebomb waiting to explode. Peter McKenna broke the tension by showing me a picture on his phone. It had Barrett with a bottle of Coors Light in his hand and a caption above saying, 'Goes down easy'. It was bizarre to think that 48 hours later I was back in the stadium again but it was the easiest way to keep my mind off things.

Later that day, I got a text from one of the producers of the *Off The Ball* radio programme on Newstalk.

'Hi, Richie, look, we were just wondering: would you come on the show tonight and have a chat?'

'What exactly do you want to talk about?'

'Ah sure look, we'll just maybe have a little chat about the season.'

Let's not beat around the bush here, lads, I thought.

'You want to talk about the sending off, don't you?'

'Yeah, that'll probably come up alright.'

I decided to do the interview. It was a real crisis communication move: get out there and tell my story. I felt it was time to draw a line under all this so I could just move on.

Things were starting to get under my skin and irritate me. One theory doing the rounds was that it had been an act of revenge for Barrett's earlier challenge. I am not a character who is hyped up on the hurling field. I am composed. Retribution is not something I ever contemplate.

WHATEVER IT TAKES

I needed all that stuff to stop rumbling on.

So I went home after work and we did the interview, pre-recorded and pushed out on air later that night.

Joe Molloy was conducting the interview which I was happy with. I knew that he felt it was a red card and he kept pushing me towards his view. In my head I felt like telling him that I didn't care what he thought, and the purpose of the interview was that people would hear my view and not his. But I remained as calm as I could. Afterwards, I didn't care how it had gone, I was just happy that I'd dealt with it, rather than have it lurking in the background, waiting to pop out in some interview further down the road.

And it was easier from there to just move on.

I let the incident drift away from me that winter, like the tide taking debris far out to sea and away over the horizon. It was now out of sight, out of mind.

A couple of months later I did appeal the one-match suspension I was handed, but it went against me. I just accepted it.

I just moved past it.

Amid the mayhem, there was a humorous postscript.

Anne later told me that she had been in the players' lounge after the game when the Tipperary players came in. She was with a few of the other wives when she saw Cathal Barrett and threw him the dirtiest look that she could. He looked back at her a little puzzled with the passive aggression.

THE FINAL RED CARD

Niamh Dowling – Cillian Buckley's wife – grabbed her.

'Anne, what are you doing?'

'I'm staring down that Cathal Barrett fella, so he knows exactly what I think of him.'

'Anne, that's Bubbles Dwyer, not Cathal Barrett!'

As deep as the hurt was over it all, you could still smile at some things.

CHAPTER 16

THE ROAD TO REDEMPTION

THE 2019 ALL-IRELAND final was the last time I played Tipperary in a Senior championship game. They were the rival that had framed my career; our meetings had featured some of my best performances for Kilkenny and most treasured scores.

Plenty kept fixating on that final. Debate raged over the red card, the scale of the defeat, and the uncertainty of our Kilkenny hurling futures. I moved on quickly and left that day in my rear-view mirror.

Once the club championship ended, I started getting ready for 2020. Typically you would hit pause and unwind for some time during the off-season, but that option never crossed my mind. There was a determination that winter to push myself to the limit in training. I had sessions six days a week. Down on the beach at Dollymount Strand or along the promenade in Clontarf, I was pushing myself further than I thought was possible. Time was no barrier, pounding the pavement at 6 a.m. or 11 p.m. didn't matter to me. Nothing interfered with it. The darker, the better, I felt; the wetter, the better. I also crammed in work at the gym, pushing myself harder and harder. I was completely driven by hurt.

And it was just so easy to train. I was never searching for any motivation, never struggling to get going. The body was in ribbons, but the mind was completely clear.

The Kilkenny set-up changed over those months. Mick Dempsey stepped away in October and Mickey Comerford from the Kilkenny U-20 team came in to replace him. Derek Lyng left to take over the U-20s, while D.J. Carey and Martin Comerford (Gorta) landed as Senior selectors.

Mick Dempsey had been excellent; he was really knowledgeable and personable. He was brilliant at his job. Mickey Comerford was also top class. He had that same level of structure and discipline as Mick possessed, meaning the weekly schedule was loaded with information. Mickey brought freshness and enthusiasm with him. Not only would he outline a training session and tell you why you were doing it, he would then meet up to do it with you.

Mickey's own fitness levels were sky high. In those one-on-one running and strength sessions with lads, he was providing a serious challenge. A great rapport was quickly built up as a result.

By the time Mickey took over, I had banked three months of hard, solid work. That gave me an edge in early season training over others. I wasn't at the same level of fitness as my early twenties but I was at levels above where I had been for the previous three years.

* * *

At the outset of 2020, we were all adjusting to the new faces around the place in Kilkenny. The transition was a bit messy at times. D.J. and Gorta were new, yet McGarry and Cody were still there. As everyone got used to a different system, it could get disjointed. We played Dublin in the first round of the league, a game for which I was suspended due to the All-Ireland final.

The Friday night before our first league game against Dublin, McGarry came over to me at training. They were excited about the shape I was in at this early part of the season and they were keen to start me.

'James, sure I'm suspended after the All-Ireland.'

McGarry took a step back. That thought hadn't crossed his radar.

Brian approached me later. 'So I hear you don't want to play at the weekend then?'

'I don't know what kind of a show you lads are running here, Brian.'

We both laughed about it. I was in a good mood as I knew the work I had put in was noticed by the management team.

Gorta was caught with work and late for training that same night. We were pucking across the pitch by the time he landed. He had been in such a rush getting there that he was still a bit flustered by the time he approached me for a chat.

'Now, Richie, what we want on Sunday is for you to stay close to goal, make those runs left and right.'

I thought he was winding me up.

'Gorta! I'm not playing, I'm suspended, I already told the lads. Do ye not talk to each other?'

We both just burst out laughing.

And I was pushed into action soon enough. League campaigns could often see me used sparingly as the years went on and the miles jumped up on the clock, but the block of winter work had left me in a good place. I played against Carlow, Wexford and Clare. I felt great and I was racking up the scores.

Then bang – Covid hit the world like a sledgehammer. Hurling was gone, all our plans smashed to pieces.

I looked at the bright side. I had picked up a back injury against Clare and figured this would mean a break for a few weeks, a chance now to get myself right and come back stronger.

But reality soon hit home. There would be no short-term fix for this.

∗ ∗ ∗

THE ROAD TO REDEMPTION

On 12 March 2020, Taoiseach Leo Varadkar addressed the country from Washington. We were to enter lockdown.

I watched the news in a meeting room underneath the Hogan Stand and no one knew how to react. Were we to go home now? What were we to do about work tomorrow? None of us had a clue as to how this was going to pan out. Online working was still an alien concept. Zoom calls? I'd never heard of them.

Everyone just left that day, confused, and over time we plotted a way to figure out this strange, new world.

At that point in my life, the priority was clear. Hurling was number one. It remained the only show in town. I had put my heart and soul into training that winter, emptying myself with that image of the first championship game in my head. Rumours were flying around that the GAA were going to pull the plug on the whole year. I was desperate to play again. I needed to get back on track.

When were the games returning? Would they ever return? No one knew.

Brian sent out a message to the Kilkenny squad. *No training, lads, stick to the restrictions until we hear anything further.*

We met as players on an online call, with Mickey Comerford there as well to advise. Thinking this was a temporary stoppage, we didn't want standards to slip. Training programmes were handed out and needed to be followed. Some lads were living together in Kilkenny, which was ideal as they could go to the Castle Park to put in the running miles together.

I was stuck in Dublin but decided to flip it to my advantage. After all, working from home meant I was in complete control of my calendar and could tailor my training to fit in sessions during the day.

In a house on Collins Avenue, I lived with Anne and some of my old college friends. We bought a bench and adjustable dumbbells, kitting out a spare room as a gym. Everywhere you looked, there was free time to be put to use, so I trained away in the house and ran non-stop in the parks nearby.

Eventually, that summer, there was white smoke. Club matches were returning first. It was a great outlet to kickstart hurling again. I could see the thinking behind the decision, but in another way I really wanted county games first.

We threw ourselves into hurling with Danesfort. In the championship first round in Nowlan Park we played Mullinavat. I scored 16 points from the middle of the field, seven from play; it was comfortably one of the best games of hurling I'd ever played. But we lost after extra time and near the end I pulled my hamstring.

Usually, a hamstring injury would have ruled me out for two to four weeks. After six weeks, however, I still wasn't right. The rest of the club season was a write-off and after nine years at Senior level we were relegated to the Intermediate grade. With the quick turnaround I was now in trouble for the start of the inter-county season as well.

* * *

It was mid-November when I was summoned down to the Hogan Stand sideline, not long before the second-half water break. We were in trouble. Galway had got a handle on this game and it looked like we would lose our third Leinster final in a row.

Brian's message was simple.

'Richie, remember the last time when you came on against these lads in 2016, you went in on Daithí Burke and you destroyed him. Just go in there and do that again.'

'No problem, Brian,' I said. My mindset had been similar, watching on. The hamstring had healed, the focus was clear. No pep talk was needed to fire me up, I just wanted to be unleashed onto the pitch.

Fifty-six minutes in and we were staring at a five-point deficit. These were the scenarios I relished. Everyone could get involved when you're up by five but how were you going to respond when the team was struggling? Hide away in the corner or go stand up in the middle?

I saw Mossy Keoghan get the ball around the middle and pop it to Padraig Walsh. The body language of the defender in these scenarios was always key. When Padraig moves forward, he puts his head up and delivers the ball into space.

If he's leaning backwards, the ball is going to be cleared up into the sky and will fall on a crowd. In this case, I could see that Padraig was on the move, so I started my run quite deep in the full-forward line, then sprinted to the right to get free, so the pass could be placed in front of me. However, Padraig drove it the other way, back across me and down on top of Daithí Burke. I had no time to stand up and give out about the quality of the ball. I could only turn and react.

The yellow sliotars – I detest them. In night-time hurling matches, the ball gets lost in the glow of the light as it drops. I couldn't see the ball initially, but I knew that Daithí could see it. His arm was up, hand outstretched, waiting to catch. Common sense dictated my next move – put my hurl in front of his hand, tip the ball and I knew that it would fall behind my head.

I gave Daithí a little nudge so as to give myself an advantage under the breaking ball. Galway's Gearóid McInerney was covering, so, having tipped the ball beyond Daithí, I just tried to hold him off with one arm and get to that loose ball first.

Out of the corner of my eye, I saw Éanna Murphy charging out of goal. Where is this lad going, I thought. He looked like he was going to try to pull on the ball so I reached in to lift it past him, ensuring he missed it with his swing, and then his momentum carried him into McInerney.

I took a touch to balance it on my hurl and then the thought struck me: no goalkeeper was at home at the Davin

End. My back was to the goal but I knew where the net was – I just had to get the ball in there as fast as I could. Any moment to pause and the chance was gone, as you're inviting a block. I flicked it, turned and watched the umpire raise the green flag.

I allowed myself a little fist pump, then jogged out and got going again. The only roars were from the subs bench, the stadium completely empty otherwise. We were back in this game.

It was the catalyst for us to take over and win. Every Kilkenny player was lifted and we got another goal within seconds, T.J. blasted home a shot. From there, we just took off. I finished with 1–2, as we won our first Leinster title in four years.

I was back playing and leading the attack for Kilkenny again.

At that moment, I didn't view the goal as anything special. All four touches were the only option I could take with the ball at the time; every flick was a sensible decision. There was no rehearsed plan; it all just felt natural. When you're hurling at that level, one of the hardest things is just being able to think clearly. Achieve that clarity of thought amid the chaos and you'll make the right decisions and gain the advantage over everyone else.

I'm still asked about that Leinster final goal and the one against Tipperary in 2011. People are fishing for more information. How did you do it? What were you thinking?

WHATEVER IT TAKES

In both situations, it was a simple reaction as the play was unfolding. There was just one guiding question at all times.

What needs to be done here to score a goal?

* * *

If you're still hurling in the weeks leading up to Christmas, it's generally with your club as you're on this brilliant journey with everyone in your community, with a county trophy already secured and embracing the novelty of days out in the province.

There was none of that in 2020. The whole country was stuck indoors that winter, us county hurlers were some of the few allowed to escape and play in a championship that just felt completely at odds to what we were used to.

It was my 14th season as a Kilkenny Senior hurler. I knew all about playing in Croke Park, but these experiences were completely abnormal. After years spent feeding off the energy from huge crowds on big championship days, suddenly that was all out of the picture. I lived off the electricity that shot around the stadium when there was a big score or tackle, the gasp at some outstanding piece of skill or a huge missed chance. Now there was just silence, save for some shouts by players and management to each other, all of whom were surrounded by rows of empty seats. It was eerie stuff. It sucked plenty of enjoyment out of hurling. In a way, it cut the pressure too that weighed down on some players. If you struggled to perform because there were 80,000 people watching you, well now there was nobody there so that excuse was gone.

Behind the scenes it was complicated on game days. There was no longer a Kilkenny team bus; instead, we all had to make our own way there by car. That didn't bother me because I lived close to Croke Park, but it was an issue for everybody travelling up from Kilkenny. Some lads didn't drive, some didn't have their own cars.

The first round, when we went to play Dublin, Eoin Cody got a flat tyre on the motorway. One of the medical team had to turn back to pick him up and the car was abandoned on the side of the road, left to be sorted out later.

In Croke Park, two big dressing rooms and a warm-up area were kitted out for each team. Plenty of space for all, but instead the Kilkenny management insisted on being extra cautious. We would tog out around the concourse on level three of the Hogan Stand. We mainly togged out on the ground and the physio benches were set up close by. We sat wherever we could. Some sat on the counters normally used at burger stands and others used the bucket seats at the back of the stands. I did some foam rolling as part of my warm-up routine on the floor of the men's toilets. Sometimes it lashed rain and showers of water would skate in on us. Lads were freezing cold and trying to beat a ball off the wall to stay warm. In the build-up to a big match, getting the group together and building collective focus was hard. We had county board officials manning the exits into the stands to stop members of the opposition backroom team from sneaking in to listen to our team talk. At times, you were looking around and the whole thing felt ridiculous but overall, I enjoyed it. There was a great sense of humility about rolling around on a toilet floor before going out to play an All-Ireland semi-final.

We were out of the 2020 championship after the All-Ireland semi-final against Waterford. We started like a train. We went nine points up in the first half and were ahead by seven at half-time. Eleven minutes in, I darted onto a ball in behind everyone, raced through and felt certain I had scored a goal as my shot flew through the air. Stephen O'Keeffe made a great save, but at least Mossy Keoghan tapped in the rebound. T.J. got another goal soon after.

David Herity had rung me the week of the game. He'd been studying Waterford. 'Remember that if you're going in on Stephen O'Keeffe, he never comes off his line, so carry the ball in as close as you can and just finish it past him.'

That was on my mind when I chased down the ball. If he had broken from his line he would have got there before me, but he stayed. I carried it in as far as I could but just didn't hit my shot far enough away from him.

When we beat Galway in that Leinster final, it had been another testament to our survival instincts. However, the joy of the end result probably led us to believe that we played better than we actually did.

THE ROAD TO REDEMPTION

Colin Fennelly and Walter Walsh were both left out of the starting team for the next game, the semi-final against Waterford. Colin was the most feared full-forward in the country at the time, while Walter was another big figure for us. They came on in the third quarter but by then the game was drifting away from us. We really needed those two lads on the pitch from the start. They were tried and tested leaders for us and they were no good sitting in the stand. Waterford were on top all over and you could see their confidence levels soaring. When the pressure was applied, we had no answer.

Old failings from a few years earlier resurfaced as we hit aimless balls down the pitch. We lacked the fluency to work the ball short and transition it from defence to attack when the pressure really came on.

Waterford won by four and if the game had gone on any longer, they would have beaten us by more. It was a severe disappointment. The loss was hard to take, as was the reality of getting no reward after a season that had dragged on through months of uncertainty.

But the real punishment came two weeks later when we had to sit down and watch the All-Ireland final, seeing Limerick win it at their ease.

Growing up in that Kilkenny hurling environment, if you lost an All-Ireland final, the target as players was to get back there the year after and win it. There was also an expectation from everyone in the county that you would do exactly that. Losing to Waterford meant we hadn't held up our end of the bargain after 2019.

We also wanted another crack off Limerick. The previous year we had beaten them in the semi-final. We were the better team and deserved it. We led for the majority of the game and any time Limerick made their way back, we stepped it up a gear and pushed ahead. But all the talk doing the rounds was that Limerick would have wrapped up three in a row if they hadn't had a slow start and slipped up against Kilkenny that day. It was a view that came mainly from supporters and pundits, rather than directly from their camp, but it really struck a sour note with us. The 2018 All-Ireland quarter-final had its own controversy with late refereeing decisions going against us, but once the whistle blew we never spoke about it again, accepting our defeat and wishing Limerick well.

John Kiely never engaged in any excuses or talk of being caught off guard by Kilkenny in that game. He was too clever for that. He was quick to congratulate us and both himself and Paul Kinnerk quickly analysed where they went wrong in that game and what they needed to improve on to get back to the top. Limerick's approach to 2020 was starkly different to the 'Kilkenny Way'.

Both teams ended the year as unsuccessful challengers in the 2019 championship but our responses to defeat took different paths. Our traditional approach to defeat was to clean out the team and get fresh blood in and this worked incredibly well in 2006, 2011 and 2014 when we had conveyor belts of talented, hungry youngsters ready to break the door down to get in. Players who, if born in any other county in Ireland, would already be household names.

2019 was different however, we had just found a bit of rhythm in games against Cork, Limerick and Tipperary and we were playing to a structure that allowed us to get the best out of our players on the pitch. This wasn't a team coming to the end of the road. It was a team that had finally got things right. Colin and I had worked well as two full-forwards playing close to goal with Adrian Mullen providing the legs to move freely into the half-forward line and beyond if needed. We were as dominant as ever on our puckouts and most importantly we looked like a team that was in control of our play and not reacting to the game plan of the opposition. There was of course room for competition from guys who forced their way in, but building on 2019 rather than starting with a clean slate would have been something to consider. The change of management team and the disruption from Covid made that more difficult.

Limerick's approach to defeat in 2019 was different. There were no major changes but they made adjustments where needed to improve things. All of their changes were done with a purpose.

Kyle Hayes, who had ended up at centre-back against us in that game, stayed at that end of the field, providing a real attacking force from the half-back line. Barry Nash provided a solution at corner-back as a ball-playing defender who revolutionised their short puckout game. Cian Lynch had been anonymous due to Conor Browne's tenacious man-marking game in the semi-final and he found himself operating at centre-forward where he got a little more freedom to implement his link-up play.

That day in Croke Park we demolished Nickie Quaid's puckouts. His trademark arrowed deliveries into the wide open spaces for the half-forward line to run on to were taken away through disciplined covering by Wally Walsh and John Donnelly on both wings and superior anticipation from our half-back line. We had even greater success on their short puckouts where we completely shut down every attempt.

Throughout all their success, Limerick have remained faithful to the majority of their team. The core group has not changed in terms of personnel but they have added elements to their game every year, leading to a team that is not just improving at the things that made them good in the first place, they are evolving as a team and continuously adding more weapons to their arsenal.

After losing the 2016 final to Tipperary, we had made a similar mistake in not giving those guys a shot at redemption. We just needed to be straight with ourselves. 'Look, we're still a top team filled with excellent players. We were beaten by a better team on the day. Let's learn from it and improve!'

THE ROAD TO REDEMPTION

Limerick did just that after 2019 and it couldn't have worked out much better. They are the standard bearers and regardless of their 2024 loss to Cork they are still the team that every other county measures themselves by.

✷ ✷ ✷

Sitting in the Hogan Stand, I could hear the calls fired towards the sideline. What started as a murmur gradually grew into something more regular and insistent from the Kilkenny supporters as the second half wore on.

'Get Richie Hogan on! Bring on Richie!'

It was August 2021 and a place in the All-Ireland final was slipping out of our grasp. We had edged the first half with Cork, having gone in a point up, but they had taken control in the second half and this red wave was crashing through us as they went six clear.

I watched on, powerless. We brought on our first sub at half-time, the second and third before the water break and the fourth with 10 minutes to go. I was still rooted to my seat.

I'd turned 33 that day. *Happy birthday, Richie. Your present is a front-row seat in Croke Park to watch the hurling.*

We had also been here eight months earlier, losing an All-Ireland semi-final to Waterford. A winter night when the cold rattled around an empty Croke Park. After that defeat, there had been no hanging around.

By late November we'd figured it was only a month until a new season started, so it was time to get straight to work again. And then the country was again caught in the grip of a Covid lockdown after Christmas, so all our hurling plans were thrown up in a heap for the second year in a row.

I had come back in 2020, proving that I could still contribute at the very top of the game. That sparked the confidence to keep going. When the league resumed in early May, however, I was struggling a little with injury, hamstring trouble this time. I wasn't too worried however until it came to the Leinster final and I wasn't included on the panel, having regained my fitness by then. I was patient and played the long game. I got my body right before the Cork game, putting my hand back up for selection. But I hadn't been picked to start; now, with 10 minutes to go, I was still on the bench.

There were fans roaring my name now. Covid had cut the attendance in half at Croke Park, so everything could be heard more clearly.

Was Brian worried about my fitness? Did he think I was finished? Maybe he didn't trust me to perform at this level anymore?

A feeling of embarrassment crept over me. Time was almost up; we'd cut the gap to three, but we were still being beaten.

Is this how bad it's gone?

Then we were saved at the death. Cork were turned over coming out of defence and Padraig Walsh flighted this brilliantly judged pass into Adrian Mullen's lap. He stepped inside a couple of covering defenders and cracked his shot home. It was a brilliant goal. We'd snatched a draw.

As everyone got ready for extra time, Brian came over.

'Richie, are you alright?'

'What do you mean? Of course I'm alright.'

'Okay, okay.'

We had been well beaten in every part of the game except the scoreboard and now there were 20 more minutes left to play. Gorta, our selector, told me to warm up. I would be coming on at the start of the second period of extra time.

'I'm ready to go now, Gorta, get me on!'

Ten minutes later the whistle blew, and the lads were on the pitch at the break in extra time. I waited for the call but nobody came near me in the stand. I was not waiting around any longer. I strapped on the helmet, ran down the steps, hopped the gate and tore across the pitch to the team huddle.

I went straight up to Brian and Gorta.

'So, where am I coming on, lads?'

They looked at each other.

'Okay, Eoin Cody, you're coming off.'

It felt like I'd had to intervene and put myself on the pitch. The humiliation of the day was complete.

WHATEVER IT TAKES

We were in a tight spot. Cork had just got a goal, with Jack O'Connor exploding down the left wing, burning past everyone, and firing in his shot. They were three up starting the second period of extra time and then they took over completely. Shane Kingston had come on and was destroying us. We were well beaten by the end; Cork won comfortably.

That night, we headed back to Kilkenny, seeking comfort for our pain in a few drinks. Everyone was floored, as it was another lost year.

For the first time, I was really questioning the point in staying involved. *It can't get much worse than this. You're going to have to go.*

My sudden demise in the pecking order had come so quickly and I couldn't get my head around it. Even though I missed some time through injury I had plenty of training under my belt at this stage. I started the 2020 All-Ireland semi-final eight months earlier in December and had come on to score 1–02 against Galway and help turn around the Leinster final a few weeks before that. And now I'm literally at the bottom of the barrel. I couldn't make sense of it.

It was the lowest point I've ever had as a Kilkenny hurler, lower even than the sending off against Tipperary.

CHAPTER 17

THERE'S MORE TO LIFE THAN HURLING

WHEN THE SELECTION calls were made during the 2022 championship, I wasn't featuring. Familiar ailments were hindering my progress; all the while, I was trying to coax my back into cooperating, praying for an opportunity to get a clear break.

Then it came.

A four-week gap had opened up after the Leinster final. After multiple back injections and weeks of rehab and fitness work, I knew this was my chance. The goal was pretty simple – be the best player on the field in training, night after night, and hope that the body holds up. I knew that if I could deliver consistently over the internal training games during that period then Brian would have no choice; I would be back in. My ability to deliver in a Kilkenny jersey had never been in question and now I had four weeks to prove my fitness and form.

During that time, it didn't matter who I was marking or where I was playing – I couldn't be stopped. The pain, both physical and mental, that I had gone through over the last 12 months had given me an edge that the others in training couldn't handle. My interactions with my teammates during that time perked up significantly; they were as happy as I was. They had seen what I had gone through to get back and, most importantly, they knew what I could bring for the team on All-Ireland semi-final day.

I wasn't getting carried away, though. I was ready to start but also knew that Brian would take a little more convincing and that a 20-minute run out off the bench was the most likely scenario. Unlike 2021, there were no doubts about my form this time, and so I felt that there would be no repeating sense of embarrassment, where I sat in the stand as the game moved out of our reach. This time I had proven beyond all doubt that I was the most in-form player in our camp and I was ready.

Instead, I spent the whole evening rooted to my seat in the Hogan Stand as we cut Clare to ribbons. Kilkenny is a small hurling community. Word spreads quickly. It was getting out that I was lighting it up in training, but that wasn't translating to game time.

A no-show against Clare, I was deflated. It felt like a betrayal of the core rule Brian had always preached: play well in training, get to play in matches.

We had a team meeting after the Clare game, in the build-up to the final against Limerick, discussing some general tactical plans for the team.

It was going to be my last game for Kilkenny. That was now decided in my mind. When I got a chance to speak privately to Brian, I had nothing left to lose. So I was completely straight with him.

'Brian, I've been one of the best players in training. You can't argue with that. So what's going on?'

'Well look, Richie, you haven't played a lot in the last year. We just don't know whether you'll be able to do it or not.'

'Brian, I can't get any game time unless you put me on the field. That's the only cure for that problem. I'm destroying lads in training and those players are playing. Either we're both not good enough to play or we both are. I just feel that you have completely written me off here.'

'Okay so. We're training on Sunday; let's see how it goes for you.'

'Right, Brian, you put me in on your best defender and we'll see.'

The challenge was set for both of us. I'd perform on Sunday in training and he'd live up to his word. I ended up marking Mikey Butler. We'd a good battle and I felt there was enough evidence there to ensure I featured against Limerick.

***

I'd spent the entire 2022 season working away in the background, believing that when the chance to play arrived, I would be ready for it. Training was tough physically and even tougher mentally, but it was nothing compared with dealing with the general GAA public during that time. When you're a veteran and your game time becomes restricted, plenty fall into an assumption that you've retired – out of sight, out of mind. On a regular basis I would be approached by someone in the street for a chat about hurling. The conversation tended to go in the same direction.

'What are you doing yourself now?'

'Are you still playing a bit with your club?'

'Do you miss not being involved?'

Often, I was too embarrassed to admit that I was still training hard and desperately trying to wring one last drop from my Kilkenny hurling career. Instead, I played along and said I was playing a little bit of club hurling but nothing too serious. At the start, my heart would sink when those conversations happened. As the year went on, however, I grew immune to it and it only fuelled my determination.

One of these interactions happened on the All-Ireland final weekend in the middle of July.

The Friday before the game, I got a WhatsApp from Bernard Brogan.

THERE'S MORE TO LIFE THAN HURLING

'You working at the game on Sunday? I have a Q&A in the Croke Park Hotel if you were around for 30 min pre game?'

I had to look at the message a few times to see if it was a wind-up. As I read it again, I laughed. *I would love to see the look on this lad's face when I come on the field on Sunday.*

I never replied. Better to let him sweat it out. Sure enough, he followed up with an apology for his ignorance a few weeks later and we both laughed about it.

Fifty-nine minutes into the final and Brian called me over. I had been warming up for the previous 10 minutes along the line, pausing intermittently to have a quick look out on the pitch or catch the replay of a score on the big screen.

'Richie, it's as simple as this. We need scores now, that's it. Go out there, get on the ball and put it over the bar.'

I looked him in the eye and nodded.

'No problem.'

We trailed by two. Adrian Mullen cut the gap and then on 63 minutes David Blanchfield fired a ball down the wing. I'd escaped free underneath the Hogan Stand, 45 yards out. I stuck the hurl up to trap the ball, gathered and leaning on the back foot, I lofted a shot away just as Sean Finn dove in with this attempt to block.

That feeling, watching the ball sail over the bar, was magical. All the frustration and anger and doubt, it was all channelled into that shot. *Here we go, the team is on a roll and I'm playing my part.* That was all it was ever about for me – how could I help Kilkenny to succeed?

It was the only shot I got off in the final and the last point I ever scored in Croke Park. The challenge just fizzled out for us. Limerick got over the line by two points.

The roar from the crowd when I hit that point will never leave me. It felt like there was a wave of emotion from the Kilkenny crowd rolling in behind me. That bond remained intact.

Countless people since, from all parts of Ireland, have felt it important to talk to me with such pride about that point. Almost as if it was their own son who struck that ball over the bar.

'Oh, I was sitting right behind that point when you hit it, everyone around me jumped out of their seat.'

There must have been a lot of people in the Hogan Stand that day with a perfect sight line.

It wasn't like the 2020 Leinster final goal against Galway, though, as this wasn't a score that propelled us to victory. It's hard to look back on a score as fondly when the team has lost.

I knew I had increased the pressure on myself to perform by demanding inclusion that day, but the flip side was that there was a release in the knowledge that it was my last day out. I knew Brian had made up his mind about me and I'd never be playing for Kilkenny again.

It was game over for me, but at least this time I had really left on my own terms.

THERE'S MORE TO LIFE THAN HURLING

* * *

After the 2022 All-Ireland I was done. I just needed to tell the world of a decision that was settled in my head. No one had been consulted. Anne probably would have guessed it, but I've never been a person who sits down with family to thrash things out when I'm about to make a decision – especially when it was a hurling matter.

It was glaringly obvious to anyone who looked close enough that I didn't have a playing future with Kilkenny as long as Brian was the manager.

But then the word filtered through to us in Italy that Brian was leaving the hotseat. As the days went on, I started to process this news and questions popped up. Could there be a chance for me in 2023? Could my body go again? Who was going to be in charge?

After we flew home, we got stuck into the club championship with Danesfort. It was just a brilliant time to be involved that October, immersed in hurling with the local lads again. We built some momentum and I got into a hot scoring run – 11 points against Conahy Shamrocks, 10 against the Rower-Inistioge, and, lastly, a dozen against Thomastown, split evenly between play and frees.

It took extra time after this epic rollercoaster of a game before we won that final.

1–36 to 4–25.

The satisfaction I felt after that win was unique. I knew my playing days with Danesfort and Kilkenny would soon be coming to an end and that days like this would probably never come again. With Kilkenny, success had always been about meeting expectation, whereas there was more of an element of surprise to this. Paddy was in goal, while I played centre-forward. We had been young lads in our early twenties when Danesfort had won the county Intermediate in 2011; we were now adults in our thirties for that 2022 success. Time brought a greater appreciation and we made sure to cherish that day in Nowlan Park.

*　*　*

All signs pointed towards Derek Lyng getting the manager job. Brian announced he was going on 23 July and, sure enough, the Kilkenny County Board announced Derek was appointed on 4 August. They acted swiftly, allowing no time for a vacuum to be filled with rumours.

Derek was the perfect choice. He had the experience from being a Senior selector and U-20 boss, as well as the track record as a player, to back up taking on the job. It wasn't easy to step up to fill the vacancy when Brian left. But Derek was a natural leader. He retired in December 2010, so we'd spent four seasons together in the same dressing room. It was at a time when I was unproven, fighting my way into the team, drinking in everything that was going on around me.

The outside world was attracted to our stars, like Henry, Tommy and J.J., but inside we knew the value of people like Derek. Derek spoke sparingly but the timing and content when he did say a few words were always on the money. He was a clear communicator who allowed for no bullshit. He was a guy who struggled a little bit with injury during league campaigns, but remained a player that was nailed on for Brian Cody's championship teams. When the year progressed, his importance grew. I had huge admiration for a player like that, those who had the ability to step up their performance in big games. It was a sign of brilliance.

We went on the Kilkenny team holiday to Thailand between that county final and the Leinster club championship. The trip was a reward for our 2022 efforts, so your intentions for 2023 were irrelevant as to whether you got a seat on the plane.

Derek rang me before we headed on the holiday. My plans were still up in the air, but he got straight to the point. There was a place for me on the Kilkenny squad for 2023. A few years wrecked by injury hadn't diluted his regard for me.

I went to the first team meeting in Hotel Kilkenny in late 2022. Two other Danesfort lads, Des Dunne and Darragh O'Neill, had been called in after great years with the club. There were 40 players in the room when Derek stood up to address us.

WHATEVER IT TAKES

I was keen to hear what tone he was going to strike. Any suggestion of a long-term project and I was gone out the door. The perception going into the meeting was that Kilkenny, after winning the All-Ireland U-20, would try and blood a few players and build a team for two or three years down the line.

I had no time for that. What use would I be sitting there getting in the way of lads who were looking to develop? My sole interest was in winning the 2023 All-Ireland, not looking towards the future.

Derek introduced the team of people he had assembled to work with and outlined their roles. And then he said very plainly and clearly that we were all in this for one reason: to win the All-Ireland final this year. As players we would do everything we could on the pitch, he knew, and as management and backroom staff, they would do everything off the pitch – all designed to go and win that title.

He could have adopted a more patient, long-term view; instead, he raised the stakes for everyone in that hotel meeting room. This was brave and welcome, because when you call out a target at the start of a season, you crank up the pressure to go achieve it.

I was sold on Derek Lyng's Kilkenny hurling vision. I would give it one more year.

The club season had left me in decent athletic shape but I had to receive a cortisone injection to get me through the semi-final and another in advance of the county final.

THERE'S MORE TO LIFE THAN HURLING

We got to work, although I had to raise this with Derek. He agreed that they needed to tailor my approach. The goal was to get me in prime condition by next summer; whatever game time that involved earlier in the year would be figured out.

The same S&C team was on board. That continuity was vital for me, as Mickey Comerford knew what I needed.

I was hungry and enthusiastic knowing that this time the slate would be completely clean.

* * *

If my final year taught me nothing else, it taught me that there is more to life than hurling. I had so much hope that had compounded for a few years and I was ready to cash in.

I was born on the eighth day of the eighth month in the eighty-eighth year of the last century. I weighed eight pounds and eight ounces at birth. I've spent my whole life hearing from those who've asked me for my date of birth about how I must be a really lucky person. For a while, when backed up with the most amazing period of success, I began to believe it. Slowly but surely, in a sporting context, that luck eroded.

My early season training had been going really well and a February league start was in the plan. I jarred my leg in training, however, which left me with a damaged hamstring, delaying my league comeback by a few weeks. I was selected to play against Waterford in the last round in Nowlan Park. Derek came to me on the Friday night before the game explaining my role and I left the field that night like a child excited to play his first game. I hadn't started a game for Kilkenny since the 2020 All-Ireland semi-final against the same opposition. *This really will be different*, I thought.

On the Saturday, Ireland played England in the Six Nations Grand Slam decider. Anne and I were going to watch the game with Herro and his wife Ciara and Cillian Buckley and his wife Niamh out in the Herity house in Ennisnag on the edge of Danesfort. I popped into Hotel Kilkenny to use the sauna for a while that afternoon just to ensure that the body was in prime shape for the following day.

Paddy's house is near Herro's and I was collecting Anne there on the way. I was running late and asked her to be outside ready to go when I got there. Usually we would swap over, especially on match weekends as I like to do as little driving as possible, but on this occasion she jumped in the passenger seat as we were only going a few miles over the road. And thank God she did.

Halfway to Herro's house Anne's head slumped down to one side and her body started to jerk slightly. I noticed this out of the corner of my eye and at first thought she was pretending. I lifted up her head and saw that she had turned completely pale, and her body was shaking aggressively. She was having a seizure. I pulled off the road into a driveway and started talking to her, trying to wake her up.

I called 999 on the car's Bluetooth speaker and jumped over to see what I could do. Her jaw was rammed shut and she appeared to be choking.

I had always assumed that I would be calm and collected in a situation like this, but I fell apart with panic. I thought she was going to swallow her tongue, so I tried to prise her mouth open with my shaking hands, but her jaws were locked too tightly. She was getting virtually no air in.

The operator answered and transferred me to the Kilkenny accident and emergency unit.

'I need an ambulance; my wife is having a seizure! I am in a place called Ennisnag in Kilkenny and I need an ambulance now.'

His efforts to calm me down frustrated me. If he could see what I could see, then he would also have understood the need for urgency.

'Listen to me. We are in a place called Ennisnag, very close to Sheridan's Pub. It is halfway between Danesfort and Stoneyford.'

'Do you have an Eircode or is there a particular monument nearby that you can describe?'

'I just told you where I am! Are you familiar with Kilkenny?'

'Sorry, I'm not familiar with Kilkenny. Could you look up your exact location on your phone and let me know?'

I looked at Anne and every ounce of colour was gone from her face and virtually no air was getting through her mouth. *By the time he gets someone out to me she's going to be dead*, I thought. So I hung up the phone and kept trying to open her mouth.

I had never seen someone have a seizure before, I wasn't aware that swallowing your tongue wasn't possible. I had lost hope at this point, the skin on the tips of my fingers had been peeled back by her teeth and I kissed her on the forehead in between talking to her and continuing to try to open her mouth.

I rang Herro, knowing he'd answer because he was expecting us and also knowing he could call the ambulance with the details needed.

He answered.

'Richie.'

'Herro, I need you to listen! Anne is having a seizure. We are halfway between your house and Paddy's. I need you to call an ambulance.'

He knew by the tone of my voice that I was serious, but I felt the need to remind him anyway.

'This is not a fucking joke! This is serious!'

'Okay! Okay! I've got it!'

Anne had settled a little. Her body had stopped jerking, and she was getting a little more air in. This calmed me a bit. I got my jacket and put it over her, and she drifted off while still breathing heavily.

Herro and Cillian arrived minutes later in the car and brought a blanket. By then the situation was a little less dramatic and I pretended that I had things under control. The ambulance arrived about 40 minutes later and Anne was asleep, unaware of what had gone on but shattered physically as a result. We went to hospital in Waterford and she was discharged the following morning. Seizures are not a regular thing for Anne. She'd never had one before and hasn't had one since; it frightened the life out of me.

I spent the night sitting on the floor of the waiting room in University Hospital Waterford before Anne's dad Jim came to collect us the following morning. I didn't give a shit about hurling for those 24 hours, and there was no way I was going to play a match against Waterford. I rang Tadhg Crowley, who is also Anne's GP, and asked him to deliver the news to Derek.

Once Anne got the all clear we settled down within a few days. A win against Waterford meant a league semi-final against Cork in Nowlan Park the following week. Derek kept his word and put me in from the start at centre-forward. I didn't feel an ounce of pressure. The previous week's events had given me an enlightened perspective on what was important. My freedom showed on the pitch and I drove the first ball over the bar within 30 seconds.

I was marking Ciaran Joyce for a while and playing really well before Niall O'Leary was send out from corner-back to man-mark me after 20 minutes. It felt like I was back where I belonged. Fifteen minutes into the second half I made a cross-field run in anticipation of a puckout, switching positions with Paddy Deegan. Paddy's marker Tommy O'Connell was in close pursuit and collided with me as we crossed. I didn't properly see Tommy, and he didn't see me, but the collision of his body into my arm hit me with this excruciating pain.

The wrist of my left arm was already heavily strapped, as I had torn a tendon previously, so there was very little flexibility there and it just snapped. I was forced off moments later. However, desperation not to be stuck on the treatment table again compelled me to keep my head down, my mouth shut and hope for the best.

That night at home in Dublin, the pain still hadn't eased. I booked an X-ray nearby in Affidea Clinic in Santry for the Monday morning and rang my boss in PwC looking for a few hours off work. The results revealed the ugly truth: a break in two places in my arm. The surgeon spoke about a cast, an eight-week wait until that was removed, with a further four before there could be a playing return. I was wise enough by now to know the difference between a surgeon's advice and what might be deemed a realistic timeline.

I left with this sense of misery in tow, clinging to the thought that I had made an impact against Cork and that would count for something in the minds of the selectors. My right hand had previously been through a similar war, and I remembered the difficulty in returning after that break. The power drained from it and there had been a real problem even holding a hurl for a period of time. I knew this would be the case again this time round.

Preventing that weakness developing was now key. This time my right arm needed to be packed with greater strength, allowing my left to just guide the hurl when swinging. When we went on a training camp to Fota Island Resort in Cork, I was doing a running session up and down the line when the lads were playing a match, swiping the hurl left and right as I went. I was also pucking the ball one-handed, tennis-racket style, with anyone who was free to fire it back to me. I lifted weights one-handed and isolated my right wrist, strengthening it as much as possible while I had the chance.

Anything to get myself ready.

* * *

I got back on track during the Leinster Championship. A game against Antrim up in Corrigan Park was the target. In a continuation of form, things went wrong after making the long trek to West Belfast.

We hammered Antrim 5–31 to 3–20 and were in control all day. At half-time, I was told that I would be brought on early in the second half, but that switch was delayed due to an injury elsewhere on the team. When I did eventually get introduced, it felt more sudden and rushed. With the first ball I collected, I fired it across to Wally Walsh, and he stuck over a point. The second ball was a short sideline cut played my way which I ran toward to touch it into my hand. I got a push from behind by my marker and I felt my hamstring pull as I put the brakes on.

I faced a real dilemma. If I put my hand up that my hamstring was torn I would never hurl for Kilkenny again. How could they chance putting on an injury-prone guy who could only last a few minutes? It would be a career-ending afternoon.

Or, given we were streets ahead on the scoreboard, I could keep going at whatever pace I could and avoid running at full speed.

I went for Option B.

It worked, up to a point.

Since I had only come on in the sixtieth minute, I was ordered into those running sessions you see done after a county game, where unused subs and lads who played little are put through their paces. I had to tell Mickey Comerford that I wasn't feeling up to it, and then broke the news during the weekend of my true injury situation.

Heading down the motorway that evening, my mood was really low. It was hard to see a way out of this injury mire I was getting bogged down in. There had been a freak nature to the arm break, but the hamstring felt more like a signal that my body was screaming to a halt.

* * *

THERE'S MORE TO LIFE THAN HURLING

I left Dublin at 6.15 a.m. on the Friday morning before the Leinster final and pointed the car towards Kilkenny. That was a trip I often made, as it enabled me to work for the day remotely in Kilkenny before heading to training that evening. I had just started working for PricewaterhouseCoopers and I was in their Kilkenny office that morning for 8 a.m., energised at the thought of the weekend ahead, particularly as I was back in contention to play.

The day was busy, wrapping up stuff at the end of a working week. At lunchtime, I popped over to get a salad in Freshly Chopped just next to the Mart in Kilkenny. I was rushing out of the car and, as I climbed out the door, I felt that familiar feeling in my back. There was no time to waste – my back was nearing a spasm, after all – so I just lay down on the ground of the car park.

Try to relax, Richie, just stay calm.

I breathed softly, aware of this crucial two-minute window to limit the damage, conscious of what anyone walking by was going to think of the sight of a Kilkenny hurler stretched out on the tarmac on a Friday afternoon, staring at the sky.

The ground was nice and cold. My knees were gently moved left and right, as I aimed to avoid tension creeping in. Slowly clambering up to walk, I knew that I had shifted to one side.

After managing to get some food into me, I returned to the office and spent the rest of the day at the standing desk.

I finished up at 6 p.m. We were close to Nowlan Park and so I headed straight there as I knew the physios would be setting up early.

I spotted John Kearns as soon as I arrived.

'My back is gone, John. It's your job now to fix it.'

John always laughs in these situations, when I come with a volley of demands and expect an instant miracle to be performed. My desperation was obvious, I suspect. John did what he could in a 45-minute session while I lay on the physio bed. Training that night was out the window, but there was still a glimmer of hope I could tog out in Croke Park on the Sunday.

Once I rolled off the table, however, it was clear there'd been no improvement. Derek came in to chat and we made a deal that I would sleep on it and give him a call. By 8 a.m. the following morning, I knew that I was gone off the squad for Sunday.

The match was an epic win for Kilkenny, Cillian Buckley scoring the most famous goal of his life. I was thrilled for the lads and devastated for myself. They headed back to Kilkenny that night to celebrate, while I just went home in Dublin, staring at the four walls and wondering if there was any break going to come my way in this year of injury misfortune.

* * *

As hard and unforgiving as the season was transpiring to be, Derek was great to me. I never felt forgotten or discarded. Sometimes, he would ask me to speak to the group, and it was clear that he valued what I'd say.

The new management all brought plenty to the set-up. I'd hurled with Michael Rice for years: a shrewd, clever fella. Peter Barry had retired from Kilkenny the year before I started. I never played with him, but his name and reputation hung in the air. Lads spoke passionately about him: how he was a driving force that epitomised all the greatest attributes of Kilkenny hurling. I knew Peter O'Donovan also from my U-21 days and he and Conor Phelan paired up to add new ideas to our style of play.

Derek was very good at listening to everybody. He would take all those views on board and then arrive at his own decision. That could differ from what most had suggested, but that was fine. As a manager, it was clear that he was going to listen to everybody and then assume responsibility. That gave us a new lease of life.

We knew the scale of the challenge we were taking on. Limerick were a formidable, four-in-a-row chasing machine at the time.

I don't know Paul Kinnerk. We've never met or spoken, I've just seen him on the sideline on match day at John Kiely's shoulder. His fingerprints are all over that Limerick team.

We'd destroyed them on short puckouts in the 2019 semi-final. Straight away, the following year, you could see that they had practised short puckouts non-stop. They removed the risk of contested possession and made sure they retained the ball. If they got 40 puckouts in a game they would hit all of them at the corner-back if that was the right choice to make. The introduction of Barry Nash was key, as they were bringing a different dynamic to it with a repurposed ball-playing forward in their defence.

It was a case of hurling problem solving. That ability to see something that is going wrong and decide they will fix it by becoming the best in the country at it. A weakness is therefore turned into a strength through relentless practice. Amidst all of the admiration that I have for the current Limerick team, that appetite for continuous improvement is what I admire most.

* * *

The purest experience of sporting enjoyment is with your childhood friends in the school yard or the local club pitch. That joyous sense of abandon pucking a ball, it's at a time when it's just fun. You remember that feeling, how good it was.

When and where was the last time you experienced it?

You don't know; you can't put your finger on it. It wasn't apparent at the time that there was a finality to it, so how could you have savoured it properly? But there was an end point.

THERE'S MORE TO LIFE THAN HURLING

Before the 2023 All-Ireland final, I knew this day represented the closing of my Kilkenny chapter. I had thought the previous year's final was my last game, but I was absolutely certain there was no further story to be written for me after this one.

I entered the game with the uncertainty that stems from having a body so susceptible to injury. Was my back going to betray me again? Waking up that morning, and moving through the pre-match routine, it all felt good. For the Clare semi-final game, I had been wrapped up in worry before I got onto the pitch; on that final Sunday, however, everything unfolded smoothly.

The usual tension and nervous energy of such a game doesn't lend itself to enjoyment. But I paused and appreciated the whole build-up. I loved stepping out in Croke Park and feeling my senses spring alive. The supporters' experience is not the same as that of a player in that way. The player feels that heat on the pitch, murky and heavy, which accompanies a full house.

Everything was heightened for me in the stadium – the sight, the smell, the sound, the touch.

When we walked the pitch an hour before throw-in, I grabbed a clump of freshly cut grass out of the ground, pressed it to my nose and just let the smell linger for a few seconds. Just to activate the senses again. I was aware that this was it. I would be gone out the door once that final whistle blew. There'd be no turning back. So I just held that grass and remembered all the times here, good and bad, and knew I wanted one last winning feeling with Kilkenny.

* * *

It wasn't to be. Hurling is not sentimental. We knew that well over the years when we beat so many teams that were desperate to win the All-Ireland. Limerick now had that control.

Before the game, I talked to a couple of the selectors and just asked for enough time on the pitch to make a difference. Ten or fifteen minutes is a compressed period, in which it's difficult to help your team and change the course a game is taking. Not enough ball comes your way to shape the outcome.

Given my injury problems, I was told to regularly warm up. As the second half progressed, I was getting tired of being on the sideline. Peter Barry saw me and said I'd be on around the sixty-third minute. He called for patience, something subs never have on the day of a game.

It was a day where Eoin Cody had cracked an early goal for us and Paddy Deegan stuck another in after half-time. That put us up 2–10 to 0–11, but when I came into the game on 66 minutes we were losing by eight points.

Limerick were a runaway train in that half, unstoppable and mowing down anything in their way. My introduction made little difference that day.

THERE'S MORE TO LIFE THAN HURLING

It was a day where everything clicked for them.

They hit 30 points by the finish. When the final whistle blew, they'd won by nine.

* * *

Just under six weeks later, I officially retired, hanging up the boots at the age of thirty-five. The first my parents knew about it was when the retirement statement was issued. Anne texted my mam a few minutes earlier so that she wouldn't find out scrolling through Instagram. Overstating the significance of a decision is not my style.

When I left the field after the 2015 All-Ireland final, I was twenty-seven and had seven All-Ireland Senior medals to my name. I didn't add any more to that tally but having the success frontloaded into the first part of my career doesn't make me feel short-changed. The meaning of those moments wouldn't be any greater if they had been shared more evenly out over the years.

By early 2024, the start of a new inter-county hurling season didn't really register with me. The schedule of games wasn't controlling the rhythms of my life any more. If I had still been capable of hurling for Kilkenny, I'd have missed it hugely. But that just was not a realistic option for me. So I pushed it aside. I tried to focus all my energy and attention – everything that I'd brought to the hurling pitch – towards my career and family.

A couple of weeks after I retired, myself and Anne sat down with the calendar and started planning. We booked flights and hotels in various windows that now popped up when my life was free from hurling duties. In 2024, we went to Amsterdam with Paddy and Claire and Paul and Eadaoin in January. At Easter, we took off to China for a fortnight – where Pa Minogue now lives with his wife Oonagh. Holidays post hurling are more relaxed. Anxiety around keeping the body in shape and primed for a new season of training is no longer there.

Going to games as a fan wasn't a big interest for me. Instead, punditry work with GAAGO and *Off The Ball* kept me in touch with the championship scene the first year I was gone, enabling me to stand on the sideline of championship games.

As a kid, I would go to every club game in Kilkenny. My father still has that passion, so does Paddy. I was different.

It is the training that I miss. The shift to fitness work on my own was a hard adjustment. I remained disciplined: early morning gym sessions near work at Spencer Dock, running that night as well.

You lose touch with the players with whom you shared a dressing room. There would be the odd message exchanged with a few, but hurling chat would be off the cards. I'd like to ask about training – curious about what type of work they're doing, more than anything – but it's pushing them into an awkward spot that they don't need to be in.

THERE'S MORE TO LIFE THAN HURLING

A lot of my really good friends with Kilkenny finished before me and have been on the retirement beat a while.

When you're living in Dublin, you're detached from life in Kilkenny. It makes the transition a little easier. If you're working in Kilkenny and you're passing by St Kieran's or Nowlan Park every day, you're getting reminders all the time. So I kept away from that.

Playing for Kilkenny had been a magnificent obsession, with soaring highs and shattering lows.

Twenty seasons were spent going across Minor, U-21 and Senior teams.

Never content with what had been achieved.

Never giving up after defeats and injuries.

Never finished.

ACKNOWLEDGEMENTS

THE GAA IS a sporting organisation like no other. I, like many other players, would not have achieved what I have without the selfless dedication of the volunteers within the GAA. As such, it is impossible for me to thank everyone individually without leaving out someone of significance.

To my mother, Liz, and my father, Seán, thank you for everything you have done for me. I know you sacrificed much of what you may have wanted in your early lives so that Paddy, Rachel, Niamh and I could have what we needed. I completely take you both for granted and it's likely that I will continue to do this. There is nothing I can do to repay the love and guidance you have given me in my life.

WHATEVER IT TAKES

To my brother Paddy and sisters Rachel and Niamh. Thank you for your support on the pitch and off it. Pushing yourselves to achieve your best inspires me to do the same in all domains of life.

I was inspired to play hurling at a young age through both sides of my family. Listening to stories about hurling from my grandfathers, Mick McCarthy and Patsy Hogan, about games and players from the past filled me with a love for the game. The fact that you both reached hurling heights before me filled me with the confidence that I could make it to the top as well.

To my nanny, Eileen. I didn't realise it then, but the decision to bring me and Paddy to the handball alley in Kilfane when we were kids was one that enhanced our lives hugely. We travelled the country and then the world, making great friends and competing at the highest level. Thank you for being there every step of the way. To my grandmother, Bea, thank you for teaching me the importance and value of kindness through your actions.

To my wife Anne. Thank you for your love and support during the toughest times on and off the pitch. The sacrifices that I have made to play at the top level were an easy decision, but for you to sacrifice so many of your personal opportunities so that I could maximise my playing career was incredibly selfless. I look forward to repaying some of that for the rest of our lives together. Anne's parents, Dolores and Jim Ryan, and the wider family, have been a fantastic support over the years.

ACKNOWLEDGEMENTS

Thank you to Brother Damien Brennan. You will never read this book, but you were instrumental in the creation of the content in it. You once said to me during one of our sessions, 'Richie, you will write a book one day'. I'm sorry for laughing at your suggestion and as usual you were right in the end.

To my aunts Linda, Una, Imelda, Pearl and Ann, and my uncles Richie and John, and all my cousins. I was blessed to have your incredible support during my career. Requests for tickets for every game filled me with strength, knowing that a large section of the crowd had my back during every game.

To Jimmy Holden, I've no idea how you became my handball coach when I was younger, but I'm delighted you did. We had the greatest times together from Kilfane to California.

To all my former teammates, coaches and the volunteers in Danesfort, thank you for the impact you had on my development since Paddy and I arrived in 2001. We have achieved great success together during my time and I'm looking forward to ensuring that continues into the next generation.

Thank you to the Kilkenny management teams of all the teams I played on, but especially the senior management and backroom teams over the years, led by Brian Cody and Derek Lyng and the Kilkenny County board and Supporters Club members during that time. Special thanks to the medical teams that kept me on the pitch for 17 years at the highest level.

To Eddie O'Donnell, thank you for providing me with the courage and opportunity to put my story on paper. Thank you also to Isabelle, Fiona, Sarah and Iollann in Gill Books for your incredible work and professionalism during the process. To Fintan O'Toole, thank you for your tireless effort and patience and for writing my story in such an articulate manner.

Finally, thank you to all my wonderful teammates over the years. Winning All-Irelands beside my brother Paddy, my cousin Mark Kelly, my clubmate Paul Murphy, my countless school friends from St Kieran's College and some of my childhood heroes enhanced the experience and enjoyment that I received from my hurling career. I will never forget the great times we had.

Richie Hogan

I first noticed Richie Hogan's hurling emergence on the underage teams in Kilkenny, and was struck by how at ease he was playing at grades above his age: a 15-year-old with the Kilkenny minor team in 2004, an 18-year-old scoring a goal in the 2006 All-Ireland U-21 final, and then moving onto the Kilkenny senior squad as a teenager. Throughout his 17-year Senior career, I was fortunate to have a perfect view from press boxes around the country. Getting to work

ACKNOWLEDGEMENTS

with him on this book and reliving those days has been hugely rewarding, and so has getting an insight into the challenges that had to be overcome to stay at the top in hurling for so long. Thanks to Richie for his time and honesty during all our chats. I hope he enjoyed sharing his memories as much as I did listening to them.

Thanks to all the team at Gill Books for making this book happen, particularly Sarah and Isabelle for their help and patience with it all.

Also big thanks to Damian Lawlor for getting the ball rolling last December.

To Paul Dollery, Denis Hurley, Denis Walsh and Declan Bogue – thanks lads for the feedback and suggestions in helping to shape the book.

Niall Kelly has always been a big support, thanks to him and all the team at The42.ie.

Thanks as always to Paudie, Norma, Fionnuala and Ronan, and to all the Desmond family for helping out.

Finally to Colette, Rían and Laoise, who I'm always fortunate to have backing me. Thanks for all your understanding and support during a hectic year.

Fintan O'Toole